A Place of Thin Veil

A Place of Thin Veil

LIFE AND **DEATH** IN GALLUP, NEW MEXICO

BOB ROSEBROUGH

RIO NUEVO
PUBLISHERS

Rio Nuevo Publishers®
P. O. Box 5250
Tucson, AZ 85703-0250
(520) 623-9558
www.rionuevo.com

Library of Congress Cataloging-in-Publication Data

Names: Rosebrough, Bob, author.
Title: A place of thin veil : life and death in Gallup, New Mexico / Bob Rosebrough.
Description: Tucson, AZ : Rio Nuevo Publishers, [2021] | Includes index.
Identifiers: LCCN 2020054097 | ISBN 9781940322520 (trade paperback)
Subjects: LCSH: Casuse, Larry. | Navajo Indians—New Mexico—Gallup—Social life
    and customs—20th century. | Gallup (N.M.)—History—20th century.
Classification: LCC F804.G25 R67 2021 | DDC 978.983—dc23
LC record available at https://lccn.loc.gov/2020054097

Managing Editor: Aaron Downey
Book design: Preston Thomas, Cadence Design Studio
Cover image: iStock.com/baona

Printed in the United States of America.

10 9 8 7 6 5 4 3 2 1

For Bren
who makes all things possible

Contents

Prologue

Ursula Casuse bursts into my sunny, corner office at City Hall without slowing to introduce herself and begins talking without warm-up. A Navajo woman in her early forties, with raven hair that cascades down to the middle of her back, she has an anguished look on her face. She is holding a frayed, yellowed copy of the *Gallup Independent* with a headline reading: MAYOR SAFE; ABDUCTOR DEAD.

Ursula radiates a frenetic energy that is unusual for a person of her culture; in my experience, Navajo people value composure and reserve, especially in public. I don't try to slow her down; I don't think I can. Instead, I zero in on her facial expressions and body language trying to get a read on whether her emotion is real or manufactured. Ursula is struggling to keep her focus, to stay on topic. She has something urgent to tell me. This, I sense, is real to her.

Earlier, I had spotted Ursula's name on my Open-Door Friday appointment list and wondered, *Is she Larry Casuse's sister?* I hoped then to get to know her and engage her in a conversation because I've become fascinated by the history of my adopted hometown and the compelling story of her brother's life and death.

After seeing the headline in the newspaper, my question from the morning is answered without any words being spoken. I know with certainty that Ursula is Larry's younger sister. But it's also clear that this meeting isn't going to go as I had hoped. Ursula is complaining about the Gallup police department, which, because I'm mayor, is now under my oversight, and pointing to the photo in the old newspaper she carries.

"The police have this photo framed in the FOP building, like a trophy," Ursula says, referring to the Fraternal Order of Police building. Her voice is strained, and her cadence disjointed and choppy.

"Let's sit," I say as I gesture toward a varnished maple conference table near two large windows with vertical blinds. I'm trying to engage her and slow her down.

"I know your brother, Don," I say. As I mention his name, I remember Don telling me something about this same photo several years earlier.

Ursula pauses, but only for a moment, ignores my comment and continues pressing her case. Some Open-Door Friday appointments are like this. Ursula talks as if she rehearsed what she's now saying for days, and it seems to frustrate her when I say anything that threatens to take her off her mental script.

She lays out the newspaper on the conference table, and as she does, the yellowed paper gives off a musty smell. There's a lot I'd like to talk to Ursula about, but that's not going to happen, at least not today. I shift into problem-solving-mayor mode and resign myself to working through this on her terms.

In March 1973, Ursula's older brother, Larry Casuse, a 19-year-old Indian activist, kidnapped Gallup mayor Emmett Garcia, a 35-year-old rising political star, at gunpoint here in City Hall. Larry died in the shootout that followed minutes later. In the weeks leading up to the kidnapping, Larry had been protesting Garcia's appointment to the University of New Mexico Board of Regents, because Garcia was a co-owner of a notorious bar bordering the Navajo Nation whose parking lot was usually full of passed-out bodies.

There's no way I would have been having this conversation but for the unlikely fact that I ran for mayor of Gallup in 2003 and won. I'm a rarity of sorts—a Gallup mayor who wasn't born here, a tall white lawyer in my early fifties wearing a bolo tie. At times, I find myself considering how strange it really is that I moved to this town that borders the Navajo Nation on the extreme western edge of New Mexico with its rugged, violent history and otherworldly landscape. I'm living a future I couldn't have imagined while growing up.

I've heard that the photo Ursula is showing me spurred mass protest marches by Navajos that rocked the town shortly after her brother's violent death. More than thirty years later, ripples from the clash—which originated over exploitation of Natives by the alcohol industry—still reverberate here.

To varying degrees, public inebriation is a chronic problem in all Navajo Nation border towns. But Gallup, more than any other, is *the* border town and, for reasons that were a mystery to me for many years, the city developed a community ethic that looked the other way from the overservice of alcohol to Indians.

Ursula seems to assume that I know the story of her brother and Mayor Garcia, and she's right. But to say I know it is an understatement; this story has entwined itself with my life. Not long after moving to Gallup, I sought details about the story. And now, at times like this, it feels as if the story is seeking me.

Inexplicably, I feel an odd connection to both Larry Casuse *and* Emmett Garcia, and I suspect that I'm alone in that respect. Everyone else in town seems to have taken sides. Like Garcia, I've been shaking up the You-scratch-my-back-and-I'll-scratch-yours political culture of Gallup, proposing good-government policies, cutting costs to fund quality-of-life and infrastructure projects, and bringing in a professional city manager from outside Gallup. But like Casuse, I'm appalled that some bars in Gallup overserve alcohol to Native people—without repercussion—until the people either pass out or run out of money. I don't get it. I don't understand how the owners of these bars, who would be viewed as pariahs elsewhere, are treated like pillars of the community here. Two years into a four-year term as mayor, I've been proposing that nuisance suits be brought against problem bars and that sales of fortified wines and 44-ounce malt liquors designed to entice alcohol-dependent people be limited. Predictably, a backlash is building.

The picture Ursula is showing me is unlike anything I've ever seen in a newspaper. "Let me take a look at this," I say leaning forward. Ursula pauses, then continues pressing her case as I stare at the photo.

Three policemen stand like deer hunters posing with a trophy buck. They're evenly spaced around the kill, and the thin officer in the middle is resting the butt of his rifle on his hip, the barrel pointed toward the sky. The officers are in full, dark uniforms—peaked hats with thin visors, embroidered badges, thick black leather belts and boots, metal shirt buttons, dark sunglasses, and cloth ribbons on the outside seams of their pants. Nothing visible in the dress of any of the officers suggests that they have just been involved in a struggle or shoot-out.

The officers stand on a dusty sidewalk in downtown Gallup in front of a store. Behind them a glass display window is missing, and bullet holes riddle another window and the shiny tile squares to the left of the store's entrance. The officers' unruffled physical appearance stands in stark contrast to the dead body at their feet.

The mangled, bloody, barrel-chested corpse of Larry Casuse sprawls within the triangle formed by the three officers. Casuse's body lies on the sidewalk face-up—his long black hair is tangled and soaked in blood. Streams of blood flow from Casuse's nose and mouth. His right arm near the elbow is bloody, and there are dark, bloody stains on his shirt in the upper chest area and on his jacket at the shoulder.

Blood darkens the sidewalk. Two small ovals of blood lay between Casuse's head and the curb and several larger pools are visible between Casuse's body and the store entrance. It appears that the body was dragged from inside the store by the police and placed on the sidewalk in plain view of the world. There are dark marks near the feet of the officer who stands to the left of Casuse's body, suggesting that he walked through a pool of blood and then left bloody footprints as he shifted positions.

At first glance the officers appear casual, but as I look closer small signs suggest they are gripped by tension—as if they know that forces far beyond their control are playing out. The arms of the plump officer on the left are bent at the elbow cocked and his hands are at his waist, clenched into fists. The eyes of the thin officer are squinting as if the photo has caught him in mid-blink. The sturdy officer with dark sunglasses, whom I know to be former Gallup police chief Manuel Gonzales, is standing erect and alert. His right arm, with hand open and palm down, is extended over Casuse's bullet-riddled, shattered body.

The gore of the photo shocks me—it seems to me that a journalistic line of some sort was crossed by its publication.

As I'm fixated on the photo, Ursula repeats her message yet again. "They display it like a trophy." Ursula wants me to search the FOP building, confiscate the photo, and reprimand the police department. The FOP building is closed to the public. Even I, as mayor, have not been inside.

"How do you know they have the photo?" I ask. It would now be thirty-two years old. She tells me that a friend and her 8- or 9-year-old nephew saw the photo when they were at the FOP building for an event.

"We have a new police chief who came from Albuquerque," I say. "I don't think he would like this, if it's still going on." I tell Ursula that I'm going to ask the city attorney, who works closely with the police, to help me. And I add that although I've never been to the FOP building and don't even know where it is, I'm going to see if I can go there personally.

By this point, Ursula is starting to run out of steam, and I test the waters to see if we can just have a conversation. "Larry and I were the same age," I say. "I grew up in Farmington and Larry and I both graduated from high school in 1971. We were both sophomores at UNM in 1973, but I didn't know Larry. We never crossed paths."

Ursula listens and nods but she doesn't respond and the look on her face remains both pleading and insistent. She gives me her phone number. I get out my calendar and we set an appointment for her to come back in two and a half weeks so that I can report on what I find to her. "Please invite other members of your family," I say. "Anyone in your family that you would like to bring with you is welcome."

After Ursula leaves, I have a few minutes to collect my thoughts before my next appointment with the representative of a neighborhood association. I've begun to realize that every story I see playing out in Gallup has an origin set in a time that came before. And the kidnapping of Emmett Garcia and Larry Casuse's violent death is a story that cuts to the core of some harsh Gallup history.

For decades before Larry Casuse walked into City Hall with a gun, townspeople in Gallup weaved their way around drunken, comatose bodies without pausing. Most who witnessed such scenes recognized that they were somehow connected to the conquest and subjugation of the Navajo people in the mid-1800s. But there exists, I am belatedly coming to realize, other trauma as well—less obvious but equally real—contributing to the perfect storm that played out between Casuse and Garcia and that still plays out on the streets of Gallup today.

PART
ONE

avajo Church, near Wingate N.M.

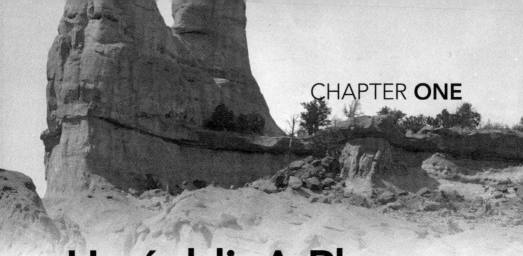

CHAPTER ONE

Hwéeldi: A Place of Suffering

It's midday on a Friday in the fall of 1969. I'm fifteen years old and walking across the Farmington High courtyard, feeling excited and self-conscious about wearing my kelly-green Farmington High letter jacket for the first time. Two cute, popular girls I barely know approach me and say, "We're going to Gallup on the activities bus. Do you want to go?"

At first, I think they're flirting and that my new letter jacket has drawn them to me. But they aren't, they're just selling tickets to the Gallup-Farmington football game, and they're good at it. I'm sold. Uncharacteristically, without calling to ask my parents for permission first, I buy a ticket.

The cities of Farmington—my hometown—and Gallup straddle the eastern portion of the Navajo Nation. They are 120 miles apart, Farmington to the north and Gallup to the south. Farmington is surrounded by farms, cottonwood trees, oil rigs, and two coal-fired power plants. Most of my family's neighbors moved to this oil and gas boomtown from

Native dancers have been an ongoing part of the Gallup's Inter-Tribal Indian Ceremonial since its founding in 1922. *Photo by Tom Mullarky from the Guadagnoli Collection*

out of state. Looking north from the town's high points, you can see the snowcapped peaks of the San Juan Mountains. They feed the Animas, San Juan, and La Plata Rivers, which flow south to converge in or near Farmington which is known as Totah, or "three waters," to the Navajos.

Growing up, I didn't know anyone in Gallup and my family never went to, or even through, our neighboring city. As a kid, I knew that there were more Indians and Hispanics in Gallup than in Farmington, that Farmington parents were worried a fight might break out whenever Gallup Little League teams came to town, and that Gallup held an annual event called the Inter-Tribal Indian Ceremonial that was kind of a big deal. I didn't know much else about the place.

Now, bus ticket in hand, I picture myself walking around the Gallup High football stadium—enemy territory—alone in my new letter jacket,

Gallup High football stadium built into a hillside, as seen here from an ultra-light plane. *Courtesy of Chris Dahl-Bredine*

jostled and challenged by a hostile crowd. I'm a tall, skinny kid who started first grade early, struggled to catch up in school and in sports, and hasn't yet kissed a girl. What have I done? But, I'm somehow eager and energized by the prospect of an imagined clash as I step onto the activities bus.

At the back of the bus, I take a seat near some students who are more acquaintances than friends. I spend most of the trip listening to their banter, oblivious to the passing landscape. When we get to Gallup it's dark, but the football field is aglow. This stadium is unlike any I've seen. The hometown stands are made completely of concrete and built into the side of a large hill like a fortress. The visitor bleachers where we Farmington kids settle are rickety and free standing. The ground drops off behind us, an unnerving black void. After half time, I get up without saying a word to the kids and parents I've come with and head across the field toward the concrete hometown bleachers, which are awash in orange and black, the Gallup team's colors.

There the scene is just as I visualized it. Clusters of dark-skinned, black-haired teenagers are buzzing in animated, swarming packs and completely disregarding the game below. Two Gallup boys with a girl trailing behind them spot me and head straight toward me. I brace myself. In a friendly tone that immediately sets me at ease, one boy says, "Hey, cool jacket. What are you doing over here?" And, so it goes.

To my surprise, the Gallup kids adopt me as a curious oddity and take a friendly interest in me—no clash at all. After spending some time with them, I work my way to the concession stand and then back to the northern end of the concourse. There I stand alone looking down on the football field bathed in bright light.

Gazing down at the expanse of green with its precise white markings and two teams locked in competition, I'm filled with a sense of vibrancy and peace unlike anything I've experienced before. Time seems to stop, and all separateness from the scene and people in front of me disappears. Like the field below me, I feel as if I'm being flooded with light.

Back in Farmington, I don't dwell on my experience above the Gallup High football field. I don't talk about it to anyone or even think about it. But I *feel* it and it subtly sinks in, affecting in turn how I feel about the town of Gallup.

A couple of months after the football game, I make a second trip to Gallup, this time as an underclassman who is part of a Farmington High basketball team loaded with talented seniors. I sit quietly listening to the seniors on the team tease each other. As we approach Gallup on our team bus, one of the guys says, "This is where they have all the drunk Indians. Let's see if we can spot some." When we reach the outskirts of town, a "game" ensues where several of my teammates spot and count drunk Indians. I sit silently observing. "There are two more," one says. "That's six and seven."

As we enter Gallup's downtown, the drunk-spotting game continues until an alarmed voice cries out, "Look over there!" We all look. An Indian man lies face down and motionless on the sidewalk, a halo of deep maroon blood surrounding his head. Another man stands by the fallen man, looking around as if he is expecting help. People walk by without pausing. The bus falls thunderously silent. Without anyone saying another word, the game is over.

On those two early trips I felt as if I had been grabbed and flung into a mysterious, awe-inspiring and perilous world, if only for moments, that were far beyond my ability to make sense of. Thirty-eight years will pass before the mysterious nature of it begins to make sense to me, when I am then at lunch with a wise old sage who moves to Gallup during the last years of his life.

The Farmington of my youth epitomized white-bread Americana, and in that way, it was Gallup's opposite. The United States had conclusively defeated evil in World War II, and our future was unlimited. America was ascendant, and Farmington was quintessentially American. None of my friends and their parents ever talked about their European ancestry or cultural traditions of a home country. It wasn't even clear to me that any of my friends even knew what European country their ancestors came from. In Farmington, we just thought of ourselves as American. Sure, there were Hispanics in town, but they were overwhelmed in number, and Navajos came to town to shop but not live. Neither group seemed to make even a slight dent in the town's dominant culture.

Observing Navajo people from a distance was a constant part of life as I grew up, and direct dealings were rare. Yet I picked up bits and pieces of Navajo culture and customs almost by osmosis. Navajos didn't shake hands as we did; they gently touched hands without tightening a grip. It wasn't "manly" by the standards of the American West, but I liked it though I couldn't quite say why. It just seemed to me to be a more appropriate way to greet a fellow human, and without thinking much about it I found myself emulating their light touch. With each other, Navajos seemed friendly and they liked to joke. With strangers they showed a quiet reserve and wariness. I had heard that when traditional Navajo men married, they moved to live near their in-laws and that it was taboo for them to speak to their mothers-in-law or even meet their mothers-in-law face-to-face. I didn't then and still don't understand how that could work.

The Navajo language was strange and altogether foreign to me; it seemed to start and stop abruptly with rising and falling tones and required a level of finesse. Navajos pointed direction not with their fingers but by pursing their lips. In the 1960s in Farmington, it seemed to me that every Navajo drove a pickup truck. And in almost every Navajo pickup truck a grandma sat on a seat or box in the bed of the truck—mid-center and facing back—in what appeared to be a place of honor. I loved that and envied the Navajo grandmas. I wished I could ride there too, and I couldn't imagine my own grandmother being healthy and rugged enough to ride in the bed of a pickup. The Navajo grandmas wore long-sleeved velvet blouses, scarves over their heads, turquoise-and-silver squash blossom necklaces, and full-length billowing cotton skirts cinched with leather concho belts. In cold weather, the grandmas draped blankets over their heads and around themselves. These elders wore expressions of steely resolve.

As a kid, I didn't encounter many Navajo people who actually lived in Farmington and I had very few Navajo classmates in elementary school. It wasn't until my sophomore year in high school, a year before my first trip to Gallup, that I made a Navajo friend.

Fred Tsosie was a year older than I, and we were both distance runners on the track team. Fred was reserved when I joined the track team after the basketball season ended. We were all competing to establish a pecking order. But after several weeks, when I pulled a muscle in the second meet and it appeared that the rest of my season was going to be a wash, Fred gently started offering advice and encouraging me. I immediately wished I had known Fred when I had started the track season. If I'd had the benefit of his advice early on, I think I might have avoided injury. He told me things that my hyped-up coaches should have told me but didn't, like how to slow down and pace myself and save my energy for key races and moments.

In Farmington, I was the kid who was always going to be catching up, having started first grade when I was five years old. When I started college at the University of New Mexico in Albuquerque, amid the tan stucco and concrete buildings, I had caught up—as both a student and a competitive athlete. But I was still embarrassingly tongue-tied around girls, dated awkwardly, and didn't have a steady girlfriend.

Basketball became my refuge. During afternoon pickup games on the hard wood courts of Johnson Gym, I played hard-fought games with former UNM stars and scrappy gym rats like myself. We formed a city league and an Amateur Athletic Union team. Larry Price, a rawboned, sharp-elbowed guy from Gallup, who was three years older than me became my best friend on the team. He had gone into the Navy straight out of high school and when he started college at UNM he was out-battling players who were three and four inches taller. He was the toughest white guy I'd met on a basketball court and we shared the bond of being late bloomers playing with former collegiate stars. And though I didn't know it yet, he was another thread to my future hometown.

The Maloofmen, with Larry Price (lower right) and Bob Rosebrough (second from left, upper row) won the New Mexico AAU tournament for six straight years in the 1970s. *Courtesy of Larry Price*

Late one afternoon in March 1973, I'm driving back to my UNM dorm room at Alvarado Hall to change clothes and study before heading off to a city league game. As I listen to Neil Young singing "Southern Man" on the radio, a bulletin interrupts regular programming. The reporter announces breaking news. The mayor of Gallup dove through the plate-glass window of a sporting goods store to escape kidnappers who had marched him through town at gunpoint. The reporter's voice is urgent and the broadcast clear and precise. One of the Indian activists who kidnapped the mayor, the reporter says, is dead.

I listen intently and wonder, *How did the mayor have the courage to dive through a plate glass window?* It's like something out of a movie.

There's no mention in the radio bulletin of the events that led up to the kidnapping, and I won't learn until many years later that the mayor's abductor is, like me, a 19-year-old sophomore at the University of New Mexico. There is, of course, no mention that the as-yet-unnamed man was one of the Gallup High linemen dressed in orange and black on the evening of my first visit to Gallup four years earlier. It's not clear what the activist's cause was, and no explanation of his motives is offered.

With the American Indian Movement takeover in Wounded Knee, South Dakota, and the shooting of a U.S. marshal still fresh in the news, I assume that the unnamed activist is a Plains Indian who came to Gallup from out of state. The bearing of Navajo men that I'd encountered growing up in Farmington evinced deference, passivity, and stoicism—even vulnerability. I had never seen a Navajo man be aggressive or violent.

The Navajos I knew picked their battles carefully and maintained a special attachment to their homeland. I had no trouble though imagining a Plains Indian traveling some distance to join in a conflict.

The radio account is a puzzle piece that doesn't fit with anything I'm currently familiar with, but it sticks in my mind. Even though key parts of the conflict between the mayor and the activist had taken place a few days earlier within easy walking distance of my dorm room, I didn't know anything about it other than what I had just heard on my car radio. I had no clue how entwined I would later become with the story.

At the basketball game later that night, I approach my buddy from Gallup and ask him if he's heard the news. He nods yes, and I teasingly shove a basketball in his chest saying, "Man, you come from a wild ass town." Without saying a word or smiling, he nods again and gives me a look that says: *You don't know the half of it.*

Years earlier, my sisters and I travelled to eastern New Mexico to spend a week with our cousins, uncle, and aunt who owned a couple of small Route 66 motels in San Jon. It was a regular summer trip for us.

One morning after we finished stripping sheets in the motel rooms, my cousin Bruce and I went out to ride dirt bikes. Several miles out into the country, we laid our motorcycles down and walked up a large sand dune surrounded by the endless plains of eastern New Mexico beneath a blue, cloudless sky—two skinny white kids standing on top of a sand dune, without a man-made structure in sight.

"We have Navajos here, too," said Bruce, completely unexpectedly. We've never talked about Navajos. I had no idea what he was going to say.

"During the summers, they come out to work on some of the farms," he continued. "The place where they were taken after they were captured is not too far from here."

As we stood looking out on the plains, I couldn't imagine Navajo people living in this landscape, a place without cedars, junipers, red-walled canyons, mesas, and snow-capped peaks in the distance. Captured? Brought to such a foreign landscape? I didn't understand what Bruce was talking about.

The Navajo creation story, Diné Bahané, describes a journey through three worlds—First World, which is Dark; Second World, which is Blue;

A Navajo woman in traditional dress with a cradleboard for her baby. *Photo by Tom Mullarky from the Guadagnoli Collection*

and Third World, which is Yellow—that lead to Fourth World, the White or Glittering World. Ethnographers describe it differently. They say the Navajo are a branch of Athabascan Indians who migrated from Northern Canada south to the Four Corners region of the Southwest, an area previously occupied by the Anasazi, or, as they are now called, Ancestral Puebloans.

All agree Navajo people have a special attachment to their homeland, Dinétah, a land of canyons and mesas, bounded by four sacred and forested mountains. There, vertical sandstone towers defy erosion, and volcanic monoliths festooned with vertical wings and needles erupt through the earth's crust; it is an awe-inspiring, stunningly beautiful and harsh land.

The Navajo people withstood conquest when Spanish settlers migrated north from Mexico, but they never had a real chance of stemming the tide of Manifest Destiny. After I began studying their history in earnest, I learned that the merciless form their suppression ultimately took was largely the result of the unrelenting ambition and driving energy of one man, James Henry Carleton, a Union general during the Civil War who

Venus's Needle in Todilto Park north of Window Rock on the Navajo Nation. *Courtesy of Bob Rosebrough*

Shiprock—also known as "Rock with Wings"—with a volcanic dike that has burst through the crust of the earth in the foreground. *Courtesy of Chris Dahl-Bredine*

had been previously stationed in New Mexico before being assigned to California. Carleton returned to New Mexico with troops from California looking to repulse Confederate invaders from Texas but arrived too late in the conflict to make his mark.

An early milepost in the saga of Navajo subjugation was the takeover of Las Vegas, New Mexico, by the U.S. Army in 1846 in the face of token opposition by Spanish settlers. The first Spanish scouting party had come north in 1539, from what is now Mexico—193 years before the birth of George Washington. The initial Spanish scouts stopped outside Zuni Pueblo, thirty-five miles south of what is now Gallup. In the 300-plus years that followed, Spanish settlers came north to settle in the Rio Grande Valley of what was to become New Mexico, Pueblo Indians revolted and drove the Spanish out, Spanish control was reestablished, and then, in 1821, Mexico won independence from Spain.

In August 1846, American troops marched west toward New Mexico on the Santa Fe Trail after President James Polk, with his eyes fixed on the riches of California persuaded Congress to declare war on Mexico, over the objection of some members, including Abraham Lincoln.

The Spanish villagers of Las Vegas, New Mexico, who were not simply Spanish in origin but a *mestizaje* group sharing European and Native Mexican heritage, were hunkered down awaiting a clearly superior fighting force. Before sunrise they awoke to the sounds of hooves and shouts only to find that Navajo raiders had kidnapped a young Spanish herdsman and taken off with their livestock.

The long-standing war between the Navajos and the Spanish settlers was not as one sided as the raid on Las Vegas might suggest. The Spaniards, since their initial settlement 250 years earlier, had been dishing out at least as much as they took from the Navajos—and the war was not just about livestock and territory. It was far more personal. The Spanish settlers had for years been conducting slave raids to take Navajo women and children. I was surprised to learn the primal depth of the conflict between the two groups; I hadn't realized that the Navajo and Hispanic people I grew up around shared a history of combat.

Ironically, the combatants had much more in common than the tribalism that pitted them against each other. Both peoples felt a deep connection to a starkly beautiful land of immense, almost surreal, vistas —a land of mystery and veiled forces both seen and unseen. From their writings and oral stories, it was evident that both bands of people listened to the voices of the earth as they followed the cycles of the sun and moon while farming, herding livestock, and hunting wild game. Everything was alive and everything was sacred to both Navajos and Spaniards—the rivers, springs, winds, plains, canyons, animals, crops, and seasons. Many in both warring camps recognized their interconnectedness with the earth and of all forms of life. Yet, in the way of humans generally, the harsh reality of tribal separateness prevailed over any numinous sense of unity. By the time the "Americans" entered the picture, a continuous state of war had existed between Spanish settlers and the Navajos.

After a systematic takeover of the territory, the Americans found themselves in charge of this land that simmered with ancient and intimate hostility. It was a place, they would find, where imported ideas simply didn't apply. As one of the early territorial governors would say a little more than thirty years after the American invasion, "Every calculation based on experience elsewhere fails in New Mexico."

This truth, I would later discover when I ventured into local politics, is borne out in modern New Mexico too—and nowhere more so than in the heart of Navajo country.

In one significant way, the Mexican–American War decidedly tipped the ongoing conflict between the Navajos and the Spanish settlers in favor of the settlers. After the settlers submitted to the Americans and became citizens of the United States, they incessantly lobbied the American army to protect them from the Navajos while their own livestock and slave raids against the Navajos continued unabated. By some estimates, twenty years after the Americans arrived in New Mexico, as many as a third or more of the Navajo people had been taken as slaves by Spanish settlers.

But it was not just lobbying by the Spanish settlers that made the Navajos the focus of the territorial government once the Americans were firmly in control of the area. The Spanish settlers had surrendered, and both they and the Pueblo Indians of New Mexico were rooted to specific areas of the land. The Navajo people, while firmly attached to their homeland, were mobile within it and defended it aggressively. Compared with the Spanish settlers and the Pueblo Indians, the Navajos posed more of a real threat to the American dream of Manifest Destiny.

The American conquest of New Mexico presented the Navajo people with a confusing new challenge. While the Americans had centralized

Resilient people living a rugged life—four Navajo women with children.
Photo by Tom Mullarky from the Guadagnoli Collection

leadership, that made them no less bewildering to the Navajos—New Mexico was a dumping ground of sorts, as the leadership in Washington, DC deposited a constantly shifting cast of generals and territorial governors. These men rotated through this hardship post hoping that it would lead to better things for them elsewhere. The Americans had one voice, but that voice was always changing.

In contrast, the Navajo people had well-established leadership that wasn't looking to go anywhere else, and their leadership wasn't centralized—the Navajos had many voices, but each of their headmen spoke only for his group or clan and not for the entire tribe. The wild swings in policy by the Americans when one leader moved on and another came in were baffling to the Navajos. The Americans, in turn, were frustrated that no one chief could speak for or assure enforcement of agreements with the entire Navajo tribe.

To my surprise, I learned that the pivotal years of the war on the Navajos—1860 to 1865—coincided almost exactly with the years of the American Civil War. I had assumed that any military resources available to the Union would have been needed east of the Mississippi during the war.

Yet the summer of 1860, just before Lincoln was elected president and South Carolina became the first state to secede from the Union, the horses of a Navajo headman named Manuelito grazed on the pastures of

Navajo headman Manuelito was
one the last Navajo leaders to
surrender. *C. M. Bell, circa 1870s,
Library of Congress, LC-USZ62-119662*

Fort Defiance in what is now northeastern Arizona, about thirty miles
from Gallup. The fort's pastures were off-limits to the Navajos but there
were no fences to keep Manuelito's horses out. Mounted soldiers shot
the horses and events began to spiral. Then Manuelito staged a raid,
largely unsuccessful, on the U.S. horse herd at the fort. Manuelito and
his father-in-law, another headman, Barboncito, attacked Fort Defiance
two hours before sunrise. A thousand warriors dealt a severe blow to the
fort before they had to retreat when the troops formed rows and began
steady musket fire on them. When Colonel Edward Canby arrived with
reinforcements, Manuelito and Barboncito drew back into the nearby
Chuska Mountains. In the months that followed, Canby scoured the
Chuskas for the attackers without success, but in forcing the Navajos to
run, he had limited their ability to raise crops and livestock.

In January 1861, a month before the Confederacy was formed and
Jefferson Davis elected as its president, Manuelito, Barboncito, several
other Navajo headmen, and Canby met at Bear Springs or Fort Fauntleroy, fifteen miles east of what is now Gallup, and signed a peace treaty.
Around this time many U.S. soldiers were deserting to fight for the Confederacy. Among those who left was Colonel Thomas Fauntleroy, for
whom the fort had been named and whose departure prompted it to

later be renamed Fort Wingate. Fort Wingate is now a small community that includes a Bureau of Indian Education school, a mobile home park, several churches, a small convenience store, and many dilapidated barracks and buildings.

The months following the signing of the peace treaty were a lull before two gathering storms: New Mexico's unique chapter in the Civil War and the all-out war on the Navajos.

During this brief peace, conflict was never far beneath the surface of relations between the Americans and the Navajo people. Navajos began to come to the forts to trade and drink. The troops began to dispense supplies of meat and flour to Navajos from the gates of the forts on ration days. Some Navajo women became prostitutes and some Navajo men became spies and guides for the U.S. troops. Ration day was festive at Fort Fauntleroy—an air of good feeling was accompanied by food, alcohol, horse races, and betting between the Navajos and the troops.

In September 1861 in the final horse race of a series—after many troops and Navajos had been drinking for hours—a Navajo horse and rider veered completely off course and the U.S. rider won. When the Navajo rider inspected his horse, he discovered that a bridle strap had been slashed. The Navajos claimed sabotage and demanded a rematch. The soldiers refused. The troops collected their wagers and began parading around the grounds flaunting their victory. Most of the Navajos thought they should cut their losses and go home, but one firebrand fueled by alcohol, like the soldiers, stormed the fort's gate to hurl threats and demand the return of the Navajo's bets.

A guard fired a shot when the Navajo tried to force entry. The fort's commanding officer ordered the artillery sergeant to bring out the howitzers and open fire. A massacre ensued. Fifteen Navajos, mostly women and children, were killed and more were wounded. Afterward, there were no more horse races at Fort Wingate and whatever tentative peace that had existed was irrevocably ended. The Navajos were thrust into what they called the "fearing time."

Before things got worse for the Navajos, a respite occurred when Confederate cavalry from Texas invaded New Mexico. These Tejanos fought their way up the Rio Grande Valley forcing Union troops, led by Canby and Kit Carson to retreat north of Santa Fe and join with a contingent of Coloradans who were itching to join the fight on the Union side. Just

Navajo horsemen racing an approaching storm. *Photo by Tom Mullarky from the Guadagnoli Collection*

east of Santa Fe near Glorieta Pass in the Sangre de Christo Mountains, in a pivotal battle that would become known as the Gettysburg of the West, a group of Coloradans guided by a New Mexico volunteer staged a flanking maneuver and came across the poorly guarded Confederate supply train. The Coloradans torched eighty supply wagons and systematically slaughtered more than five hundred Confederate horses and mules, leaving the Tejanos in a foreign, hostile land without support or allies. They had no choice but to ingloriously retreat.

Meanwhile, the Navajos used the U.S. Army's engagement with the Tejanos as an opportunity to press their raids on Spanish settlers. With the Tejano retreat, Canby turned his attention back to the Navajos and began planning a military campaign to push them into a portion of their homeland where they could be confined to a reservation as so many other tribes on the continent had been. But before he could achieve this goal, Canby was promoted to the rank of general and transferred back east to fight in the Civil War. The fate of the Navajo people would take a dramatic turn for the worse.

Canby's replacement was General James Henry Carleton, a complex, remarkable, but delusional man. Carleton had some attributes that had made heroes of other men in the American West. He was strong-willed, intelligent, and ambitious. But he was also a Christian idealist and a perfectionist who was incapable of admitting a mistake or changing his mind. His own soldiers described him as rigid and peculiar.

During Carleton's first stint in New Mexico, for five years at several forts in the 1850s, he had been generally disdainful of the territory and its people. He'd come to believe that the never-ending Navajo war was the main cause of what he perceived as New Mexico's perpetual state of backwardness. When the Tejanos invaded New Mexico, Carleton marched back from California, where he was then stationed, with 1,500 troops, but he arrived too late and was left to help with mopping up.

Carleton became convinced of two matters that now appear absurd. When he was first stationed in New Mexico, Carleton had become fascinated by an area where a stand of cottonwood trees grew along the Pecos River on the territory's eastern plains. The place was called Bosque Redondo or "round forest." On my trips to eastern New Mexico as a kid, nothing about that landscape appealed to me, and I felt sorry for my cousins who lived there. To Carleton, it was an idyllic place for "true civilization" to grow.

Carleton was convinced that the solution to the "Navajo problem" was to move the entire Navajo tribe to Bosque Redondo where they would, he thought, become Christian farmers. And he was certain that once the Navajos were gone, their homeland would offer up a wealth of gold and precious metals to an influx of prospectors like those he had witnessed in California.

When Canby was promoted and reassigned back East in the summer of 1862, Carleton was named the military commander of New Mexico. He moved to Santa Fe where he exercised absolute rule over the territory for the next four years. During those years, if an idea became fixed in Carleton's mind, for better or worse, it became an indisputable reality for the people of New Mexico.

How much of Western history's worst episodes can be attributed to the insecurities of men of hubris? Carleton was not a West Point graduate as were many of his peers, and he'd made it his life's calling to catch up with his more well-connected colleagues. Solving the "Navajo problem" in New Mexico would, he thought, finally bring him the recognition that had eluded him.

Carleton ordered Christopher "Kit" Carson, an army colonel to Fort Wingate to prepare for war on the Navajos. In the months preceding the order, Carson led a successful campaign against the Mescalero Apaches, during which he soured on Carleton's shoot-on-sight orders. Carson, five-foot-six and illiterate, was an iconic figure in the west—a fur trapper, wilderness guide, and Indian agent—who was known to the Navajos as Rope Thrower. Carson resigned from the U.S. Army, on February 3, 1863, rather than follow Carleton's order; he had joined the army to fight Confederates, not the Navajos.

For reasons unknown, Carson, whose resignation Carleton refused to accept, later relented, and in the summer of 1863, as the battle of Gettysburg was being fought in the east, he headed west with 1,000 men toward the canyons, mesas, and mountains of the vast, rugged Navajo homeland—an area 250 miles east to west and 150 miles south to north. Together with other U.S. Army officers, he led a force that included New Mexico volunteers and Ute warriors, hereditary enemies of the Navajos. Carson knew the area well; he had gained information about the strongholds in Dinétah from Navajos who had shared information with him over the years that he would now inevitably use against them.

Kit Carson was a fur trapper, wilderness guide, and Indian fighter.
Courtesy Palace of the Governors (MNM/DCA), Neg. No. 007151

Carson had no intention of chasing Navajo warriors around their vast homeland as Canby had done two years earlier after the battle at Fort Defiance. Instead, he employed a scorched-earth strategy designed to deprive the Navajos of the resources they needed to sustain life in a harsh land. When Carson's forces came upon an empty Navajo settlement, they destroyed hogans, burned crops, and killed or captured livestock. Carson's Ute warriors guarded water holes and salt sources. Because I grew up on the fringes of the Navajo homeland, witnessing both its ruggedness and fragility, it was obvious to me years later as I read of Carson's exploits that his military strategy was ruthless, cruel, and certain to succeed.

The Navajo campaign was a war of attrition, fought without decisive or major battles. Amazingly, it resulted in only one U.S. casualty during its entirety. The same could not be said for the Navajo side.

Carleton progressively turned up the pressure as he micromanaged the campaign from a distance in Santa Fe. He sent out regular missives to Carson and demanded that Carson, despite his illiteracy, respond in kind through the assistance of an aide. In October, two Navajos appeared at Fort Wingate with a truce flag. They brought an offer to build hogans near Fort Wingate under the eyes of the soldiers and to send a group of chiefs to Santa Fe to sue for peace. Carleton was undeterred; the Navajo people, he said, had to leave their homeland and go to Bosque Redondo or face continuing war.

By December, after months of being deprived of food and shelter, the Navajos' condition was desperate. But Carleton pressed on; he ordered Carson to attack the heart of the Navajos' homeland, Canyon de Chelly—a place of stunning, almost mystical beauty, and a place that would come to hold a special significance to me. When I read about the account—about 150 years after it happened—of the conquest of the Navajos at this place through military force, it seemed to me the equivalent of cutting a beating heart out of a living creature.

The Navajos had been on the run for six months without the shelter of home and facing the relentless destruction of their food sources. When the Navajos mounted an attack on a U.S. pack herd carrying supplies, Carson sought a delay in the attack on Canyon de Chelly. Carleton would have none of it. He ordered Carson to attack without delay. In freezing cold with six inches of snow on the ground, Carson followed orders and sent one part of his force into the canyon from the east. He then led the remainder of his forces to the canyon's western end. Inside the canyon, Carson's troops continued to destroy hogans, food caches, and livestock and in a crushing blow to the spirit of the Navajo people, they destroyed a 5,000-tree peach orchard that dated back to the time of the first Spaniards in the Southwest.

Skirmishes erupted, but for the most part the Navajos continued to evade Carson's troops. Three hundred found safety on top of Fortress Rock, deep in the canyon, but in the end Carson's troops swept Canyon

Kit Carson (lower center) and James Carelton (lower right): The reluctant field commander and the unyielding architect of the war on the Navajos. *Courtesy Palace of the Governors (MNM/DCA), Neg. No. 009826*

Canyon de Chelly, the heart of
the Navajo Nation, shown from
above. *Courtesy of Chris Dahl-
Bredine*

de Chelly, destroying everything that could not be hidden. There were
now few places in the Navajo homeland that were safe, and there were
several more brutal months of winter to come without food. During the
course of the Canyon de Chelly attack, the first major surrender of sixty
Navajos took place. It was the beginning of a flood. Over the course of
the winter in early 1864, starving Navajos began surrendering in waves
at Fort Defiance and Fort Wingate. By March 3, eight hundred Navajos
had surrendered. Now began the tribe's Long Walk to Carleton's chosen
relocation point in Bosque Redondo.

The Long Walk was not one mass movement of Navajo people, as I had
always thought, but a series of unremitting marches by clusters of Navajos
who started out in a state of utter exhaustion and malnutrition. It's estimated
that eventually 9,000 Navajos would start the Long Walk and five hundred
would die along the way. An unknown number of Navajos never made the
walk, finding shelter instead in strongholds like the Chuska Mountains and
the remote western region of Dinétah near Navajo Mountain.

Navajo captives at Bosque Redondo, or Hwéeldi, a place of suffering.
Courtesy Palace of the Governors (MNM/DCA), Neg. No. 038191

Carleton appeared to genuinely believe in his plan and did everything in his power to make his social experiment at Bosque Redondo a success. But after the first few promising months, when the Navajos dug irrigation ditches and the first plantings began to thrive, it was simply not to be. What followed seems in retrospect like a series of Old Testament plagues.

Within the first year the entire "round forest" of cottonwood trees that had drawn Carleton's attention to the area in the first place was consumed in the construction of nearby Fort Sumner. This left no timber for hogans. Then Navajos contracted severe dysentery from the slow-moving Pecos River, their only water source. Syphilis broke out among the Navajos and the soldiers. Comanches raided the unarmed Navajos. In the final blow, cut worms, not common in the West, destroyed an entire 3,000-acre crop that all parties had pinned their hopes on.

To the Navajo people, Bosque Redondo became known as Hwéeldi or "place of suffering." To Americans, it became an ordinance facility to which scarce provisions had to be continually shipped. A project that had originally been envisioned as being self-sufficient had become a bottomless money pit.

In succeeding years there was more of the same: scurvy, measles, floods, hailstorms, and more crop failures. By 1865—the year Robert E. Lee surrendered at Appomattox, President Lincoln was assassinated, and

Navajo captives under guard at Bosque Redondo suffered scurvy, measles, floods, hailstorms, syphilis, and crop failures. *Wikimedia Commons*

the Thirteenth Amendment abolishing slavery was passed by Congress and then ratified by the states—Carleton's social experiment at Bosque Redondo was recognized as a failure. Facing open criticism by New Mexicans about the conditions at Bosque Redondo, General Carleton was removed from his post in September 1866 and ordered to report to duty in Louisiana. The *Santa Fe New Mexican* rejoiced, "It appears that our territory will be free from the presence of this man Carleton who has lorded it amongst us."

The new superintendent at Bosque Redondo said, "Would any sensible man select a spot for a reservation for 8,000 Indians where the water is scarcely bearable, where the soil is poor and cold and where the mesquite roots twelve miles distant are the only wood for the Indians to use?" Still it would be another two years while the post-Civil War wheels of bureaucracy turned before the Navajo people were allowed to leave the Place of Suffering.

The task of negotiating a treaty with the 7,304 surviving Navajos fell to General William Tecumseh Sherman, no stranger to scorched-earth military campaigns. He led "Sherman's March to the sea," a 300-mile Civil War march through Georgia, from Atlanta to Savannah, which left a sixty-mile-wide swath of destruction.

Indian commissary and Company Quarters, Fort Sumner, New Mexico, near Bosque Redondo. *Courtesy Palace of the Governors (MNM/DCA). Neg. No. 001815*

What Sherman found in Bosque Redondo appalled even him. "I found the bosque a mere spot of green grass in the midst of a wild desert," he wrote, "and that the Navajos had sunk into a condition of absolute poverty and despair."

On May 28, 1868, Sherman offered the Navajos a historic choice: He would transport them to watered, well-timbered, game-rich land in the Arkansas River Valley of Oklahoma in Indian Territory, land set aside for Native Americans, or he would allow them to return to a reduced version of their homeland.

Barboncito replied for his people. He told Sherman that the Navajos wanted to return to their homeland, not move to Oklahoma. "When the Navajos were first created," he said, "four sacred mountains and four rivers were pointed out to us, inside of which we should live, and that was to be Dinétah. Changing Woman gave us this land. Our God created this land specially for us."

The next day the Navajos at Bosque Redondo unanimously voted to return to their homeland. A reservation map was drawn up that included far less land than their original homeland and not one of the four sacred mountains—Mount Blanca to the east, Mount Taylor to the south, the San Francisco Peaks to the west, and Hesperus Mountain to the north. But it was an extensive domain, almost the size of Ohio. Barboncito accepted, saying, "It is the very heart of our country."

On June 1, 1868, a treaty was signed that promised the Navajo people tools, seed, three sheep per family, and one teacher for every thirty children. During the reading and translation of the treaty an extended discussion took place about the return of Navajo captives held as slaves by New Mexicans. When asked how many Navajos had been taken by and were living with Spanish settlers, Barboncito replied, "Over half the tribe."

Sherman offered some promises that were not, however, incorporated into the language of the Treaty, according to the written record of the negotiations. "We will do all we can to have your children returned to you," he said. "Our government is determined that the enslavement of the Navajos will cease and those guilty of holding them in slavery shall be punished."

Within two weeks the Navajos were assembled and prepared to walk back to Dinétah—roughly 2,000 fewer than the original number had survived the Long Walk and the years at Bosque Redondo. Their column was escorted by four companies of cavalry and as it left Hwéeldi, the convoy stretched for ten miles. On July 5, the Navajos marched through Albuquerque, forded the Rio Grande, and climbed the nine-mile escarpment that rises from the western bank of the Rio Grande.

As the returning Navajos crested the rise, Mount Taylor, or Tsoodził, the Navajos' sacred mountain of the south came into view. With their land now in sight, many of the Navajo survivors fell to their knees and cried tears of joy and sorrow.

They were home.

CHAPTER **TWO**

Coal: A Long Silent Pause

In the oval commons at the University of New Mexico law school, two of my classmates are talking in low, hushed tones, assuming I am too preoccupied to hear them. Not far from us, two other classmates are playing a boisterous game of Ping-Pong. The commons surround a circular classroom outside of which I am snuggled down in a large leather chair reading my Business Associations textbook and taking notes.

"What is Bob doing? Why is he moving to Gallup?" says one.

"I don't know," the other replies. "Gallup's the armpit of New Mexico."

As I secretly listen, I'm more amused than offended. In fact, I'm not offended at all. While I'm insecure about many things, my plan to move to Gallup after graduation from law school isn't one of them. It's one of the things I feel real peace and certainty about.

Growing up in Farmington, I sensed that there was an established order to things. If I stayed there, I would succeed up to a point but not beyond. My prospective life there or in Albuquerque, I felt, would be largely preordained and it wouldn't matter how much or how little effort I put into it. Gallup felt entirely different to me. Everything there seemed both possible and precariously uncertain and up for grabs. And I liked the idea of that.

Gallup represented the one facet of my future that offered excitement and adventure at a time when I was otherwise making time-to-settle-down decisions and readying myself for my adult life. Over the course of law school, I had fallen in love with a classmate who seemed flattered that I was smitten and gave me flirtatiously mixed messages. But it became clear that, at best, I was only third or fourth on her list. This had mired me in a deep depression that in the close confines of law school was retriggered every day.

Midway through my third year, another classmate took pity on me and set me up on a blind date. Thirty-five days later, I was engaged, and soon thereafter bought a gray, four-door family-man Ford Granada to replace my beloved ragtop CJ5 Jeep.

My fiancée, Beth, is a legal assistant in a downtown law firm who grew up in Tulsa and went to college in Oklahoma. She is from a Republican, Catholic family; I'm from a Democratic, Protestant family.

Like me, she's a responsible rule follower who is rebounding from another relationship. She tells me that she had a boyfriend at Oklahoma State who was fun loving and liberal and who drew her out. But it didn't last. I ask her why not. "My father didn't like him," she says. Both of us are encased in protective shells and neither of us draws the other out, but we're both responsible, socially acceptable to our families, ready to be married, and eager to escape failed loves.

Beth, like my openly disapproving law school friends and parents and sisters, has doubts about the move to Gallup. But I'm resolved and energized by the prospect. In contrast to most of my decisions at that time, which are primarily products of my analytical mind, the move to Gallup seems firmly rooted in my chest.

Newly married in the spring of 1979, my wife and I load our overnight bags into the gray Granada and head for Gallup to spend the weekend with my future bosses—two well-connected, up-and-coming young lawyers—to plan our move to Gallup in the fall.

Leaving Albuquerque, we cross the reflective mirror of the Rio Grande and its gentle gorge, which is lush with cottonwood trees. We start the long climb west of the river.

As we crest Nine Mile Hill, the view is immense, almost too much to fully take in. Horizontally striated mesas, each a different size and shape, are randomly dotted with dark green junipers and cedars. There is no hint of water anywhere. Though stunningly beautiful, the landscape appears uninhabitable.

Sixty miles distant, Mount Taylor, an ancient volcano, looms on the horizon. A sloping pyramid rising above the tabletops, the mountain is dark in contrast with the tan- and rust-colored mesas.

Foreign words appear on the highway signs as we approach Taylor: Canoncito, Mesita, Laguna, Acoma, and Cubero. Route 66 billboards shill for tourists, promising jackalopes, moccasins, pecan rolls, fireworks, pottery, and coonskin caps.

As we near Taylor, the surrounding mesas are bigger and closer. On flanks near the road, there are huge boulders—some the size of a small house—and the tops of the mesas are capped by a layer of black lava. The roadway enters a canyon where it's choked by a twenty-foot-high, torturous lava bed that, other than the highway blasted through it, seems impervious to human travel.

At one point amidst the lava beds we glimpse a stand of cattails and a slow-moving, narrow stream about the size of a small irrigation ditch— the only water we'll see on the two-hour drive. My wife is subdued and quietly observant.

Mount Taylor now towers above us on the right, revealing several summits that are entirely forested except for the southwest flank of the main summit that's swept bare of trees by prevailing winds and covered in snow.

Beyond Mount Taylor, as we enter the Navajos' ancestral homeland, the landscape shifts. For the next sixty miles, green forested slopes rise to the south to form the Zuni Mountains. To the north, a series of detached, separate mesas soon combine into a continuous line of rust-red cliffs.

Twenty-five miles from Gallup, we cross the Continental Divide and begin to see the intrusions of American industry onto the landscape. A refinery obtrudes on our right as we descend from the divide, and soon on our left, munition igloos sprawl in repetitive patterns across the earth at Fort Wingate Army Depot, where 115 years earlier Navajos were gunned down after the contested horse race. Another refinery appears on the right, improbably located in front of the most beautiful section of red rock cliffs, a pair of vertical sandstone spires, and a pyramid-shaped peak.

An irregular, jagged sandstone monocline, or hogback, rises as a barrier before us. A huge V has been blasted out of the hogback and appears

The Red Rocks—Pyramid Rock and Church Rock prior to Route 66, I-40, and the refinery. *Courtesy Palace of the Governors (MNM/DCA), Neg. No. 088274*

to be the future course of the interstate, but signage diverts us onto old Route 66 and we pass through a narrow, naturally formed gap.

Over the 140 miles on the interstate, we've traveled continuously through landscapes with vistas extending up to thirty miles. Now as we enter Gallup, that changes. The extended vistas are gone and the land-scape closes in, becoming more immediate, more urgent.

The two young lawyers I will be working with, Tim and Jay, gradu-ated three years earlier from UNM and have taken over the practice of an old-time Gallup lawyer who passed away. Beth and I meet them and their wives at Jay's house. While the women go on a separate tour of the town, the three of us lawyers head to lunch at the Eagle Cafe in downtown Gallup. One block west of the café's location, I would later learn, was the place where Larry Casuses's body was dragged out onto the sidewalk to lie in a pool of blood.

On Route 66, in downtown Gallup, all the stores face north toward the railroad tracks and the swath of leveled land that is to become a sec-tion of I-40. Old-timers call the two blocks between First and Third Street "Front Street." Because there are no south-facing buildings, Front Street looks like a man-made cliff. Large, gaudy signs form a visual cacoph-ony that blares: HANDCRAFTED INDIAN JEWELRY, GENUINE NATIVE ARTS AND CRAFTS, POTTERY, KACHINAS, CASH

PAWN, DEALERS WELCOME. Signs shout in triplicate: NAVAJO, HOPI, ZUNI, and WHOLESALE, RETAIL, JOBBER.

Two Native men weave down the sidewalk in dirty Levis with shirt-tails splayed. Mud-splattered pickup trucks stream by large plate-glass windows framed by retracted wrought-iron security gates. The faded words "Kitchen's Opera House" are visible above a western-wear store. In the restaurant, Tim, Jay, and I are seated near a family of traditionally dressed Navajos. When the Japanese waitress arrives to take their order, I hear the familiar sound of the Navajo language as the customers place their order.

Throughout the weekend, as Tim and Jay talk about their cases, their clients, and the community, I'm jealous. It's clear that through their lives as lawyers in this town of 20,000 people, they have immersed themselves in the community. And I'm eager to do the same.

Gallup seems to be a unique place with a mix of people that, to my limited knowledge, is not replicated elsewhere in America. Although Gallup epitomizes New Mexico's tri-cultural heritage—Hispanic, Native, and Anglo—it's much more than that. For one thing, *Anglo* isn't exactly the right word. Many whites in Gallup, I will learn, are from Southern and

The West 200 block of Railroad Avenue in Gallup's early days. The avenue was later known as either Front Street or Route 66. *Courtesy of Octavia Fellin Public Library, Gallup, New Mexico*

When first built in 1895, Kitchen's Opera House was one of best and largest buildings in New Mexico. *Courtesy of the Octavia Fellin Public Library, Gallup, New Mexico*

Eastern Europe, not England. They're descendants of Slavs, Italians, and Greeks who immigrated to Gallup to mine coal and harvest timber in the Zuni Mountains in the late 1800s and early 1900s and who later started lumber yards, restaurants, insurance companies, and grocery stores. And the diversity of Gallup doesn't end with the three main cultures. There's also small numbers of Chinese, Japanese, and African Americans, as well as Arabs and East Indians.

Later, toward the end of a full day, Tim, Jay, and I drive a few miles north of Gallup and turn off onto a rough, rutted dirt road that takes us through a canyon and then up to a high rounded mesa covered with cedars, junipers, and piñons, a spot that affords a 360-degree view of the rugged landscape surrounding the town.

On the drive up, black coal, red dog gravel, and gray tailings piles are strewn alongside the road, together with the bleached stone, steel, and timber bones of long-abandoned underground coal mines.

The canyon we are driving up is named for the Gibson mines that operated for twenty years in the early 1900s until an underground fire shut down the last mine. The Gibson mines were only four of the 147

Navajo women take in the Red Rocks west of Gallup near the Arizona state line. *Photo by Tom Mullarky from the Guadagnoli Collection*

underground mines in the Gallup area, all of which are now abandoned.

We drive above the vestiges of the coal mines up to the outlook. The serrated sandstone hogback to the east and a two-tiered set of high, green-topped mesas just beyond draws my gaze. Due south, Route 66 is humming with activity. A bulldozed, barren strip of land, one of the few remaining uncompleted sections of I-40, parallels 66. Long freight trains periodically trumpet as they lumber through the valley between the two great roads. The city of Gallup spreads and melds into the contours of the land below us to the south.

Tim is a descendant of one of two prominent Gallup families that bought up 26,000 acres—forty square miles—of land from the Gallup American Coal Company in a private auction after World War II. The extended, and now increasingly fractious families formed a limited partnership. By the late '70s, the partnership group has grown to number thirty or forty people, who hold ownership interests that varies among them in percentage.

"This is like Bonanza," Jay says to Tim. "You own everything for as far as the eye can see."

"Well, maybe 1 percent of everything we can see," says Tim and they laugh.

My gaze settles on a 250-yard gap in the hogback where Route 66, a double set of train tracks, and a deep arroyo mark the best pathway for transcontinental travel for hundreds of miles either north or south of Gallup. The west-facing hogback is beginning to light up with a reddish glow as the sun nears the horizon.

I'm struck by the way successive generations in Gallup have each sought to make their mark in this place and on this vast landscape, much as I am now doing in my small way, starting my law practice and married life here. How did the men who left the mining remnants live, and what hardships did they endure? What legacy did they wish to leave?

Joe Esparza is one of the first people I meet after I move to Gallup. He is the youngest son of a Mexican coal miner, who witnessed the toll that underground coal mining in Gallup took on the early miners. Joe and I hit it off quickly. He is about twenty years older than I and working as a project manager for a local Catholic non-profit organization that provides housing, food, and tuition assistance to Indian people in the Gallup area. Joe's office is one block north of mine, and I first meet him in a small nearby restaurant.

Joe likes to tease me. His boss is my age and he's always telling me that the younger people like me don't appreciate the need for hard work, organization and discipline. I'm the surrogate Joe gets to say things to that he can't say to his boss. He always wears a coat and tie, and he carries black, blue, and red pens neatly arranged in his shirt pocket. I tease back, telling Joe that his attire is woefully inadequate and slovenly because he doesn't have a green pen in his collection. I buy Joe a green pen that he adds to his arsenal, and every time we see each other I make a comment about it that triggers our next round of banter.

Joe invites me to his house on a Sunday afternoon. As we're sitting at the dining-room table with Joe's wife Betty and their family, I ask Joe what is was like to grow up in Gallup.

Joe tells me he grew up near the Gibson mine—the mine I drove past with Tim and Jay. He tells me he was four years old when his family moved from Gibson into Gallup, and that he can still remember a row of houses and a general store owned by the mining company up on a hill.

Joe says that his father was thirty-three when he first came to the United States and landed in Morenci, Arizona. After working in the mines in Morenci, Joe's parents went back to Mexico, had several more kids there, and then came back to the United States and to Gallup. Joe was the youngest of fourteen children.

"They never spoke English," says Joe. "My dad could understand English a little bit and he could write his name, but he never spoke English. My mom and dad suffered."

Joe pauses for a long time and his family is silent and motionless. "How would you say it?" Joe says. "They didn't starve to death, but they went without eating so that my brothers and sisters would have something to eat when they were traveling. How my dad did it is beyond me. His brother died in the mines and my dad took on the responsibility for his family. He would also send money to Mexico to families down there. He supported three families on his meager wages at the mines."

Joe Esparza's father, Luis, (second from left) and mother, Maria, (fourth from left) and the four oldest of the fourteen Esparza children. *Courtesy of Octavia Fellin Public Library, Gallup, New Mexico*

"They had nothing, Joe's mom and dad," Betty adds. "Speaking no English. It's amazing and yet they managed to help other families. Joe and I sit here, and I say, 'Joe, how did they do it? How in the world did they do it?' I don't know."

Joe describes visiting his father in the hospital after he was hurt in a mine when Joe was small. His father's foot was discolored and shiny, elevated, and held in place by cables. The black lung didn't show up until later.

Betty says two of her extended relatives died in the mines. Betty's father was injured in a mine and she describes her father sitting on a couch with a hurt leg, and how he used to limp. Sitting at the Esparzas' table in their modest and cozy home it's hard to imagine that Joe and Betty were so closely tied, through family, to such danger and harm.

After my conversation with Joe and Betty, when I have a chance, I start asking Gallup's old-time Slavs, Italians, and Mexicans what the mines were like. Many of the successful people I know in town are descendants of immigrant miners; like the Esparzas, they also talk about the danger and hardship of underground coal mining and the sacrifices made by their coal-mining parents and grandparents.

And as it was with the Esparza family's story, there is a point during each conversation when a long, silent pause occurs. Because of these conversations, I come to regard the mining areas strewn with tailings piles, timber, steel, and brick to be hallowed ground—just as much as Hwéeldi.

The first mines in the Gallup coal field broke ground in 1880, one year before the Atlantic and Pacific Railroad arrived, and the sequence of the mines' development wasn't a coincidence.

Coal deposits underlie about one-fifth of New Mexico, but Gallup is one of the few places where deposits coincide with the route of a rail line. The coal in the Gallup field was found in the Mesa Verde Group and ranked from subbituminous B to high-volatile bituminous B, a middle grade of coal below anthracite in quality. Coal seams in Gallup generally range from three-and-a-half to seven feet in thickness.

When coal deposits are located near a railroad, the mines and the railroad feed on each other and create a cycle of mutual benefit. After the

The early Gallup railroad depot. When coal mines were located near a rail-road, they combined to create a cycle of mutual economic benefit. *Courtesy of Octavia Fellin Public Library, Gallup, New Mexico*

Early Gallup as viewed from the north. *Courtesy of Octavia Fellin Public Library, Gallup, New Mexico*

Civil War, former soldiers with mining backgrounds were sent to scout for coal along the proposed rail line through the gap in the hogback just east of what is now Gallup. The coal found there provided fuel to propel the railroad's engines and became a sizeable portion of the railroad's freight.

David Gallup (right) was the local railroad paymaster. On paydays, railroaders would "go to Gallup." *Courtesy of Octavia Fellin Public Library, Special Collections and Archives, Gallup, New Mexico*

The Gallup field was the westernmost source of coal on the A&P line, which served a potentially huge market for coal on the Pacific coast.

Gallup, in fact, was named after the railroad paymaster David L. Gallup, a native of Mystic, Connecticut. On paydays, railroad employees would "go to Gallup," and so named the town. David Gallup, whose family tree includes poet Emily Dickinson, both Presidents George H.W. and George W. Bush, and George H. Gallup, the founder of the Gallup poll, didn't live long in the area. He moved back East to work as a controller for the Santa Fe Railway and became a well-known figure in the New York financial district.

Beth and I find a small two-bedroom house on a hill just south of Route 66. Once we move to Gallup, as I drive to work every day I take in a panoramic view of the mesas to the north, where the first coal mines were located. In the valley below, trains rumble through, paralleling the stream of cars, trucks, and semis on I-40.

In 1880, fortune seeker Thomas Dye found what he was looking for on one of Gallup's north-side mesas—a south facing slope that exposed two thick coal seams. Dye broke ground for the town's first coal mine, sold coal to the railroad for two or three years, and opened a saloon in town.

Dye, who reportedly killed both his mother-in-law and sister-in-law and claimed their deaths were accidental, brazenly sold liquor to Indians in violation of federal law, and eventually the U.S. Cavalry surrounded his saloon and arrested him. He was found guilty of violating liquor laws and sentenced to four years in the penitentiary.

Dye's saloon was one of many. In 1911 there were twenty-two bars in Gallup, serving a population of only 4,000 people. Alcohol, gambling, and prostitution helped coal-mining immigrants blow off steam, but the abuses, particularly of alcohol, posed a problem to the Navajos, whose homeland surrounded Gallup at the time of the first coal mine. The Navajo people were only sixteen years removed from their starved surrender to Kit Carson's troops and twelve years from their walk back from Bosque Redondo after their four-year imprisonment. The still-fragile survivors were not equipped to handle the frontier town excesses, and some folks in Gallup, like Dye, were eager to profit from their vulnerability.

When I move to Gallup there's still an overabundance of bars, but their customer base is markedly different. The bars, particularly those in Gallup's downtown where I go to work, are filled almost entirely with Native people rather than immigrant coal miners and railroaders.

Back in 1880 when the railroad arrived, production in the Gallup coal field exploded. The influx of men, money, and equipment was staggering. In 1882, 220 miners produced 33,373 tons of coal. Three years later, in 1885, 700 produced 97,755 tons of coal. By 1888, 300,000 tons of coal were produced. From 1900 to 1910, coal production averaged 500,000 to 600,000 tons per year. The numbers tell me how frenetically busy Gallup must have been in those early days.

I'm not surprised to learn that very few Navajos worked in the underground mines given that their creation story says they emerged from a world below and I assume they would not want to return.

Underground coal mining was a job for immigrants, and they came to Gallup in successive waves. First northern Europeans arrived: Englishmen, Scotsmen, Irishmen, Germans, and Austrians. Then came eastern and southern Europeans: Slavs, Italians, and Greeks. Then Mexicans. The descendants of those immigrants, I found as I started meeting clients in my new office, remain the bedrock of the community. One of my first clients was a Greek man in a business dispute who startled me with his tenacity. He was determined to fight with a former business partner over $170, far

Five Japanese miners and a small Japanese boy (Edward Shibata) with the Navajo Mine foreman, superintendent, and doctor in the 1910s. *Courtesy of Octavia Fellin Public Library, Gallup, New Mexico*

less than the legal fees he would incur in the dispute. It took every ounce of persuasion I could muster to convince him to grudgingly settle the dispute.

During the winter months, the miners would only see the sun briefly before going down into the dark timber-framed shafts, or later as they emerged after a ten- or eleven-hour day. Once down in the underground slopes, the miners would load their coal car and place a marker on it. A mule would haul it up toward the surface and trapper boys worked as traffic cops to keep the mine cars moving steadily. Shot lighters placed dynamite charges into the coal seams at night to give explosive coal dust and gases time to settle before the miners returned in the morning. Once a tunnel reached 100 feet in length, ash or ground gypsum was blown into the newly excavated area to settle dust and reduce the chance of explosions or fires.

Some of the mines grew to great size. The shaft for the Gamerco mine just northwest of Gallup was 800 feet below ground. There were thirty miles of mine track and underground lights. Two hundred mules spent their lives underground pulling cars up to the hoist. Underground barns for the mules were constructed at every level of the mine.

Only remnants of these mines remain when I arrive in Gallup in fall

In the year 1919 alone, there were twenty fatalities in Gallup area mines.
Photo by Tom Mullarky from the Guadagnoli Collection

1979. Frequently after work I drive north out of Gallup, turn off the highway about a mile south of Gamerco, stop by the flea market, then run up the Gibson Canyon road to the north-side overlook. As I run back down, a huge concrete smokestack and mounds of red dog gravel excavated from the Gamerco mine shafts dominate the western view.

Danger and death were a constant in the lives of Gallup coal miners. The coal mine fatality tables prepared by the state of New Mexico reported twenty-six deaths during the twenty-three-year lifespan of the Gibson mine alone. I read that men with names like Applegarth, Tetshai, Visconti, Rodriquez, Petrovich, Rocco, Mynovich, Garcia, and Micholetti fill a column of coal mining fatalities. A parallel column lists causes of death: dust explosion, blast from an adjoining room, fall of rock, fall under a mine cart, asphyxiated by a mine fire, struck by derailed mine carts, and struck by locomotive.

In the year 1919 alone, there were twenty fatalities in Gallup-area mines. And there was always the fear that something even worse might happen. A number of miners from the Raton field in northeast New Mexico moved to Gallup, telling stories of the explosions in 1913 that killed 261 men and another explosion in 1923 that killed another 120.

Underground coal seams in Gallup generally ranged from three-and-a-half to seven feet in thickness. *Photo by Tom Mullarky from the Guadagnoli Collection*

The fifty-five-year era of underground coal mining in Gallup was volatile and tumultuous. The physical danger was an ever-present threat, and there was also a contentious human element between the coal companies and the miners, between the different ethnic groups, and between strikers and scabs. During one of the first real estate transactions I negotiated as a lawyer, a middle-aged Hispanic man involved in the deal mentioned that his grandfather once used the word *Bolshevik* while telling him about a coal strike in the 1930s. His reference to Bolsheviks startled me. Over ten years would pass before I understood it.

One of the first reported strikes at a Gallup mine occurred in 1891 and caused a decline in production; in 1901 a strike shut down the Gibson mine for fifty days. During good years, the number and size of mines in the Gallup field allowed miners to move from mine to mine if they wanted to, but the coal market was volatile. Demand fluctuated sharply during the World War I years, then slumped severely after the war. After WWI, many European miners quit and were replaced by untrained Mexican workers or by mining machines.

Given its proximity to coal fields and the railroad, and the blast of economic energy the combination generated, Gallup offered business opportunities for European and Asian coal miners, some of whom were eager to escape the dangers of the coal-mining jobs that brought them to America. Money and opportunity were abundant and commercial competition was fierce. Immigrant coal miners brought the customs and heritage of their home countries with them—and an ethic characterized by thrift, hard work and a burning desire to advance, which spurred them to start businesses for themselves. Outsiders who observed Gallup in the era of the underground coal mines described business and professional men battling and scheming in a life-and-death struggle over money and property.

At the time, Gallup overwhelmed Navajos. Shortly after enactment of the U.S. Constitution, federal laws were passed that banned the sale of liquor to Indians and it remained illegal until 1953, when Indian veterans who served in WWII began pushing for equal rights.

But while it was illegal to serve alcohol to Indians in Gallup's early days, bootlegging to Navajos was common and lucrative. After I met with a Gallup old-timer in my office one day, he lingered and told me stories of how many people in Gallup got their start in business by bootlegging alcohol to Navajos. He pointedly didn't mention names.

The Allison Coal camp in 1915, one of several camps that sprung up west and north of Gallup. *Courtesy Palace of the Governors (MNM/DCA) Neg. No.*

New Mexico National Guardsmen were called in to Gallup in the 1930s following a hasty declaration of martial law by the governor. *Photo by Tom Mullarky from the Guadagnoli Collection*

The money that wasn't taken from Navajos by bootleggers or sharp business practices frequently ended up in the hands of the courts. One prominent Albuquerque lawyer appointed by the governor to investigate business practices in Gallup during the coal-mining era reported that Indians jailed for intoxication were customarily fined the exact amount of money that remained in their possession on their release.

But even as some European and Asian coal miners began looking for a way out of their jobs underground, there was much life—and conflict— yet to play out in the Gallup coal mines.

In April 1917, the Industrial Workers of the World, or IWW union, which had lost a bid to represent the miners in a strike, was accused of plotting to blow up the Gibson and Allison mines, two of the highest producing mines. The governor declared martial law and sent the National Guard into Gallup for six months to oversee the area mines, which were vital to America's World War I effort.

A year earlier, in the pre-dawn darkness of March 9, 1916, the Mexican revolutionary general Pancho Villa led his troops across the U.S.–Mexico border into Columbus, New Mexico, which was then a bustling army outpost and frontier town. Villa's troops torched buildings in Columbus and killed eighteen Americans before suffering a hundred casualties and retreating. Villa's scruffy band of fighters had been waging civil war in Mexico for several years. There had been other cross-border raids but the one on Columbus was the biggest and it provoked President Woodrow Wilson to send 100,000 National Guard troops to protect the border there and to hunt Villa down. A year-long pursuit never found him.

In the midst of this unrest, the Gallup American Coal Company began recruiting miners from Mexico, such as Joe Esparza's father, to break the 1917 strike. The coal company let the Mexican coal miners build adobe homes on a tract of land west of Gallup's downtown but it retained title to the land where the homes were built. The area came to be known as Chihuahuita—"little Chihuahua." Seventeen years later the neighborhood would be the epicenter of a violent conflict between the coal companies and the miners.

In 1918 A. T. Hannett, a lawyer and a Democrat, was elected mayor of Gallup by a twenty-vote margin, and he was reelected in 1920. Hannett's great nephew was one of the best students of my law school class, and after I moved to Gallup, I sought the chance to learn more about the former mayor who was reputed to have sided with the working man and fought the vested interests of his day.

Hannett, who was from New York, arrived at 2:30 in the morning on May 1, 1911; a traveling shoe salesman had told him that there was a great opportunity for a lawyer in Gallup. During his first weeks in town, Hannett went to Kitchen's Opera House to see a prize fight on the second floor. After the fight, he went downstairs for a drink that was interrupted

A. T. Hannett was a Gallup mayor, New Mexico governor, champion of the working man, and author of *Sagebrush Lawyer. Library of Congress, Prints & Photographs Division, LC-DIG-ggbain-30359*

when a "short foreigner" came in with a sawed-off shotgun and blew the head off the man standing near Hannett. The man collapsed like an empty sack and blood and brains flew, causing Hannett to vomit. Hannett decided to make Gallup his home.

I came across Hannett's 1964 memoir, *Sagebrush Lawyer*, not long after landing in town. "Coal miners, lumberjacks, railroad employees, sheep-men, cattlemen, sheep herders, cow punchers, Indians and Indian traders made Gallup a typical frontier community," he wrote. "Saturday night brought to town a motley array of human beings. From the coal mining camps came every nationality, including Italians, Greeks, Slavs, Cornish Cousin Jacks, Irish, and Scotts. The Orient furnished a few Japanese. The lumber camps in the Zuni Mountains had their quota of Finns, Scotsmen, Swedes and Norwegians."

Hannett described widespread bootlegging to Indians. He defended one bootlegger who had an Indian trading post and also ran a bakery. The client, a Frenchman known as Sloppy Jack, baked wooden molds of half-pint whiskey bottles into loaves of bread. When the bread was done, he removed the wooden mold and inserted half-pint bottles of bootleg whiskey. Sloppy Jack was convicted, and as he was about to be carted away by the federal marshal, he cried out to the judge, "You can't do this to me—I'm a businessman"—a position that would be echoed by successive generations of bootleggers and bar owners in Gallup.

Before he was elected mayor, Hannett made a name for himself as a trial lawyer battling the coal companies. His memoir describes the tumultuous coal strikes of his time. Hannett said that coal companies hired known criminals, deputized them, and sent them out to terrorize the miners and anyone else who opposed them.

Then-editor of the *Gallup Independent*, W. H. Hanns, was openly critical of the coal companies' strike-breaking tactics and challenged the constitutionality of mass deportations of union employees. During the 1917 coal strike, Hanns was arrested by a battery of heavily armed gunmen who had been deputized by McKinley County Sheriff Dee Roberts. He was brought before the Council of Defense that presided during martial law and was charged with inciting a riot. Hannett says that Hanns and several other innocent citizens were loaded onto a railroad car and shipped out of town. Reading the account, I found it hard to imagine an editor from the *Independent* being so vulnerable. The family that owned the *Independent* when I moved to Gallup was powerful and reputed to be among the top twenty-five wealthiest families in New Mexico—and they dished out far more pain, through scathing editorials, than they received.

Besides the coal companies, Hannett clashed with other authorities in Gallup at the time, notably the sheriff and district judge. He filed a lawsuit charging that the sheriff had hired an ex-convict and sued to have the sheriff removed from office, but the judge sided with the sheriff and accused Hannett of washing dirty political linen in court.

Hannett later got into a fistfight with the sheriff in the waiting room of a bank and fought a deputy sheriff who pulled a gun on him in his law office. At the time, many of the deputies were paid by the coal mines and worked part time as security guards for the mines. Hannett escaped from yet another deputy who stuck a six-shooter in his stomach at the Post Office—a Gallup old-timer came to Hannett's rescue and snatched the gun from the deputy's hand.

As mayor, Hannett empowered the citizenry of Gallup during a 1918 coal-mining strike by calling a town meeting and deputizing 150 city residents. In addition, he helped organize a relief society that gathered food, clothes, and money for the striking miners and their families. Hannett's opponents accused him of making a power grab and political grandstanding. But, reading about him not long after moving to Gallup, I frankly admired him.

When the sheriff's deputies tried to test the city's authority, the deputized city citizens surrounded and disarmed them and put them in jail until the coal companies paid their fines and moved them out of town.

During the last year of Hannett's tenure as mayor, in 1922, yet another strike was called. Hannett's political rival, the Republican Gregory Page, asked the governor to declare martial law and Hannett fought back. In a letter to the governor, he said nothing would justify sending troops to Gallup. The governor sided with Page and declared martial law anyway.

Hannett's efforts on behalf of the working man made him a strong candidate for governor, and in 1924 he was elected governor of New Mexico, served a two-year term, and then moved to Albuquerque to practice law. When the next big coal strike hit Gallup, Hannett's adversaries held sway, and, without his counterbalancing support for the miners, events would unfold much more harshly.

The market for Gallup coal was beginning to sputter in the early 1930s. Demand for coal dropped for five straight years after the stock market crashed in October 1929. The Great Depression that followed the crash wasn't the only problem; oil and electricity were now cheaper then and far more efficient. Hours for mining work were being cut back, and wages were also being cut; the non-mining work some of the coal companies offered, like making adobe blocks on company property, paid even lower wages. Underground coal mining in Gallup—a doorway to the American dream—was still dangerous and was now becoming a dead end.

During the Great Depression, new rules for unionization were established amid fear of a new political threat—communism. In the spring of 1933, the National Miners Union (NMU), which was reputed to have ties to the Communist Party of the United States, won the right to represent the Gallup miners.

Gallup was headed for its ultimate coal strike—now a life and death struggle for both sides. The miners were desperate, determined, and organized; their ability to feed their families was at stake. The mine owners and civil and law enforcement officials were equally determined—they believed that the very existence of the companies that fueled Gallup's economy was being threatened by un-American political ideologies.

On August 28, 1933, in the middle of the 12th Inter-Tribal Indian Ceremonial, the NMU miners formed picket lines at the five major mines near the town. An NMU labor organizer named Martha Roberts locked arms with thirty women, four abreast, and led six hundred miners, singing, in a march on the Gamerco Mine.

The reaction was immediate. Without a single act of violence, the New Mexico governor declared martial law at the request of Sheriff Dee Roberts, the Gallup mayor, mine owners, prominent town businessmen, and the NMU's rival unions. It appeared that the governor's response had been planned well in advance. Martial law was declared at 2 p.m. on August 30, and by 11 p.m., 250 National Guardsmen from Albuquerque, Roswell, and Clovis had arrived in Gallup.

The guardsmen surrounded Gallup and set up checkpoints at the east, west, north, and south entrances to town. The military commander issued a mass-gathering ordinance that prohibited meetings of five or more persons without a permit. Machine-gun posts were set up at strategic positions

Martha Roberts, the firebrand National Miners Union labor organizer, rallying the miners during a strike. *Photo by Tom Mullarky from the Guadagnoli*

in town and at the mines. Guardsmen patrolled the area on horseback and conducted random searches of cars with three or more people.

Over the course of the next four months, conflict erupted constantly. NMU miners drove to Santa Fe for a demonstration in the plaza that drew 1,000 miners and spectators. Back in Gallup, three men were stabbed in a strike flare up, and two miners were wounded by an early morning shotgun blast from an unidentified assailant. A sheriff's deputy was beaten and stabbed following a visit to a striker's home. Eight strikers and organizers were arrested and charged with assault. Strikers rioted near the Gallup courthouse and engaged in hand-to-hand fighting with guardsmen. A mob hurled stones and swung clubs. Six more organizers and miners were arrested.

After the arrests, negotiations to end the strike began in earnest, and a settlement was reached just before Thanksgiving. Outside strike organizers were released from jail on the condition that they leave New Mexico for at least one year. A crucial term of the settlement, which would have important repercussions later, was that miners who no longer worked for the coal companies but lived on company property were allowed time to find other housing before facing eviction.

Striking coal miners and their families in the Spanish-American Hall shortly before the 1935 riot that left two coal miners and the sheriff dead in an alley. *Photo by Tom Mullarky from the Guadagnoli Collection*

A week after the strike ended, National Guardsmen rounded up the outside labor organizers and hauled them out of state. Four days later, Prohibition ended nationwide. In Gallup, the National Guard went home before Christmas, and martial law was lifted.

In Spring 1934, despite the housing protections won by the miners in the strike settlement, a deal was struck between State Senator Clarence Vogel and the Gallup American Coal Company whereby the company sold Vogel a large tract of land that included the Chihuahuita neighborhood where many Mexican miners had built homes following the 1917 and 1922 strikes. Vogel, who was not bound by the terms of the strike settlement, raised prices and filed seventy-five eviction suits. When I moved to Gallup, one of my bosses, Tim, was helping Vogel's son sell some of the miscellaneous pieces still owned by the family after his father's death. I sensed an uneasiness in Tim concerning his client and the way in which the Vogels had acquired their landholdings, but I didn't then know any of the details.

In his role as a state senator, Vogel successfully worked to defeat an anti-eviction bill that the coal miner's union introduced in the New Mexico legislature.

In 1935, Victor Campos was the first Chihuahuita coal miner to have an eviction notice nailed to his door. An unemployed miner who could not read or write English, he nonetheless recognized the legal effect of the paper. On April 1, sheriff's deputies, who were selected and paid by coal companies and who worked primarily as mine guards, moved a bed, an armchair, and a coal stove from Campos and his family's home and placed them outside in the dirt. Campos's and a couple of union members waited until dark and then tore down boards that had been nailed to his front door and moved his belongings back inside. Within an hour, Campos and his friends were arrested and taken to jail on charges of breaking and entering.

Four days later, following Campos's arraignment and bond hearing, a crowd of around one hundred coal miners rioted and clashed with McKinley County Sheriff Mack Carmichael and three of his deputies in an alley in downtown Gallup. The alley was one I walked down every other week or so on my way to lunch at an Italian restaurant.

The sheriff and his deputies were trying to take one of Campos's friends, Esquiro Navarro, a union organizer, back to jail after the bond

Victor Campos (left) was the first miner removed from his home in Chihuahuita in 1935 by the mass evictions filed by State Senator Clarence Vogel. Campos is pictured here, years later, with two relatives. *Courtesy of Gabe Campos and Octavia Fellin Public Library, Gallup, New Mexico*

Following the 1935 coal riot, a group of "special deputies" gathered on a downtown street corner with machine guns. *Courtesy of Peter Procopio*

hearing. A large crowd of miners had gathered in front of the courthouse, and the sheriff and his men attempted to avoid them by taking a rear exit into the alley. Sheriff Carmichael and an undersheriff were escorting the prisoner down the alley and back toward the jail, with two deputies trailing behind, when a hundred miners and family members circled around into the alley and rushed forward in an effort to free Navarro.

Navarro began jostling the sheriff and undersheriff, trying to break free. One deputy threw a poorly aimed tear-gas canister that landed in the middle of the crowd, causing half the miners to press forward toward the lawmen rather than retreat. In the aftermath of the riot, Sheriff Carmichael and two miners were dead. One deputy, "Bobcat" Wilson, had two bullet wounds, and the deputy who threw the gas canister had been beaten. Six men and one woman in the crowd of miners were wounded. The gun of the deputy who had been beaten was missing, and Navarro had escaped. Gallup turned into an armed camp. Fifty-five coal miners were arrested within two hours, and more than one hundred people were placed in protective custody. Ultimately,

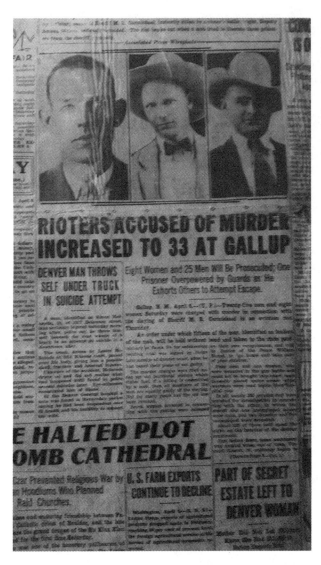

Deputy Hoy Boggess, Sheriff Mack Carmichael, and Deputy Howard "Bobcat" Wilson on the front cover of the *Denver Post* following the 1935 coal riot. *Courtesy of Bob Rosebrough*

ten miners stood trial in Aztec, New Mexico, facing first-degree murder charges for Carmichael's death.

More questions arose from the trial than were answered. The eyewitness testimony of the undersheriff and two deputies was expected to be crucial. After the testimony of the undersheriff and the deputy who threw the tear-gas canister, none of the ten defendants had been identified as having shot Sheriff Carmichael. Courtroom observers expected the remaining deputy, Bobcat Wilson, to resolve the unanswered questions. Inexplicably, the prosecution rested without calling Wilson to testify.

The jury found all ten miners not guilty of first-degree murder. Three defendants were found guilty of second-degree murder and the remaining seven were cleared of all charges, but five of the seven who were cleared were turned over to immigration officials and deported. The jury also made a request of clemency for the three convicted miners. On appeal, the New Mexico Supreme Court overturned one of the three convictions and four years after the trial, the governor granted pardons to the remaining two miners on the condition that they leave New Mexico.

When I read about it, neither the trial nor verdict made sense to me. I knew Aztec, which was just fifteen miles from my hometown of Farmington, to be an ultra-conservative community that would not have sympathy for rioting Mexican coal miners with reputed Communist affiliations. And it made no sense to me why Bobcat Wilson wasn't called to testify when the prosecution hadn't yet produced a witness who could identify any of the defendants as having shot the sheriff. It also made no sense to me that the prosecution sought first-degree murder convictions without producing a witness who could identify a shooter.

Something was missing—and a couple of decades will pass before I learn what is.

CHAPTER **THREE**

"Larry Wayne Casuse Is Dead."

A Gallup magistrate judge with a thick Greek accent is trying to talk my wife into working as a clerk for his court. We're sitting in a small conference room outside his office. His words are coming out like machine gun fire—some barely understandable to us—as my wife, wide eyed and reserved, listens politely. The judge's short, heavy-set body and face are in constant motion as he makes his pitch. When he's done, he says goodbye abruptly and leaves the room like a whirlwind. Beth, stunned, turns to me and says, "What just happened?"

"He wants you to work for him and because you were polite and didn't say no, he thinks you've accepted the job." Her eyes grow wider, and a look of concern and skepticism crosses her face.

I tell her that the judge is a legend in Santa Fe, that he is reputed to be the most effective political lobbyist in New Mexico. His lobbying efforts at the state capital on behalf of New Mexico's magistrate judges have been so successful that the state's Supreme Court, which has not fared as well as the magistrates, has recruited him to lobby on their behalf as well. He's used to getting what he wants.

The judge, Paris "Pete" Derizotis, is one of many larger-than-life characters I've been running into in Gallup as my wife and I settle into our

63

Shiprock as viewed from the top of the Chuska Mountains. In the early 1860s, Navajos found refuge on top of the Chuskas while evading American troops. *Courtesy of Brian Leddy*

new life here, and I find these men fascinating. My wife is less enthralled with these characters than I. She decides to take a job as an administrative secretary for the private hospital's CEO at the time, who fortunately for my wife was not a larger-than-life character.

The Gallup businessmen and officials I've been encountering—men whose names include Kauzlarich, Gurley, DePauli, Glascock, Lebeck, Muñoz, Zollinger, and Colaianni—are unlike any group of people I've ever met. They are all strong-willed and assertive, with an eccentricity or two. And each, in his own way, seems to feel that he runs the town.

I'm meeting a steady stream of new people every day at work, some with stories that surprise me. A gentle, soft-spoken elderly Navajo man who wants to renegotiate a business lease for a rural post office tells me that he was a Code Talker in WWII. The son of a Gallup auto dealer tells me that the secret to the dealership's early success was that his father started bartering with Navajos and taking in livestock and Indian jewelry for vehicle payments. An elderly Italian barber who needs a will talks about trying to break a $20 bill to buy a 5-cent candy bar in New York City after getting off a boat and being processed at Ellis Island.

And the places! After seven years away in college and law school, I am back in the Four Corners, near all my favorite places: Chaco Canyon, the Bisti wilderness, El Morro, Navajo Dam, Shiprock, Mount Taylor, Durango, Telluride, Ouray, the San Juan Mountains, Moab, Canyon-lands, Arches, Cedar Mesa, Lake Powell, Monument Valley, Valley of the Gods, Canyon de Chelly, the Hopi Mesas, the Grand Canyon, the Petrified Forrest, and the Painted Desert.

I can backpack in the canyons of southeast Utah in the spring and mountaineer in the San Juan Mountains of southwest Colorado in the summer and early fall, something that invariably sustains and renews me. At least once a month during climbing season, I drive up to Farmington to meet my regular climbing buddies, Ernie and Ike, and head to the mountains. On Saturday mornings we get an early start and climb for an hour by the light of our headlamps. When the sun starts coming up, we often stop and take a break to drink some water. When I pass my bottle around—filled with Gallup's highly mineralized well water—Ike takes a big swig each time and immediately spits it out.

"Gallup water!" he says, "That shit just makes you thirstier."

Basketball, as it did in college, becomes a way for me to immerse

Spider Rock in Canyon de Chelly at sunset. *Photo by Bob Rosebrough*

myself in my new surroundings. Larry Price, my college basketball teammate from Gallup, moves back home and takes charge of organizing teams.

Christopher Reeve northeast of Gallup while filming *Superman*, in which Superman cries in anguish at Lois Lane's death in an earthquake crevasse and flies furiously around the earth to reverse time and rescue her. *Courtesy of Lisa Rodriguez*

He says, "There's too many good players in Gallup for one team, so I've divided them up. You'll be the big guy on my team."

The tall guy on our rival team in Gallup is a year older than me. He played for a junior college in Kansas on scholarship. We've seen each other in action in regional tournaments but we haven't yet gone head-to-head. When I was still in my third year of law school, he was cast as the body double for Christopher Reeve in the 1978 *Superman* movie. In the movie's climactic scene, Superman shows up too late and fails to save Lois Lane from suffocating in a crevasse created by an earthquake. Superman cries out in anguish and then flies around the earth to reverse time so he can return to rescue Lois. I learn that the scene was filmed three or four miles northeast of Gallup, in what is now known as Superman Canyon.

A couple of weeks before the basketball season is set to start, as I feel tension building over the approaching clash, my rival-to-be dies in an auto accident while driving to Lake Powell. A season-ending tournament is named in his honor.

Gallup also seems to attract famous people. In the 1940s and '50s, the town was an on-location shooting spot of choice for Hollywood Westerns. Movies like *Only the Valiant, Ace in the Hole,* and *Escape from Fort Bravo* were filmed around Gallup, and stars like John Wayne, Katharine Hepburn, and Gregory Peck, among many others, were a regular presence in town. Candidates for president, like Dwight Eisenhower in the early '50s, and movie stars, like Robert Redford, were drawn to Gallup by the Inter-Tribal Ceremonial.

Dwight Eisenhower (center, back to camera) at Ceremonial in 1952 during his first campaign for president. *Photo by Tom Mullarky from the Guadagnoli Collection*

I discover that a locally owned bookstore in Gallup, Buffalo Medicine Books, is frequented by bestselling authors Edward Abbey and Tony Hillerman. The owner, Ernie Bulow, a big burley white-haired man who has immersed himself in Navajo culture, has collaborated with Hillerman, and Abbey regularly asks Bulow to keep him company when he travels for book signings.

At Jerry's Café, a popular Gallup eatery, the manager tells me that Glenn Fry and Don Henley of Eagles fame drop in when passing through on Route 66 and that on one visit, Henley took a seat in the always-crowded restaurant without realizing he had cut the waiting line. An old Navajo grandma walked up and banged her fist on the table in front of Henley, prompting him to jump up apologetically and yield the table.

And Bob Dylan's name comes up frequently. In the early '60s as he was bursting onto the music scene in New York City, Dylan gave several interviews in which he offered jumbled, fictitious accounts of growing up in Gallup.

Ernie Bulow, who has a knack for befriending famous authors, with Tony and Marie Hillerman. *Courtesy of Ernie Bulow*

In a 1962 interview with Billy James of Columbia Records, Dylan, then 20, talked about his running away from home a lot and said he'd spent "about three-quarters of my life around the Midwest and one-quarter around the Southwest—New Mexico. I lived in Gallup." In other interviews, Dylan gave in the '60s, he made cryptic, inconsistent references to Gallup.

In 1963, *Newsweek* researched Dylan's origins and poked holes in his fictional biography. The magazine reported that Dylan grew up in a conventional home and went to conventional schools. "He shrouds his past in contradictions," *Newsweek* reported, "but he is the elder son of a Hibbing, Minnesota appliance dealer named Abe Zimmerman, and as Bobby Zimmerman, he attended Hibbing High School, then briefly the University of Minnesota." Yet I find that in Gallup there are still people who swear that Dylan grew up here, although no yearbook photo or any other scrap of paper has ever been produced to support the claim.

There's a western-wear store located along Route 66 in Gallup with a sign in large white letters that says ZIMMERMAN'S. When the topic comes up, I find myself saying, "I think Dylan drove through on Route

66 at some point and saw the Zimmerman's sign and all the cowboys and Indians on the street here and decided that a childhood in Gallup would do more for his image than a small town in Minnesota."

To make sure I'm not too far off base, I ask the owner of Zimmerman's if there's any connection. He tells me that the original owners, from whom he bought the business, have died, but their son lives in Albuquerque and he claims no relationship to Dylan.

One year after I move to Gallup, I'm sitting in my office on a Saturday morning catching up on some files. My bosses Tim and Jay are in an adjoining office and I can clearly hear their voices coming through the air conditioner vent just above my desk. Tim is telling Jay that he's going to move to Santa Fe. Tim's wife is not happy in Gallup and Tim and Jay are not happy with each other. Their voices are strained and rise at times but never break into a shout. It's unsettling to listen to them talk.

I'm more compatible with Tim, who will be leaving. My relationship with Jay, on the other hand, has been strained and awkward from the start, but he's a hardworking guy with a savvy business sense and I know that Tim's departure represents a professional opportunity that I otherwise would have had to wait several more years for. A few days later, Tim's departure is made public, and Jay and I announce our new partnership.

Jay, who went to college at the University of Kansas, grew up Protestant but has since joined the Catholic Church, and he has the zeal of a convert. He actively recruits like-minded Catholics, many who are also KU grads, to move to Gallup, and uses his business and church connections to help them find jobs. Jay's activism in church helps our law practice. The Catholic Church, I'm finding, is more prominent and influential in Gallup than it is in Farmington and Albuquerque because of the larger number of Italians, Slavs, and Hispanics in town who are church members.

My wife is also Catholic, but I'm not, and the difference has been a source of tension between us. I was raised Presbyterian, but denominational differences aren't that important to me. They seem very important to Beth, however. We try alternating churches weekly for a while and then compromise by going to the Lutheran Church where we have friends, but that ends when the Lutheran minister gives a sermon that my wife perceives as bashing Catholics.

I like the priest at the Catholic church nestled below the huge sandstone hogback that erupts from the broad valley just east of Gallup. Father Frank is a quiet, peaceful man who became a priest late in life after retiring from a business career in the Midwest. I decide to convert to Catholicism, a decision that is more pragmatic than heartfelt.

Father Frank gives me a book as a confirmation present—*To Know Jesus Christ* by Frank Sheed—and I find myself thinking, *I'll never read it.*

I ask him instead how I can acquire a copy of the Canon Law of the Catholic Church and he says he will get me one. Reverting to type, I'm thinking, *If you just get me the rules, I will follow them.*

My wife, who is two years older than I, is eager to have children. Jay and the junior partner we've recently added to our practice already have children, and I would also like to have kids, but I'm not in as much of a hurry as my wife. My primary focus is developing my law practice, and that's going well.

One of my favorite clients is a real estate agent, Paul McCollum, whose office is near ours. Paul was the city manager of Gallup for many years, and he is unfailingly upbeat and friendly. After a meeting in my office, Paul lingers to visit and makes a reference in passing to former Gallup Mayor Emmett Garcia's abduction in 1973 that takes me by surprise and makes me realize that Paul was the city manager at the time.

I haven't thought about the abduction since listening to the radio bulletin about it in the UNM parking lot back in 1973, but the story had made such a vivid impression on me that my memory of the event quickly comes back as Paul and I talk. I ask Paul what he remembers, and he's glad to tell me more about this dramatic event in Gallup's turbulent history.

As Paul talks, I'm amazed at the number of people he mentions that I've already met here in Gallup. Listening to a living participant brings the story to life for me and makes it real in a way I hadn't anticipated. Up to now, the story has seemed larger than life to me, so much so that I never expected to run into ordinary folks who had been brushed by it.

Paul tells me that Larry Casuse and an accomplice kidnapped a fellow student at UNM and made the student drive them to Gallup's city hall. Mayor Garcia was meeting with three men to talk about his reelection bid. To my surprise, Paul identifies the men as my insurance agent Harry Mendoza, the Culligan Water man Red Abeita, and the magistrate judge Pete Derizotis, who had tried to hire my wife.

Gallup's current mayor, Frank Colaianni, was the operating partner of the problem bar, the Navajo Inn, now closed, whose practices Casuse was protesting against. The district attorney who investigated the matter and filed criminal charges against Casuse's accomplice is now the district judge before whom I regularly appear.

Paul tells me that Emmett Garcia moved away from Gallup and now lives in Arizona. He tells me that the Gallup chief of police at the time of the abduction, Manuel Gonzales, who had tried to stop the kidnapping in city hall, trailed Casuse and Garcia down to Route 66, and pulled Garcia away from the storefront after he dove through a glass door, retired early. Paul says that Chief Gonzales doesn't speak publicly about the incident, but he still lives in Gallup. I realize that I also know the younger brothers of Mayor Garcia and Chief Gonzales, both of whom still live and work in Gallup.

As Paul sits at the small conference table in my office describing people and events, I realize that the story that briefly captured my attention years ago is readily accessible to me now. And I realize that Larry Casuse, who'd been my age, was a Gallup High graduate, not an out-of-state activist as I'd assumed. What drove a young man like that to abduct the town's mayor? How did the kidnapping escalate to the point that the town's police killed Casuse?

Shortly after my conversation with Paul I find myself talking with a lumbering, heavy-set reporter from the *Gallup Independent*, a man whose hair always seems uncombed and whose shirt tail is perpetually untucked. He tells me that in the early '70s he was a cub reporter living in Kentucky and working the crime beat. He met a former Navajo policeman living in Kentucky who told him that he should move west and cover the Navajo Nation.

"He told me that Navajos speak in sign language and that I would need to learn it," says the reporter rolling his eyes. "I bought Iron Eyes Cody's sign language book and began studying." Shortly after the reporter moved to Gallup to work for the *Independent*, he realized that the Navajo policeman in Kentucky had been pulling his leg. While still new to the area, he found himself reporting on the abduction of Garcia and the death of Casuse; he wrote two of the three front-page articles that appeared in the *Independent* the day after the incident. Among other things, he tells me that the coroner declared Casuse's death to be a suicide, but that several eyewitnesses disputed the coroner's conclusions.

I'm fascinated and eager to learn as much as I can about the story. When I suspect someone might have any knowledge about Casuse or Garcia, I ask about the case. In part, I'm trying to flesh out the cryptic radio bulletin I'd heard while sitting in my car at UNM in 1973, but in part I'm also trying to crack what seems to me to be a code that will help me better understand my new hometown.

A few years after my conversation with Paul McCollum, the former city manager, I meet a high school teacher, Frank Bosler, who knows one of Casuse's younger sisters and is collecting documents and information about the abduction that he hopes to develop into a screenplay. A month or so after I meet him, Bosler calls me one evening and asks me to come to his house. It seems like he wants something from me or wants to suggest something to me, but he doesn't come out with it. Maybe it's just that he wants to talk or that he finds the magnitude of the story too much to grapple with alone. I tell him that I recorded my conversation with McCollum and that I'll get him a copy of the transcript.

We talk for more than an hour in his dimly lit living room, which is strewn with papers and books, and then, without prompting, he takes me to his kitchen where a large plastic storage bin on the floor is filled with cassette tapes, newspaper articles, and photographs. He fishes out a copy of a letter Casuse wrote to his father a few months before the abduction and a cassette tape of a live radio broadcast of the standoff and shootout on Route 66. He says he has duplicates of both, and hands them to me.

Later, the reporter from the *Independent* drops a copy of a *New Yorker* magazine article on the abduction at my office with an attached note that mentions the title of a memoir written by a former president of the UNM Board of Regents that contains a chapter on the abduction. I locate a copy of the regent's book, which focuses on the turmoil and student protests during the Vietnam War years of the late '60s and early '70s. The book's slipcover features a black-and-white photograph of troops with battle helmets and gas masks, carrying rifles with bayonets and facing off against students.

One chapter is titled; "Kidnapping a Regent," the regent being Gallup Mayor Garcia. The book includes a photo of Larry Casuse speaking at a public meeting. Casuse has a broad, handsome face with dark complexion. He looks comfortable and confident as he speaks; a crowd of people is seated behind him. His wavy, black, shoulder-length hair, parted in the

Larry Casuse speaking to the UNM Board of Regents in 1973. Board president Calvin Horn said, "I knew he was not a publicity seeker or working for personal gain. He was different." Albuquerque Journal, *February, 1973. Used by permission of the publisher.*

middle, is held in place by a neatly folded bandana headband. He wears wire-rim glasses and a faded Levi's jacket.

I call Manuel Gonzales, the retired police chief that McCollum mentioned and ask if he will talk to me. Gonzales is friendly and polite—he says that he'll think about it, but he hasn't been giving interviews or discussing the matter publicly. He says of Casuse, "He died for something he believed in," but he doesn't elaborate. I don't expect him to call back and I decide not to pressure him. But from the various sources I've spoken with and investigate, I begin piecing together this keystone story.

A couple months before the police dragged his lifeless body through the shattered glass of a storefront onto the sidewalk, Larry Wayne Casuse came home to Gallup from the University of New Mexico at the tail end of his Christmas break. Gallup in early January is not a pretty place. Snow begins to accumulate on the north side of buildings and then packs into glazed ice. Pickup trucks pour into town from a maze of rutted, dirt roads on the vast Navajo Reservation; once in town, they shed a rust-red mixture of clay and dirt from their undercarriages, which disintegrates into a fine dust and coats sidewalks, cars, buildings, and plants. By the end of winter, before harsh spring winds sweep through, the entire town is coated in a fine, all-encompassing layer of dust.

When he returned to Albuquerque to start the second semester of his sophomore year, 19-year-old Larry Casuse sat down and wrote a letter that began, "Dear Daddy." Casuse's letter was intended to reassure and comfort his father at a time when Casuse himself was facing overwhelming pressures. His father was a full-blooded Navajo from the Mexican Springs area of the reservation twenty miles north of Gallup, and his mother was Austrian. Casuse's parents had met in Germany toward the end of World War II, and they had recently divorced.

Casuse, who had not seen his father on his Christmas trip home, mailed one copy of his letter to his father at an address in Mexican Springs and another to an address in Arizona. He told his father that he'd brought gifts for his six younger brothers and sisters and that he'd hung around Gallup for four days before returning to Albuquerque. He said his grades had dropped. This had to have been a real disappointment to Casuse, who was a bright young man with a history of doing well in school. He assured his father that he would bring his grades up in the next semester.

Just weeks earlier, before Christmas, Casuse had been tried and convicted at the courthouse in Gallup of a felony—he'd left the scene of an accident involving the death of a young Navajo woman who had walked out in front of his car late at night on a dark, unlighted highway just north of Gallup. Casuse took the young woman's death hard, and his friends said that he was stricken with guilt and grief, but his letter to his father mentioned none of that. He told his father that he had a new trial coming up on January 25 and said that he thought everything would be all right. Given the history of the case to that point, Casuse's optimism appeared unrealistic. Perhaps he was just trying to put his father's mind at ease. After commenting on the weather, he signed off with, "Your son, Larry."

From my talks with Frank Bosler, and the *Independent* reporter, and from reading the *New Yorker* article, I learned that it wasn't until Casuse moved from the Silver City area of southwestern New Mexico to Gallup near his father's home, and started high school, that he first felt the sting of racial prejudice. Larry, more than the other Casuse children, looked distinctly Navajo.

While the preceding generations in Gallup had experienced a remarkable melding of nationalities as immigrant Italians, Croatians, Mexicans, Greeks, and Japanese worked, played, and went to school together, most Navajos continued to live out in the county and hadn't been part of the melting pot. Few Navajo children attended Gallup schools. For the most part, they were educated in Bureau of Indian Affairs boarding schools out on the reservation. The boarding schools were dying out and Navajos started being bused into town, a process that was not without friction.

Casuse played football in high school and took up wrestling as a light heavyweight. His closest friends were the other Navajo football players. He was active in the Indian Club, which organized the first powwow ever held at Gallup High, and he was pictured in the high school yearbook wearing a feathered war bonnet. As a junior and senior in high school, Casuse immersed himself increasingly in Navajo culture.

When he moved on to UNM in Albuquerque, he became politically active in a variety of Native causes—this was at the same time his mother left his father for a white Gallup businessman. Casuse joined the university's Kiva Club, an Indian student organization, and was elected its president. He also participated in protests of the annual Gallup Inter-Tribal Indian Ceremonial, which many Indian activists felt exploited Native craftsmen. Casuse's activism coincided with the rise of the American Indian Movement, members of which occupied Alcatraz Island in 1969 and, four years later, took hostages in the siege at Wounded Knee, South Dakota.

Larry Casuse was a Gallup High football player. *Courtesy of Don Casuse*

Larry Casuse (far right) and fellow Gallup High Indian Club officers. *Courtesy of Don Casuse*

Just before Casuse's sophomore year, the driving accident occurred in which he hit and killed the young Navajo woman. After the accident, Casuse put the woman's lifeless body into the trunk of his car and drove toward the home of a state police officer he knew. But before he reached his destination, his car got mired in mud on a side road. Casuse was charged with driving under the influence of alcohol and leaving the scene of an accident involving death. Jailed in Gallup for several weeks that summer, Casuse was then released to go back to school in the fall. A trial was set for December, and the alcohol charge was dropped before the trial.

Calvin Trillin, writing for the *New Yorker* after Casuse's death, said that the case seemed to turn on whether Casuse had been searching for help or trying to dispose of the body just his car got stuck. Casuse's friends and family felt the death and prosecution affected Casuse deeply. Some observers said that he appeared increasingly tense during public appearances, and that his remorse about the death was so strong that he could not speak of it without weeping. But Casuse believed that the criminal charges had been brought by the Gallup authorities to punish him for his political activism. Many shared his point of view.

Just before Christmas 1972, Casuse's lawyer, a public defender from Navajo Legal Aid, inexplicably waived his client's right to a jury trial, tried his case to a district judge, and lost. Just after Christmas, a new legal services lawyer agreed to represent Casuse and filed a motion for a new trial on the grounds that Casuse's first lawyer had been ineffective. Among other things, the motion argued that Casuse's first lawyer had failed to confer with Casuse before trial, had neglected to present any evidence, and had not adequately cross-examined witnesses. Usually, a motion of this nature would be strongly opposed by a district attorney, but for reasons not apparent from the public record, the prosecutor voluntarily agreed to a new trial, which was set for January 25 and then reset for February 14.

At the beginning of 1973, Gallup Mayor Emmett "Frankie" Garcia, like Casuse, was beginning to suffer his own wave of misfortune. Just after New Year's Day, around the same time Larry Casuse came home to see his family, Garcia's wife grew sick and was diagnosed with lupus. Although she would go on to live for many years, doctors told Garcia at the time she only had weeks to live.

In February, New Mexico's Governor Bruce King offered Garcia one of the most prized political appointments in New Mexico—a seat on the UNM Board of Regents. Garcia, who had been elected to a two-year term as mayor in March 1971, was a 35-year-old rising political star who had been shaking things up in Gallup. He arrived at the office early,

Emmett Garcia's supporters lift him in victory the night of his election as Gallup mayor in 1971. *Courtesy of the* Gallup Independent

stayed late, and pushed his staff hard with a steady stream of ideas and projects. He also took a step toward tackling Gallup's alcohol problem, something that elected officials in the town generally shied away from. Garcia wasn't going to do anything radical, but he had begun rounding up city, county, and state money in anticipation of matching a large federal grant for an alcohol rehabilitation program.

Gallup's public intoxication problem was no secret; part of the foundation and fabric of the town was access to alcohol. Over the years, Gallup had become the watering hole of choice for the dry Navajo reservation, and in the early 1970s several national publications featured extensive exposés on the town's crowded drunk tank, deaths from exposure, and other human suffering tied to the alcohol industry.

The last two weeks of February were hectic for Garcia and Casuse and started ominously for both. On February 15, Garcia was involved in a head-on collision in Arizona. He somehow managed to survive the crash but he was bruised, beaten up, and left temporarily walking on crutches.

The day before Garcia's car accident, Casuse went to trial again—this time before a jury. The jury deadlocked 11 to 1 in favor of the prosecution, and the judge declared a mistrial and set a third trial on short notice.

Meanwhile, the process to seat Garcia as a UNM regent was moving ahead. Just six days after Casuse's deadlocked trial, Garcia went before the New Mexico senate's Rules Committee, where the two separate storms that were swirling around Garcia and Casuse joined and gained strength. Casuse appeared before the committee to speak against Garcia's appointment. He told the senate committee that Garcia owned the Navajo Inn, a notorious so-called Indian bar twenty-four miles northwest

Calvin Horn (far left) and the University of New Mexico Regents. *Calvin Horn and UNM Regents, 1971, UNMA 108, Calvin Horn Papers, Center for Southwest Research, University Libraries, University of New Mexico*

A field representative for the New Mexico Commission on Alcoholism presents Gallup Mayor Emmett Garcia with a license plate commemorating January 1972, as alcoholism prevention month. *Courtesy of the* Gallup Independent

of Gallup on the boundary of the reservation. On most days, the gravel parking lot and grounds surrounding the bar looked like the aftermath of a war—strewn with limp bodies that looked lifeless. Pictures had been taken and passed around of Navajo men passed out face-down on anthills.

Casuse told the senators that Garcia was a "false person" for simultaneously selling liquor to Indians while also serving as a director of the Alcoholic Rehabilitation Center in Gallup. Calvin Horn, the president of the UNM Board of Regents, attended the confirmation hearings and was taken aback by the tone of Casuse's comments. He later wrote in his memoirs, "Larry was quiet in his presentation, but every word he spoke against Mr. Garcia's appointment seemed spit out of his mouth."

Garcia defended himself, telling committee members that he owned only a one-third interest in the bar and had no part in its management. He said he had sold his controlling interest six years earlier and, at the request of the two buyers, retained an interest only to break a tie if they became involved in a dispute.

The final battle of the confirmation took place on February 23 when the UNM regents were to meet to swear in Garcia, with TV cameras present. The Indian Students' Kiva Club held a rally that was attended by about two hundred people to protest Garcia's appointment thirty minutes before the regents meeting and burn a rag doll figure of Garcia in effigy. The crowd then filed into the meeting room. When the matter was called for discussion, Casuse pushed his way to the front of the group and was recognized by President Horn.

"I sat there and looked at Larry's intense face as he spoke," Horn later wrote. "He didn't appear to be speaking to the regents, the crowd, or even the TV cameras. His mind seemed far away. I wondered what was in his thoughts. I knew he was not a publicity seeker or working for any personal gain. He was different."

Casuse again labeled Garcia a "false person" and condemned the regents, Garcia, and the state senate. "We're going to get the human beings together and put an end to people like Emmett Garcia," he said. Then according to Horn, "in quiet dignity he stood and retired to the back of the room. Larry had brought the crowded room to stony silence." The regents unanimously approved Garcia's appointment to the board. After the meeting a coffin was placed on the university mall marked with Garcia's name.

Horn thought about Casuse during the following week and considered dropping in to see him at the Kiva Club but decided he would "visit with Larry in the future."

That future would never arrive.

A week after the regents meeting, on March 1, 1973, Larry Wayne Casuse walked into city hall in Gallup with a gun. Accompanying Casuse was another young Navajo man, Robert Nakaidinae. Two days earlier, AIM activists had taken hostages in Wounded Knee, South Dakota, at the beginning of a prolonged siege. Garcia, who was only weeks away from reelection as mayor, had been talking shop with three of his political lieutenants: Harry Mendoza, Red Abeita, and the city's alcohol coordinator, Pete Derizotis. Mendoza, who thirty years later would become one of my political archrivals, and Abeita had left Garcia's office by the time a secretary came in and announced visitors. The excitable Derizotis was still there and he popped up and told Garcia,

University of New Mexico Kiva Club members burn Mayor Garcia in effigy.
Courtesy of New Mexico Daily Lobo

"I'll get it." Garcia heard Derizotis saying, "No, no, no, Larry. You can't do that," in the outer lobby. There was a commotion and Casuse and Nakaidinae appeared in Garcia's office; Casuse was brandishing a pearl-handled .32-caliber revolver.

(left) Larry Casuse photographed in the days leading up to the abduction of Mayor Garcia in February 1973. *Courtesy of the* Gallup Independent. *Front page, March 2, 1973.* (right) Robert Nakaidinae, the hapless accomplice, received a light jail sentence. Albuquerque Journal, *March 3, 1973. Used by permission of the publisher.*

According to the former city manager Paul McCollum, the scene then played out like a TV drama: Garcia grabs Casuse and they wrestle. At one point, Casuse pulls the trigger but the gun doesn't fire. With Garcia holding him from behind, Casuse cocks the gun and pulls the trigger again, this time sending a bullet through the mayor's desk, chair, and the wall behind. Garcia tries to negotiate, but Casuse breaks loose, points the gun at Garcia's head, and orders him to his knees. The Gallup police chief, Manuel Gonzales, bursts in with his gun drawn, but Garcia orders him to follow Casuse's instructions. Casuse orders Gonzales to unload the bullets from his gun and hand it over to Nakaidinae, who handcuffs Garcia's hands behind his back.

Without ever taking the gun away from Garcia's head, Casuse marches Garcia out of city hall and down Second Street toward the two-block row of north-facing buildings on Front Street on Route 66, with Nakaidinae following.

Most accounts say that Casuse intended to take Garcia across Route 66 and the railroad tracks to the Gallup Indian Center but was deterred

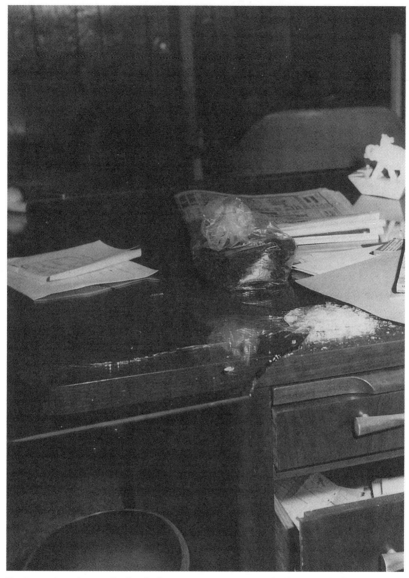

Broken glass from a bullet hole on Mayor Garcia's desk at city hall. *Courtesy of the* Gallup Independent

by a passing train and then sought refuge in Stearns Sporting Goods on Front Street—a gun and hunting store, loaded with rifles, pistols, shotguns, and ammunition.

The aftermath. Inside Stearns Sporting Goods store following the shootout.
Courtesy of the Gallup Independent

When the trio arrives at the store, they find it closed, with a note posted on the glass door. Nakaidinae, as directed by Casuse, uses Chief Gonzales's gun like a hammer to break the glass and get inside. Every law enforcement officer in the area swarms to the site.

Traffic on Route 66 is diverted as news of the kidnapping spreads instantly through town. Gallup radio station KGAK radio dispatches a news reporter who begins a live broadcast across the street from the scene. Inside the store, Casuse and Nakaidinae begin gathering and loading weapons. A policeman walks brazenly in front of the store's plate-glass windows, and Casuse sends him scrambling with a warning shot into the ceiling.

In a pivotal moment, Casuse hears noises at the back door of the store. He tells Nakaidinae to watch Garcia and goes to investigate. It's not long before Nakaidinae takes his finger off the trigger of the shotgun and moves to lay it on a counter. Seizing the opportunity, and with his hands still handcuffed behind him, Garcia kicks Nakaidinae and bolts. Nakaidinae recovers and fires the shotgun in the direction of the fleeing mayor.

Listening to the cassette tape Frank Bosler has given me, I hear the KGAK radio reporter positioned outside the store interviewing Paul

A lone shotgun leaned against the shelves inside Stearns Sporting Goods after the shootout. *Courtesy of the* Gallup Independent

City officials and policemen huddle in the alley behind Stearns Sporting Goods. *Courtesy of the* Gallup Independent

Stearns Sporting Goods, as viewed from north of Route 66, after the shootout. *Courtesy of the* Gallup Independent

McCollum. The reporter asks the city manager, "Do you have any idea what their griefs are?"

Seconds later, as McCollum is answering, radio listeners hear glass breaking in the background as Garcia bursts out of the building and lands on the sidewalk. Someone yells, "Watch out! Watch out!" while Garcia makes loud, primal, yelping sounds in short bursts. He is frantically pleading for help while he gasps for air. Manuel Gonzales, who is tucked down just outside the storefront, grabs Garcia and drags him to safety.

"A man has just apparently been shot and thrown out . . . thrown out the window," says the reporter. "We can't tell at this time . . . we can't tell if it's the mayor." The reporter is also struggling to breathe. His words are interrupted by gasps as he describes shots being fired.

"The man appears to be conscious," the reporter says. "He lifted his head. His hands are tied behind his back. We don't know at this time . . . another shot is fired. Chief Gonzales has a rifle. Now, the chief had been disarmed earlier. The chief just fired a bullet into the building. Shots are coming rapidly out of the building."

A bullet-riddled car parked in front of Stearns Sporting Goods. *Courtesy of the* Gallup Independent

Inside Stearns Sporting Goods after the shootout, looking out. *Courtesy of the* Gallup Independent

Moments later, McCollum returns to the reporter, saying, "The mayor's okay. The only thing we know is that he is all right. He came out through the window. He has a wound. Whether it's caused by a bullet or caused by breaking glass, we don't know at this time, but we are talking to him around the other side and his family is over there."

Radio listeners hear more yelling and more gunfire and whistles as the reporter interviews McCollum. A tear-gas bomb is shot into Stearns Sporting Goods. Nakaidinae comes out with his hands over his head and he is directed by police to lie flat. Policemen pour into the store and drag out a body covered with blood.

The reporter begins walking across the street toward the shattered storefront. He says, "There is no movement from the body of Larry Wayne Casuse. From this reporter's opinion and distance of about thirty feet, Larry Wayne Casuse appears to be dead by this reporter. He is covered by blood in the face and there appears to be little doubt that Larry Wayne Casuse is dead."

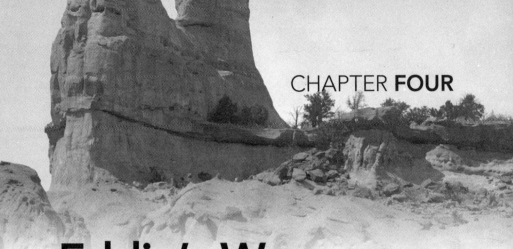

CHAPTER **FOUR**

Eddie's Way or No Way

In the late 1980s, after I've been in town almost ten years, I'm sitting with my wife and young family in a wooden pew at a small Catholic church tucked below a towering sandstone cliff. I'm shifting, getting ready to stand and walk toward the altar to receive communion. My wife lightly touches my forearm and whispers, "You can't go up."

I stare at her blankly, not understanding.

"You ate a donut, before we left the house," she says. I think she's telling me that I broke the rule that requires fasting for an hour before taking communion. I'm surprised and miffed as I keep my seat while she goes up to the altar and returns. I try to remember whether the rule requires fasting one hour before church begins or one hour before communion. And I'm wondering why she's brought this up now, in the middle of the service, rather than at home when I picked up the strawberry-frosted donut from the tray on the counter. I'm starting to chafe at the very rules I once sought from Catholicism.

As pressures continue to build in my marriage and law partnership, I'm completely inept at diffusing them. I just put my head down, ignore

(left) Matt on his first camping trip to Cedar Mesa in southeast Utah. (right) Amy and Megan on the Durango and Silverton Narrow Gauge Railroad train on an overnight camping trip. *Courtesy of Bob Rosebrough*

my wife's and law partner's resentments, stuff down my own resentments, and push on.

My wife and I now have three kids—curly-haired Matt; cherub-faced Mark; and high-energy, daredevil Megan. A fourth child, calm and curious Amy, will follow. Our evenings are largely devoted to feeding, reading books, bathing, picking up, and putting kids to bed. As a result of the pressures at the office and home, at times I feel overwhelmed by everydayism.

I try to incorporate some fun into our routine. On Saturday mornings, the kids and I go to Maria's restaurant downtown, a block from my office, to sit in a wooden booth near the sunny front window and eat pancakes while my wife gets a rare chance to sleep in. When the kids get a little older, we start going up to Cedar Mesa in southeastern Utah in the spring to car camp on a high mesa with stunning views of Monument Valley and the San Juan River gorge. In the summer, the kids and I take the narrow gauge train from Durango into the mountains for short, easy, overnight camping trips.

Every workday, I go to my buttoned-down law office amid banks, insurance companies, city hall, title companies, real estate agencies, and optometry offices. The historic courthouse where I've learned to be a law-yer is only a block from our office. The area near my office feels entirely different from Front Street on Route 66. The surrounding tan-brick and earth-tone-stucco buildings seem comfortable to me while Front Street just two blocks north is rough and raw.

My partner, Jay, and I bring in a third partner, and what seems to be an ever-shifting cast of associate lawyers and summer law clerks. Two older Hispanic women, who have worked as legal secretaries for years in Gallup, and a young Anglo woman crank out legal documents for us.

Our law practice is going very well and we're building a reliable base of clients, although I lose my first two jury trials, both tough cases. During a recess in my third jury trial, where I face a senior Gallup lawyer who likes to tell young lawyers that he never loses, the judge says in a low voice, "You're going to win this one," while the older lawyer is present but distracted. And, although it's the jury's decision not the judge's, he turns out to be right; the jury comes back in our favor. As an encore several months later, I win a difficult divorce trial against the same lawyer after he refuses to discuss settlement prior to trial.

Most of my time at work, though, isn't spent in the courtroom. Each week I meet a stream of new people who are buying homes, drawing up estate plans, starting businesses, and making business deals. And I always seem to have several cases that ground me in the harsh reality of my chosen town.

I represent a father in a child custody dispute, for example. The mother on the witness stand before me is losing her fourth child. She has lost her first three children, each from a different father and each lost in a different way. The mother is crying; tears stream down her face and real emotion chokes her voice. She has an extensive history of alcohol dependence. She says, "I love my baby. I want to be her mother." She promises to fulfill requirements set by the court that, thus far, she has broken repeatedly. She seems to mean what she says but she hasn't been able to live it. After being left in a dangerous situation, her baby was placed in foster care and the mother hasn't visited her daughter once, yet she is asking the judge to give her full custody.

A bar serves a young Navajo man to the point of intoxication and then keeps serving him more. Early in the morning before sunrise, still drunk and on his way home, the young Navajo man drives head-on into the vehicle of an older Navajo couple halfway between Farmington and Gallup, and the husband dies. After reaching a settlement with the drunk driver's insurance company, I bring a dram-shop lawsuit against the bar, alleging that the bar served the driver after knowing that he had already reached the point of intoxication. We win a jury trial against the bar, but never collect a penny because the bar files bankruptcy and the Court of Appeals reverses the jury's decision—because the policemen who tested the drunk driver hadn't properly calibrated the breathalyzer machine.

At the office, tension is mounting. I'm irritated by my partner's daily rehash of the comments of a bombastic new radio personality, Rush Limbaugh, but I don't say a word about my irritation to him. When he makes a critical comment about Martin Luther King Day during a morning break at a coffee shop, I break my silence. I defend Martin Luther King Day and he defends Columbus Day, while two of our friends sit silently, wide-eyed, appearing to wonder if our conversation, and partnership, are going to blow up.

Not long afterward, my partner, who makes most of the major decisions at the office, wants more playing time on our basketball team, of which I'm the informal coach. He genuinely seems to have hurt feelings, but this time it's one of the few aspects of our relationship where what I say goes, and I listen but ignore his complaints. There's a constant silent tension both at home and the office. Other people's rules and expectations are closing in on me.

Athletics and mountaineering, which are becoming harder and harder to fit into my schedule, are my release from the stress of daily life. During the winter, our city league basketball games are on Wednesday nights, and on Sunday afternoons we go to Gallup's branch of UNM (where one of the guys has a key) and we play full-court games until we are blissfully exhausted. Now that we have kids, I start getting up early in the morning in the dark to get a run in before the kids wake up. During the summer, on every third or fourth weekend, I drive up to the San Juan Mountains to backpack and climb. I can't seem to get enough of the mountains, and I progress to more technically difficult peaks. Over the course of a year and a half, I write a climbing and hiking guide to the San Juan Mountains, a project I enjoy—both the writing and the people I meet along the way.

To train for the hard climbs, I start rock climbing and bouldering on the cliffs and crags around Gallup as another release from the daily grind.

Bob Rosebrough climbing Arrow Peak in the San Juan Mountains. *Courtesy of Ernie Stromeyer*

During the winter, when the mountains are snowed in and it's hard to train outdoors in Gallup, I start playing racquetball at lunch at the Gallup Fitness Center, in part to squeeze in a workout during a time that doesn't cut into my family obligations.

Tension also prevails in Gallup, in particular about the town's public drunkenness problem. Everyone knows it's a problem, but the constant refrain I hear from old-timers is, "It will never change." And nothing more. There is never any discussion about right or wrong, alternatives or solutions. Simply: "It will never change."

During my rushed noon-time jaunts to the Gallup Fitness Center in the late 1980s, I begin running into Eddie Muñoz, a legendary former mayor of Gallup.

Muñoz is nearing 60; I'm in my mid-30s. And we are plainly different. Muñoz is short, stocky, and Hispanic; I'm tall, thin, and white. Beyond appearances, Muñoz is reputed to be pugnacious and domineering, while I'm a first-born child who is eager to please, overly responsible, and deferential—up to a point.

Over the lunch hour, while I play racquetball, Muñoz lifts light weights and takes a sauna. We exchange short, clipped greetings in passing that begin with me saying, "Hi, mayor"—it's the start of a delicate, and at times contentious dance we perform until the last days of his life and, as implausible as it may sound, for a few days thereafter.

Muñoz has a reputation; he is universally described as strong-willed and aggressive. Some describe his actions while serving as mayor from 1958 to 1969, the longest mayoralty in Gallup's history, as self-serving. His run ended four years before the abduction of Mayor Garcia. The most common thing said about Muñoz is, "It's Eddie's way or no way," and when people talk about him, they use words like *stubborn* and *fighter*. Now in 1987, it's rumored that Muñoz is planning another run for mayor.

Different versions of a story float around town about a fistfight during Muñoz's first stint as mayor and a recent clash with the current city manager, whom Muñoz, it's said, wants to fire if elected.

Beth and I have moved to a larger house in a more prominent neighborhood, and I now live two houses south of Muñoz, but we rarely cross paths as neighbors. An area of brick near Muñoz's front door is a lighter shade of red than the surrounding bricks. I overhear a Catholic friend saying that the lighter-colored area was left when Muñoz took down a tile portrait of Our Lady of Guadalupe, named for an appearance in Mexico of the Virgin Mary, when he started attending a nondenominational Christian church called The Door.

Muñoz fascinates me; he, like so many in Gallup, is a larger-than-life figure. More than anyone I know he seems to live life on his terms regardless of whether others approve. I'm intrigued by him but inept about how to approach him. I come close to talking to Muñoz about his pending run for mayor a couple times at the Fitness Center, but the words never quite leave my mouth. Gallup politics are beyond me—there's just so much that's still foreign and unapproachable. And, I've got a full plate going without getting involved in politics.

Gallup's alcohol problems seem completely beyond my influence, but Muñoz's impending run for mayor is threatening to shake up the firmly entrenched status quo. One prominent businessman tells me, "Eddie asked to meet with us up at the Country Club. He said he is going to take on Gallup's alcohol problem. He seems serious about it." The businessman seems puzzled, as if he is considering how things are going to play out now that Muñoz's indomitable will is focused on Gallup's intractable problem.

Muñoz is a self-made man. Many years later in a conversation with his wife Margaret, I learn that as a kid Muñoz had a red wagon that he loaded with tamales his mother cooked and clothes she laundered for neighbors, and he delivered them for her. When he started school, Muñoz didn't speak English and he would later say that he was spanked a lot for speaking Spanish. Muñoz's parents were from Juarez, Mexico, and his father was a section hand for the railroad. They lived in several New Mexico railroad towns before landing in Gallup.

Muñoz lied about his age to get into the Merchant Marines at the age of 16. During World War II, Muñoz's father was walking home from a friend's home when he was hit by a teenage drunk driver from a prominent Gallup family and died instantly. Muñoz couldn't come home from the war and didn't have enough money to pay for his father's funeral. A local Gallup judge dismissed the criminal charges against the teen driver and Margaret would later say that the tragedy, and the judge's decision, left Muñoz bitter toward politicians.

After the war, Muñoz worked as an electrical lineman for the city of Gallup, then started working at a service station. His first year, he worked from 5 a.m. to 11 p.m. day in and day out, and when an opportunity came up for him to buy a station, he jumped at the chance. Soon thereafter he bought a second station.

Muñoz had a close friend who owned a drugstore. Margaret, then just a girl, worked as a soda jerk there. She also babysat the drugstore owner's kids when he and his wife went out on the town with Muñoz. Margaret, six years younger than Muñoz, was from a prominent Spanish-American family that had lived in New Mexico for generations. Muñoz and Margaret eventually fell in love and married over the opposition of Margaret's family, who disapproved of marriage to a second-generation Mexican-American. Many of the Hispanic families in New Mexico dated their ancestry back for centuries to the Spanish settlers in the Rio Grande corridor and northern New Mexico. But in Gallup, many Hispanics came from Mexico in the early 1900s to work in the coal mines; they were considered by some of the longtime Spanish-origin families to be of a lower caste.

Margaret's uncles were the county assessor and county judge and they delivered the Mexican and Spanish vote for the political faction that ran Gallup at the time.

Despite his disdain of politicians, or maybe because of it, Muñoz stumbled into politics when he went to pick up his lawyer, Al Lebeck, one day. Lebeck—my adversary twenty-five years later in the first jury trial I won—had helped Muñoz start his businesses. They were supposed to go fishing, but Muñoz found that Lebeck and some colleagues were having a meeting about the upcoming municipal election. Lebeck and the other men were putting a slate of candidates together called the Greater Gallup ticket and they only had until 5 p.m. to file their declarations of candidacy. Lebeck's group asked Muñoz to run for city council with them.

Muñoz felt he needed to ask Margaret's uncles before deciding whether to run. He went to one of the uncles, who told him not to run.

Eddie Muñoz during his first stint as mayor of Gallup. *Courtesy of Octavia Fellin Public Library, Gallup, New Mexico*

Muñoz went back to Lebeck and said, "He doesn't want me to do it." Then he added, "But I'm going to do it." Muñoz was the only person on Lebeck's slate of candidates who won.

In later elections, Muñoz and Lebeck got more of their group elected. They recruited other World War II vets to join the Greater Gallup ticket, and the faction became known informally as the Young Turks.

Muñoz ran for mayor in 1958, won, and was dominant from the beginning. According to his city manager, Paul McCollum, when Muñoz said that he would do something, it got done.

There were frequent rumblings among political opponents that Muñoz and Lebeck, who became city attorney, used inside information to make land purchases and acquire wealth. The two were very close both politically and personally, and some considered Lebeck to be a mastermind in both business and politics.

After serving as mayor for twelve years, Muñoz was defeated in a close, bitter election by an accountant who ran on the slogan "It's time for a change."

Although he grew up Catholic, religion wasn't important to Muñoz during the first half of his life. "He was not particularly religious," Margaret would tell me. "He couldn't understand; he grew up in the era of priests who stood with their backs to the congregation."

Margaret, however, met some evangelical Christians at a city prayer breakfast and started attending their church, The Door Christian Fellowship. She said Muñoz didn't mind, "We let each other do what we liked." Over time, Muñoz was influenced by Margaret and their daughter Connie, who later became a Christian missionary in South Africa.

The scene at The Door on Saturday nights featured music and testimonials. The first night Muñoz attended The Door, the son of one of his friends, who had been converted by Connie, was giving personal testimony; Muñoz had known the young man when he was going through problems and was involved with drugs.

During the young man's testimony, Muñoz felt he was filled with Holy Spirit and he stood up and said, "This is so amazing. I never knew God was real."

Muñoz donated property to The Door for a new church building northwest of town but only after his partners in the land ownership,

Eddie Muñoz at a
church service during his
second stint as mayor.
Albuquerque Tribune

including Lebeck, blocked a proposed donation in a residential area. Everyone got mad at Muñoz's desire to donate land to the church, but Muñoz stood his ground.

With time, Muñoz found peace with his father's death. He knew a woman who had married into the family of the teen driver who'd hit and killed his father. Muñoz told the woman that he wanted to tell the driver that he had forgiven him, but she told him that the driver had died from alcoholism. Muñoz became friends with the family of the teen driver and later vacationed with them in Mexico.

The death of his father was not the only alcohol-related loss Muñoz suffered. One of his brothers, Raymond, lost sight and hearing on his right side in an accident caused by a drunk driver. Not long afterward, Raymond was crossing a street to sell raffle tickets to fund a trip for a Little League team. A state policeman involved in a high-speed chase hit and instantly killed him. Because of his earlier injuries, Raymond hadn't seen or heard the police car approaching.

And one of Muñoz's friends, Frank Gallegos, owned a bar on Gallup's north side called Eddie's Club. The two families were so close that they traded turns taking each other's kids to school. "He drank himself to death," Margaret said of Gallegos.

After Muñoz announces his political comeback, I'm intrigued by his reelection bid and alcohol-reform platform. One time, I come close to volunteering to help his campaign but don't. Muñoz, it seems to me, has a firmly established set of friends and supporters that he's content to rely on. I admire his assertive leadership, but he seems unapproachable as well as invincible. Sure enough, in 1987, he wins his bid for reelection after an eighteen-year hiatus.

Muñoz's first order of business after the election, as promised, is to fire the city manager, an out-of-town, Anglo professional whom I've come to know casually. Muñoz hires the son of one of his longtime friends instead. The fired city manager comes to see me, and I agree to represent him in negotiating a severance package. Shortly after I contact the new city manager with a proposal, I get a call from a friend who says, "Eddie Muñoz is asking around town about you. He's trying to get a read on you." But the incoming city manager and I successfully negotiate my client's severance without Muñoz's direct involvement.

When Muñoz is reelected in 1989, the most recent census set Gallup's population at 18,167. The Gallup police department made 31,253 pick-ups for public intoxication that year—most of the pickups were of multiple repeaters. On average, Gallup police are picking up sixty to seventy public inebriants each weekday and two hundred each day on Fridays and Saturdays. The people picked up are piled into a concrete-slab holding tank and periodically a newspaper photo runs showing their bodies jammed into the undersized cell as they sleep off their inebriation. The rate of alcohol-related deaths in Gallup at the time is twenty times higher than the national average.

Public drunkenness has become a daily sight for me by now. Every day I see inebriants weave past on the sidewalk with glazed eyes, slurring their speech, almost all nonthreatening to the point of being deferential. About once a week an intoxicated person, invariably a man, bursts into the lobby of our office and makes a scene, demanding money or begging for it.

Sporadically, I see something I can't unsee or hear something I can't unhear. One winter day, my partners and I go out the back door of our office to drive to lunch. We see a man in a dark coat and Levi's weaving into the small parking area behind the office as snow begins to fall. When we return an hour later, the man is sitting on a gas meter, leaning back against a brick wall. He is passed out cold, covered with two inches of snow, his pants at his ankles and a frozen turd dangling halfway out of his ass.

Not long thereafter, a friend asks me, "Did you hear about the woman who died on Coal Street last week?"

"No, what happened?"

"She tripped and fell face down," he tells me. "She was so drunk that she didn't try to break the fall. She landed face down, cracked her skull and bled to death on the sidewalk."

Mother Teresa in Sacred Heart Cathedral in the late 1980s. As one of my friends in attendance said, "When you hear it from her, it seems to make sense." *Courtesy of Martin Link*

When I'm with my kids, I'm never worried about their safety, but I'm constantly keeping an eye out to avoid situations where harsh images will startle or upset them.

A year after Muñoz's 1987 reelection, the public drunkenness in Gallup has begun to attract attention from the outside world. Mother Teresa visits Gallup twice and establishes ministries for her Missionaries of Charity in Gallup. "There is just as much need here as in New York, in Washington, DC, and in Calcutta," she said. On one of her visits, the diminutive future saint stands on a step stool behind the podium at Sacred Heart Cathedral to speak to a standing-room-only crowd.

I ask a friend who attended the talk about her impressions of the future saint. "She talked very simply," my friend says. "She said, 'God is love.' Pretty simple, but when you hear it from her, it seems to make sense."

Other goings-on in Gallup at the time are of a less mystical nature. In early 1988, the *Albuquerque Tribune* rents an apartment in town for six months and sends a 27-year-old reporter with Taos Pueblo and Navajo ancestry, along with a photographer, to Gallup to live and work full time in Gallup on a series of articles about the alcohol problems. The *Tribune* reporter starts following three Navajo boys from Chinle, Arizona, near Canyon de Chelly, who live in Gallup in an old boxcar on the banks of the main arroyo, the Rio Puerco, that runs east to west through town. The Chinle Boys, as they call themselves, just hang out in Gallup and drink all the time. They are part of a fluctuating cast of around three hundred or so people who live the same lifestyle. A second reporter works on the series while still living in Albuquerque. Beginning on September 26, 1988, the *Tribune* runs the weeklong series of articles titled "Gallup, A Town Under the Influence."

Every article in the eight-page A section of the paper for the entire week is devoted to Gallup's alcohol problem. The series will later win multiple journalism awards. But the project editor, a former legislative editor, is spurred by a goal other than winning awards; he wants to find out whether intensive public service journalism can help overcome the liquor industry's stranglehold on the New Mexico legislature.

Around the same time the *Tribune* is running its series, Gallup's private hospital is holding a workshop for its managers. The hospital has been struggling to retain doctors and other employees. Gallup's alcoholism problem is cited repeatedly. The hospital board president keeps asking the hospital staff and volunteers, "How long are you going to step over the bodies? How long are you going to put up with this?"

Someone in a breakout session suggests a protest march to Santa Fe, the state capital. Instantly, the idea captures the attention of the group. Every other idea pales in comparison. The hospital creates a committee to pursue the march and quickly decides that Mayor Muñoz should be involved.

Muñoz is initially lukewarm about the idea of a march; he thinks it is a little over-the-top and questions whether anyone will show up. He says there'll be just five people out there.

Around Thanksgiving the speaker of the New Mexico House of Representatives and the president pro tem of the state senate come to Gallup in response to the publicity generated by the *Tribune* series. Both are longtime political allies of the state's powerful liquor lobby and they are coming to meet with Muñoz and tell Gallup what the legislature will *not* do. The legislative leaders give their standard litany: Gallup has always had this problem. Gallup is always going to have this problem. All you can do is try to keep a lid on it. Just keep a lid on it.

The legislator's rhetoric sets Muñoz off. He walks out of the meeting and tells the hospital organizers that he wants to leave the next day for Santa Fe, even though the legislative session is still a couple months off. Muñoz is furious. Built like a pit bull, he puts his head down when he is angry and just charges ahead. Now he doesn't care *who* else shows up. He and Margaret are going to walk to Santa Fe, alone if they have to.

Muñoz and the hospital's CEO, David Conejo, become the public leaders of the Walk to Santa Fe and several administrators, two of whom are assigned to wrangle the legislature, plan the logistics. A slate of bills is drawn up proposing the closure of drive-up liquor windows, the implementation of a 5 percent liquor excise tax to fund alcohol treatment, and a $2.5 million appropriation for a detox facility to replace Gallup's holding tank.

Shortly before the 1989 legislative session starts, a man who had been drinking at the Silver Spur Bar on east 66 in Gallup leaves the bar and begins driving with a blood-alcohol level of 0.323, more than four times the legal limit. The man hits another car head-on, killing himself and all three occupants in the other car, including a Navajo baby girl—Jovita Vega. The march organizers contact the baby's mother, who agrees to let the walk use her baby's name—it will be called the Journey for Jovita.

One more point of convergence that bodes well for the walk comes after some local Navajo residents and churches twelve miles north of Gallup at Tohlakai form a movement to protest the transfer of a liquor license to the doorstep of the Navajo Nation, at a gas station where there had been a history of homeless men with high blood-alcohol levels freezing to death. Several months before the walk was organized, Muñoz came out to meet with the organizers of the protest and helped them develop a successful strategy. After they blocked the transfer of the liquor license, the Navajo organizers joined forces with Muñoz and the hospital to rally Navajo support for the walk.

But the walk awakens a dark counterbalancing force as well. A couple of children's bicycles disappear from one walk organizer's front porch. Soon thereafter he answers the phone, and a man says, "We got the bicycles—next time we will get the kids." A female hospital administrator answers a call and a man tells her she will lose her job and that she should reconsider her involvement in the walk because she can't protect her children all the time. A Navajo walk organizer from Tohlakai receives a call from his second-grade daughter's school saying that a stranger unsuccessfully attempted to check the organizer's daughter out of school. The organizers report the calls to police and start keeping a closer eye on their children's whereabouts.

The Walk to Santa Fe kicks off on February 17, 1989, a beautiful Sunday afternoon with 150 marchers gathering at a McDonalds on Gallup's east side while the Gallup High Band plays. One skeptic says, "Yeah, wait till Monday morning and see if anybody shows up" but the next day 150 people show up again for the next twenty-mile segment of the route. Different people join the march each day, and most days there are never fewer than 120. And some days, when the Navajo communities along the route pour out, 400 or 500 people walk together, so many that the highway patrol gives the marchers escorts both in front of and behind the group.

Gallup is 205 miles from Santa Fe; the marchers have figured on walking twenty miles a day for ten days, and then finishing up with a short walk from the outskirts of Santa Fe to the steps of the Roundhouse, New Mexico's capitol, on the eleventh day. Every day Muñoz and the hospital CEO, David Conejo, walk in front of the marchers, Muñoz with

The Walk to Santa Fe. Eddie Muñoz (right with walking staff and wide-brimmed hat) and Margaret Muñoz (center with white shirt and cap).

a walking stick, Teddy Roosevelt hat, hunting vest, and hunter's pants held up by suspenders. A local baker from Gallup brings an accordion and plays marching cadences he learned in the army, and the marchers sing in unison as they walk.

Muñoz's feet blister badly but he walks through it. Margaret Muñoz drives the couple's RV behind the marchers for those that need help. She later tells me, "At night his feet had blisters the size of quarters that were bleeding and swollen. He was diabetic. He put his feet in an ice bucket and then lay on the couch in the RV with his feet up on pillows to reduce the swelling. He would lie on the couch thinking about strategies to combat the alcohol problem in Gallup and say, 'These plans come into my head that can never be. I keep getting insights as to what we should do, these ideas.'"

About fifty miles into the walk, the group runs into an approaching snowstorm. They stop on Route 66 at a tourist trap with a fast-food restaurant as it starts raining and snowing. The hospital organizers confer and worry that some of the Navajo women are not dressed for the weather. Conejo gets up and makes an announcement that any walkers not dressed for the storm need to get on a bus and go home. As they finish their meal, the organizers look up to see the owner of the store passing out plastic bags to the Navajo women who proceed to cut holes in the bags to wear them as raincoats. One of the organizers chokes up at the sight and begins crying. Muñoz lightens the mood by calling out, dubbing the group "knights in shining plastic."

The winter weather inspires both conflict as well as moments of tenderness between walk organizers and the Navajo grandmas who are stalwarts of the march. One organizer tries to talk a shivering grandma into riding with Margaret Muñoz in the Winnebago. The grandma raises a walking stick, shakes it, and speaks in Navajo. The organizer asks a translator if he offended the woman. "Yeah," the translator says. "What she just told you was 'Get out of my way, white guy. I lost my husband, my oldest son, and my youngest niece to this demon, this black thing.'" The grandma then makes a spitting sound and walks off.

The walk generates spur-of-the-moment participation by many Navajos as the route passes their communities. They leave their homes in the middle of winter without any planning and are sometimes unprepared. Several Navajo women wear rubber snow boots or galoshes that cause severe blisters. In the town of Grants, roughly halfway between Gallup and Albuquerque, the march stops to buy walking shoes for several of the women. The Navajo women are resilient, as were their ancestors who made marches sometimes twice as long 125 years earlier in far worse conditions.

Food and lodging are well organized for the marchers as local communities along the route, particularly Navajo communities, provide meals and open the doors of chapter houses, schools, and churches to give the walkers a place to sleep. "My God, the meals," one organizer later tells me. "There was posole and then mutton stews, and then the breads, and then the lamb, and then someone would bring in hams, and somebody would be flipping burgers and hot dogs for the young ones."

The overnight lodging was meager. The Muñoz's Winnebago carried bedrolls and blankets that were laid out on the floors of chapels and chapter houses. "I remember being so tired and then going to these school houses along the way where we slept, and you would open the door and all you would smell is dirty socks and Bengay," one organizer tells me after the march. "I never smelled Bengay again without thinking of the march."

While the march is overcoming obstacles and moving forward, things are not going as well in Santa Fe where two of the organizers are running back and forth for committee hearings on the walk's legislative agenda. It looks like nothing is happening. Regarding the drive-up-window bill, legislators are telling the organizers, "That's unconstitutional; you can't do that. That's restraint of trade." Of the excise tax on alcohol they say, "You can't do that. That's selective unfair targeting that will never pass."

The organizers assigned to the legislature begin to feel anxious about the legislative prospects. It looks as if they're going to have a great march but that not a lot is going to happen. They have a sense that it could all be for nothing.

Things begin to change, though, when the marchers get to Albuquerque and news coverage grows. The marchers are in a narrow line, two by two, on Central Avenue with the Gallup baker playing his accordion when a Navajo woman trips and falls forward; as she does, she grabs the baker's sweatpants and pulls them down to his knees. The baker quickly recovers, missing only a couple of notes and looks up to see two Albuquerque TV cameramen filming it all.

Rally on the capitol steps at the end of the Walk to Santa Fe. One organizer of the event, Judy Conejo, said, "There were people for as far as I could see." *Copyright The New Mexican, Inc. Reprinted with permission. All rights reserved.*

Both Albuquerque newspapers, the *Journal* and *Tribune,* together with the TV stations give the walk extensive coverage and both papers editorialize in favor of the walk's legislative agenda. One *Tribune* editorial describes the power and influence of liquor lobbyists in Santa Fe and then asks, "Who do you think will win? Those with the immense courage of the human spirit, or the best argument that money can buy?"

Muñoz and Conejo are the public faces of the walk. During interviews, Muñoz gives the emotional side of the story and tells touching stories, and Conejo explains the problem factually and details what the group hopes to accomplish in the legislature. "They were a really good team," one organizer later says. "Two guys with big egos, but they were caught up in a mission."

The marchers aren't expecting to see New Mexico's governor, Garrey Carruthers, in Santa Fe. Carruthers is at a governor's conference at a swank out-of-state resort, but when an aide tells him about the media attention and the growing number of marchers, he changes his plans and comes back to Santa Fe. On the final day of the walk, February 27, 2018, there are 1,400 marchers, and the procession stretches for two miles. On the steps of the capitol the marchers are met by the governor.

"We got to the steps of the Capital, "and I turned back and there were people for as far as I could see," Conejo's wife Judy later says. "The thought just went through my mind, *If I were to die right now, it would have been enough.*"

The president pro tem of the senate, who had infuriated Muñoz during his visit to Gallup before the legislative session, stops all other legislative business and gives the walk "the privilege of the Senate" letting the marchers present their case to the combined membership of the New Mexico house and senate.

During the joint session, both the mother of the baby Jovita and the widow of the drunk driver who killed Jovita speak. "One of the ladies was talking," an organizer later says. "As she concluded and turned, the other stood up. I really didn't know what was going to happen. I thought, *Is she going to tear into her?* But as she stood up and took that first step, they turned to one another, they made eye contact, and only as a mother or a sister would feel, they did not say any words to one another. They just embraced. People gasped. There was silence."

Vega and Christie hug on the floor of the New Mexico Senate. One of the event organizers, Herb Moser, said, "They just embraced. People gasped. There was silence."
Copyright The New Mexican, Inc. Reprinted with permission. All rights reserved.

The day after the walk, at our office in Gallup, one of my partner's Catholic buddies shows up early in the morning talking excitedly about the walk. "It was me," he says, "walking with a bunch of Navajo grandmas! Can you picture that?" Without telling any of us, he had taken the day off from work, driven to Santa Fe, and joined the marchers for the final four miles to the Capitol. I immediately feel regret, knowing that he's done exactly what I wanted to do but didn't. I never considered doing the entire walk. There was no way I could have pulled that off, but I did want to join for a day or two. No one had approached me about participating, and I never gathered the nerve to suggest the idea to my wife or partner. I feel disappointed in myself and silently resolve not to pass up another opportunity like this to stand up for a cause so worthy.

In Santa Fe, the legislative session continues after the marchers return to Gallup. Before the legislature adjourns, the walk's entire legislative agenda—the ban on drive-up liquor windows, the 5 percent excise tax on alcohol, and the appropriation of money for a new short-term detox facility—are passed and signed by the governor and become law.

After the walk, although Gallup's alcohol problems remain at critical levels and there are plenty of political battles left to fight, four words—"It will never change"—seem to vanish from the community vocabulary. And they begin to vanish from my own vocabulary too.

Muñoz has blown the lid off Gallup's alcohol problem. Will it stay off?

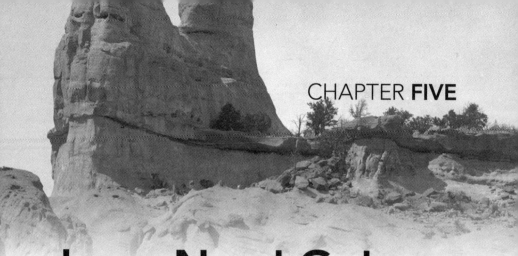

CHAPTER FIVE

Leap Now! Go!

The tips of my feet are balancing on opposing sides of a vertical rock chimney. I'm looking up at the crux move (the hardest part of a climb) on Lizard Head, a towering volcanic spire that bursts from a high, rounded prominence in the San Juan Mountains. My mountaineering buddy, Craig, is feeding me rope as I test each hold on my way up toward a small overhang. With a metal camming device in hand, I extend my reach to its limit, slot the device in a fist-sized crack below the overhang, and let out a yell.

"Are you okay?" shouts Craig forty feet below.

"Yes," I shout back, "This is great!"

I ready myself to make the move I've visualized for over a year. With the camming device protectively in place, I gather myself, absorb the moment and the surreal nature of this place, reach for a hold, and pull up and over the bulge.

Earlier, at dawn, Craig and I skied cross-country through a thick forest and high meadows, post-holed up the huge mound from which the spire extends, and gathered ourselves and our gear beneath a large, broken dihedral at the southern base of the spire. Taking turns climbing and belaying on the first pitch, we ascended sixty-five feet of rotten rock to a small platform and climbed a large crack to an airy ledge from

Bob Rosebrough slots a metal camming device into a fist-sized crack to protect the crux pitch on Lizard Head. *Courtesy of Craig Pirlot*

which we finished the pitch on a wildly exposed ten-foot traverse on solid rock.

We un-roped and scrambled up a rotten talus slope to the second, final pitch, with the chimney and crux overhang, to gain the small rocky summit and a 360-degree view of thirteen- and fourteen-thousand-foot peaks with the snow of late spring still on their flanks. There I'm feeling wildly, fiercely alive, as if I'm exactly where I'm meant to be. This climb has taken me to a place and to a physical challenge at the limits of my ability—it's the culmination of years of focus and effort.

During junior high in Farmington as a tall, gangly kid, I wasn't good enough to make any of the school athletic teams, but beginning in high school, I threw myself completely into basketball. There was the thrill of faking out the safety with a misdirection pass and my first dunk—was it really a dunk?—after hundreds of failed attempts. Then, in time, there were brief, peak experiences when it all came together, ripping a rebound and letting out a guttural yell in the intramural finals for the law school team and jamming a rebound dunk into the basket at the AAU regionals in Wichita, Kansas.

Basketball was just the first in a series of athletic passions. Next came distance running and long miles up Chokecherry Canyon in

Ike Weaver approaches Snowdon Peak on a winter climb in the San Juans.
Photo by Bob Rosebrough

Rappelling a technical route in the San Juans. *Courtesy of Ernie Stromeyer*

On top of Vestal Peak in the Grenadier Range of the San Juan Mountains.
Courtesy of Ernie Stromeyer

Farmington, around the golf course next to the law school, and up Gibson Canyon to the overlook behind the Gallup flea market; there were tight hamstrings, aching arches, and the occasional, blissfully euphoric runner's high.

Next came racquetball and early-morning and lunchtime games at the Gallup Fitness Center—rushing to and from work, breaking into an intense full-body sweat, feeling the sting as the blue rubber ball hit the back of my leg, watching every move of my opponent, conserving energy to pounce and unleashing a lethal forehand, sending the ball screaming inches above the floor down the passing lane.

Then came mountaineering and predawn hikes at a rhythmic, meditative pace, with the world confined to the illuminated circle of my headlamp—kicking up snowfields with ice ax in hand and crampons on my feet, earning 360-degree views above timberline. The climactic moments when a rope is broken out and I reach the crux and then inch across a ledge, testing the soundness of every hold while calming the fear I feel at the dizzying drop at my feet.

Next came cycling—skinny tires, Lycra shorts, sharing a pace line to break a headwind, burning quads, and a sore neck. Long miles are spent pumping rhythmically up hills sitting upright and then standing

 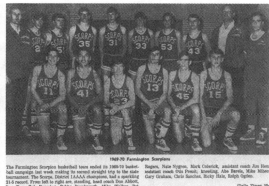

1969-70 Farmington Scorpions

The Farmington Scorpion basketball team ended its 1969-70 basketball campaign last week making its second straight trip to the state tournament. The Scorps, District 1AAAA champions, had a sparkling 21-5 record. From left to right are, standing, head coach Don Abbott, Ron Foss, Bob Downing, Bobby Rosebrough, Mike Walker, Pat

Rogers, Nate Nygren, Mark Colerick, assistant coach Jim Henn, assistant coach Otis Pronit; kneeling, Abe Barela, Mike Mihee, Gary Graham, Chris Sanchez, Ricky Hale, Ralph Ogden.

(Daily Times Ph

(left) Bob Rosebrough as a senior at Farmington High. *Courtesy of Bob Rosebrough.* (right) Bob Rosebrough (top row, fourth from left) as a junior at Farmington High. *Farmington Daily Times*

to dance on the pedals; steep descents are negotiated in a tuck position at speeds that make the front wheel vibrate. During races I conserve energy while drafting another wheel with the hope of breaking away on a hill or getting the jump in a sprint.

In these ways, I felt able to express my bigger, truer self and be free of the everydayism—the repressed emotions and constraints of my life. And in nature, I blossom. Everything there is real, unpretentious, and free of egos and ideologies.

Ten years after I move to Gallup, I am invited to lunch by a couple of my friends, two downtown businessmen. They're attempting to recruit me into another realm of competition—this one not physical. I've incrementally developed an interest in Gallup politics, which up to now has been an enigma to me. My two friends want me to become the president of the Gallup Downtown Development Group, which aspires to renovate our downtown and stimulate business growth. I suspect the position would thrust me onto a collision course with Mayor Muñoz, who owns a strip mall on the east side of town and is planning another, much larger strip mall on the north side of town. Following the Walk to Santa Fe, Muñoz won a second two-year term in the spring of 1989. He opposes downtown development and says that no part of town should get more public benefits than any other part of town. I see it differently; I believe that a downtown is the heart of any city and that Gallup's downtown, which is reeling from the loss of businesses that moved to a new, covered mall a few years earlier, needs a boost.

I agree to take on the task. But first, although I know it's a longshot, "I want to reach out to Mayor Muñoz," I tell my friends, "and try to win him over."

"It's worth a try," says one of the businessmen. "You don't have anything to lose."

The city has been planning a downtown walkway that will connect the two east-west streets south of Route 66 and make the area pedestrian friendly. But the project has been going nowhere. Muñoz and a local bank president—one of the most respected men in town—are butting heads. The bank president doesn't like Muñoz's alcohol reform agenda; he thinks the publicity is bad for Gallup. He starts an advertising campaign, with the theme "Special People, Special Place" and at the unveiling ceremony he openly bashes politicians who give Gallup a black eye by focusing on the negative. He doesn't mention Muñoz by name, but everyone in the room knows who he is talking about. The bank president, like many in Gallup, seems to prefer that no one call attention to our alcohol problem. It seems to me that his views are clouded by the fact that the problem generates money that is then deposited into his bank.

Muñoz and the bank president choose the downtown walkway project to square off. Even though both the bank and the city both initially supported the project before Muñoz's election, and the city has spent a lot of money condemning and demolishing a building and constructing the walkway right up to the bank's property, *both* men now oppose the completion of the project. The bank president says the bank won't give an easement to the city, and Muñoz says he won't accept an easement if it's given. A tan, slump-block wall stands in the middle of the proposed walkway.

I enlist a friend whose deceased father was a longtime supporter of Muñoz, to set up a meeting with the mayor. My friend, Muñoz, and I gather for an early breakfast at a restaurant on Route 66. Muñoz listens and is cordial, but noncommittal. Days later, I learn from the assistant city attorney that Muñoz is continuing to actively oppose the walkway project.

With the bank president and Muñoz dug into their positions, my plan is to persuade the bank board and the city council to override them. The bank board quickly agrees to reverse the president's position, but the city council has a public protocol that Muñoz participates in as the presiding council member.

Muñoz and I battle in two public meetings. In one, he stops me mid-sentence and demands, "Stop pointing your finger at me." Not realizing that I am, I nod acquiescence, drop my hand, and continue. The council eventually votes to accept the easement from the bank, over Muñoz's objections, and within a week the slump-block wall comes down. Several community members and friends start suggesting that I consider running for mayor, and while I find the suggestion flattering, I think the prospect would be daunting.

After the walkway fracas is behind us, Gallup collectively returns to fighting over alcohol. Muñoz's secretary receives a call at home in which the caller threatens that if Muñoz doesn't get off the liquor industry's case, the caller and others will blow up his office. Muñoz describes the call during an interview on NBC's *Today* show, and two of Gallup's local liquor dealers, in turn, threaten a defamation lawsuit against Muñoz. Liquor dealers circulate petitions calling for a grand jury investigation into alleged misuse of funds by the city related to the Walk to Santa Fe, but such a jury is not convened.

The sheriff's department plans a sting operation; several under-cover agents are recruited to drink well past the point of intoxication in a monitored environment and are then taken around town to bars where they try to buy a drink. Twelve of Gallup's bars serve the under-cover agents, despite their obvious intoxication. The DA's office files sales-to-intoxicated-persons charges, the liquor-dealers lawyer up, and the cases get bogged down in court. The liquor dealers file suits alleging that both the ban on drive-up windows and the 5 percent excise tax passed in response to the Walk to Santa Fe are unconstitutional "special" legislation because they apply only to San Juan and McKinley Counties, but the court rules against the liquor dealers in both suits and eventually, after referendum elections, both the drive-up window ban and the excise tax become law.

The *Gallup Independent*, which previously editorialized in favor of the Walk, now has a new editor who's singing a new song: Gallup's alcohol problems are no worse than anywhere else, he writes in an editorial, and community leaders should focus on the positive and spend less time dwelling on the negative.

I really didn't like facing off with Muñoz in the walkway battle; I respect his doggedness and courage, and I still regret sitting on the sidelines during the Walk to Santa Fe. But my attempts to break down the personal wall between Muñoz and me haven't worked. I'm hoping my next move with the Gallup Downtown Development Group, measures to combat public drunkenness in the downtown district, will put us on the same team.

Gallup's downtown has historically been the epicenter of its alcohol problem. After meeting with each of the downtown bar owners and persuading some but not all of them to voluntarily give up package liquor sales during business hours, I propose a zoning ordinance that will have the force of law. I also propose to ban Gallup's blood plasma center, which provides money often used for alcohol purchases, from the downtown district.

I assume Muñoz will support the proposals, given the general anti-alcohol stance he has taken, but to the consternation of some of his supporters, he opposes them, again because all commercial districts in town, he says, should be treated equally. After I jump through hoops at a series of meetings with the Planning and Zoning Commission, with large supportive crowds at each meeting, the P&Z Commission delays making a decision. Instead, a rare joint session of the P&Z Commission and City Council is called.

The joint meeting has purportedly been called to give the commission and council the opportunity to ask for more information. I lay out the Downtown Development Group proposal yet again and then I stand for questions, but none come. I continue to stand, quietly waiting and feeling anger rise in me. The P&Z Commissioners and the City Councilor members seem to me to be cowards, wasting our time and making us appear at their meetings unnecessarily. I blast both the commission and council, telling them exactly what I'm thinking, then walk out. A friend, a guy I play racquetball with at lunch, walks out with me. He points to a bench where we sit and talk. There is an odd look on his face, one I've never seen before. He seems to be simultaneously embarrassed for me and proud of me. As I cool off, I'm just embarrassed. I assume our proposals are dead.

The next day my law partner tells me that he talked to Phil Garcia, a P&Z commissioner and the manager of Gallup Title, the company that provides title insurance to home buyers. "Phil said you blew up last night," my partner says. "It really took him by surprise. He said he's never seen you even come close to losing your temper before."

I call Phil and say, "Can we talk?" I walk a block to his office.

"If you're willing to apologize to Jim [the commission chairman], I think we can get this back on track," Phil says. He tells me that the commissioners support our proposals but are laying low, trying to force Muñoz and the city council to take a public position.

"Some people are going to be upset with us if we approve this," he says. "We were trying to get the Council to take a position—to know whether our vote will do some good or whether we are taking a tough stand for nothing."

I tell Phil I'll call the commission chairman. Before I leave, he says, "You know, we've been stuck doing things one way for a long time. I told the chairman, 'It's time we listen to some of the new people in town and try something different.'"

Muñoz, though, is still the key. I call several people who supported Muñoz in the Walk to Santa Fe. "Please talk to Mayor Muñoz," I beg them. "This is going to die without his support." A few days later, Muñoz's secretary at city hall calls me and asks if I can meet him. She gives me a time.

In the sunny corner mayor's office at city hall, Muñoz gets right to the point. "If you drop the plasma center from your regulations, I'll support your proposal," he says. I agree. Within a minute, I'm out of his office. The liquor dealers still oppose the regulations, but the deal is done, and both the commission and council enact the zoning regulations against package liquor sales during business hours in the downtown. It's a big win.

The national media continues to cover Gallup. NBC's *Today* show, with Hugh Downs and Jane Pauley, runs a two-part series depicting Gallup as an alcohol war zone. It opens with a scene of a man passed out along Route 66. Throughout the program, there are shots of frozen bodies, policemen escorting staggering men into vans, and sleeping prisoners passed out in rows like sardines in the Adult Detention Center holding tank. No mention is made of the Walk to Santa Fe or its legislative successes.

ABC's *20-20* follows with a segment called "Dying for a Drink in Drunk Town." It includes videotape of the Walk to Santa Fe along with scenes of alcohol fatalities and public inebriants being rounded up by police. At one point while the reporter, John Stossel, is interviewing a Navajo tribal councilman, a passing intoxicated Navajo man starts accusing the reporter of "picking on" Indians and Stossel argues back. City police officers are shown making daily rounds to pick up street alcoholics. Muñoz appears in one segment and says something that makes me cringe.

"There's one!" he says pointing out an inebriated man while riding with a reporter at night. The second I hear those words on TV, I know there's going to be trouble. The episode makes Muñoz appear to be over-eager to help the national media show Gallup's worst side. I know the segment is going to generate yet another backlash. Days later, a waitress in a Gallup bar starts circulating recall petitions against Muñoz, and it doesn't take long for her to get enough signatures to force an election.

Muñoz calls me, and many other people in town, to ask for support in the recall election and I and others agree. Our conversation, like the one we had in settling the downtown zoning dispute, is quick and to the point, with no small talk. I agree to give a quote for use in one of his ads and I donate $100 to help pay for an ad, but we never meet in person or talk again about the recall.

Muñoz survives the recall, barely, with 51.76 percent of the vote, and word spreads that he's not planning to run for reelection in 1991. Some of my friends renew their suggestion that I consider running, but one businessman who'd encouraged me backs off gently. He says, "I'm not sure that your job as a lawyer will combine well with being mayor." I think he's just being diplomatic—I assume he's troubled by my blowup at the meeting of the council and P&Z Commission and no longer thinks I have the temperament for the job.

Shortly after the downtown zoning battle and the recall election, our local Council of Governments, a tri-county community development agency with its headquarters in Gallup, secures a large planning grant from the Robert Wood Johnson Foundation. A task force for what is called the Fighting Back Initiative is formed, which is charged with applying for a multiyear implementation grant. The object of the planning task force, which includes many Navajo people, is to create a grassroots community-based plan to reduce the demand for drugs and alcohol in the area. The executive director of the COG asks me to consider being a cochairman of the steering committee. I'm conflicted, almost tormented for weeks, by the choice between serving on the task force and running for mayor, until I take the time to do something I rarely do.

At my desk at work, I clear my mind and pray for guidance. After a few minutes of fervent silent prayer, I open my eyes and gaze around and, though I don't hear a voice or experience an epiphany, there's no more conflict. I want to serve on the steering committee, and I have no regrets about giving up the idea of running for mayor.

But as cochairman of the Fighting Back Initiative steering committee, I'm largely inept, ineffective, and unnecessarily combative. I become embroiled in a brief turf war with Muñoz and in a protracted, contentious battle with the executive director of the Council of Governments, when my request for budget information is ignored. One of the task force members writes a personal letter to me saying that she feels I see things in black and white and that I have trouble considering other people's perspectives. She tells me that she agrees with me on the substance of the two disputes, but she feels there is a better way for me to handle them.

I reply that I've considered her comments but that I have no interest in changing my approach. We're right, I tell her, and we'll become energized as a group if we fight and win together.

As the task force slogs along, hindered by a lack of clear direction and turf wars, I gain a few insights and make connections with some Navajo people that I wouldn't otherwise have encountered.

During a day-long task force session, our facilitator has us form small groups for discussion. An outspoken middle-aged Navajo woman begins talking in an aggressive tone about the litany of wrongs that Americans have inflicted on Navajos, including their internment at Bosque Redondo. When she finishes, I tell her the past wrongs she's talking about really aren't my problem; I am volunteering my time to help fix a problem I didn't create. "I wasn't around in 1864," I say. After an awkward pause, the conversation tepidly resumes but goes nowhere.

I begin to consider that I may need to rethink my point of view. I realize that, while I'm prone to righteous indignation at times, I have a problem when people express negative emotion to me. When it comes to emotion, it seems I can dish it out, but I can't take it.

An elderly Catholic nun, an Anglo, who has worked in the substance abuse field for decades asks me for a word after one meeting.

"There are three basic groups of Navajo people," she says. "Some still live a traditional Navajo lifestyle, some have transitioned to a modern lifestyle, and some are stuck somewhere in the middle. The first two groups of people do pretty well. The ones who are stuck in the middle between a traditional life and a modern life without being grounded in either world are the people we see struggling." I find myself thinking how hard it would be for me to adopt the lifestyle and values of a culture that had subjugated and imprisoned my ancestors by force. I don't think I would do well at that.

In yet another meeting, an eloquent young traditional Navajo man asks to speak to the group about the concept of *hozho*. He draws a large circle on a whiteboard and draws images of people, animals, a rainbow, food, money, cars, and books, and as he talks, he uses words like *walking in beauty*, *balance*, and *harmony*. Pointing to the different objects in the circle, he talks about how important it is for Navajos to find balance with each aspect of life. To a Navajo, he says, religion is not a separate concept that is accessible at select times or in select places. It is ever-present. The world in its entirety is holy and every aspect of a traditional Navajo's life—eating, breathing, walking, tending livestock, sleeping—is treasured.

I'm struck by the depth of his sincerity and moved by the sorrow he feels for Navajo people who are trapped in a cycle of alcohol abuse. "They are outside of themselves," he says. "They have lost harmony; they have lost balance."

Amidst occasional moments of depth and compassion, the task force grinds on and on for another year or so, with turf wars and conflict far more common than interludes of insight. At the public presentation of our task force proposal to the Robert Wood Johnson Foundation, Muñoz, who by then is no longer mayor, attends and presents me with a turquoise tie clip in the shape of a ram; he tells me, and the assembled crowd, that the ram symbolizes a fighting spirit and that he appreciates my efforts. The foundation panel tells us that they are impressed by our written proposal, which has been produced almost entirely by the Council of Governments staff.

But I'm embarrassed that our proposal is staff driven and that I and the other community members have contributed little to it. And while I'm pleasantly surprised by Muñoz's public gesture, I really don't think I deserve recognition. If anything, I would enjoy just going to lunch and having a conversation with Muñoz, but it never occurs to me to suggest that to him. Our grant application is approved, but I'm tired, frustrated, and burned out; I don't participate in the implementation phase of the initiative.

Not long thereafter, during the summer before I turn 40, my wife and kids and I go on a weeklong vacation. But first we go to see my wife's relatives in Oklahoma. While in Tulsa, I ask about local cycling races and find out that the state championships are being held the next day. On the spur of the moment, I decide to enter.

The course is a fourteen-mile circuit north of Tulsa, around lakes and over rolling, lush green hills that we are to ride three times. I'm grouped with a dozen masters riders, and as we take off, we ride at a slow pace—too slow. After a few miles, I find myself thinking: *This pace is ridiculous. Why are we going this slow?*

There is no answer. About ten miles into the first circuit, I decide to push the pace myself, and I take a long, hard pull. When I pull over to let the next rider take the lead, I find that there is no next rider.

I'm by myself, far in the lead, with thirty miles of race to go—a lone rider ahead of a fading pack. *Go! Don't look back! Go!* I feel adrenaline surging through my body. Every nerve ending is tingling at the prospect of forging ahead and trying to ride solo to victory. And I do; it's a cyclist's dream. I finish the next thirty miles a minute and a half ahead of what has become a frothing, surging pack.

At the end of the week, my fortunes are to turn. My family and I stop in Carlsbad Caverns, then drive to Silver City for the Tour of the Gila, a three-day stage race over the rugged Gila Mountains. Here I'm grouped with a large conglomerate pack that includes young national-class riders with lean, hard bodies, as well as seasoned masters riders. The courses aren't rolling; they're severe, sustained climbs done in the summer heat of southern New Mexico. I haven't ridden since Oklahoma, and I start the final and hardest stage tied for fourth in my age group with a rider from Arizona. The day is cloudless and brutally hot. I'm tired and sore from the first two days of racing. I hope I get through this. I feel fragile—like an eggshell.

After twelve miles of flat riding, we begin the first of two huge climbs. My rear gears start skipping, and I lose the lead pack at the base of the climb. Another rider and I try to close the gap to the lead riders, and after an exhausting effort we catch a pack of ten that has splintered from the now small group of leaders. With my gears continuing to slip and shift, I hang on the back of the group of ten to the top of the climb.

At the base of the next climb, my group breaks into pairs and solo riders. I'm neck and neck with the Arizona rider and struggling to keep up. I'm starting to lose ground, but I hang on, keeping him in sight. My breathing is becoming labored, my shoulders slump, and the circular rhythm of my feet slows to piston-like stabs.

At the top of the second climb, the Arizonan pulls away and is gone. I have nothing left. I'm shattered—completely exhausted and dehydrated—but the race is not done. There are ten miles of rolling terrain to the finish. Straggling riders are beginning to zip by me. There is nothing I can do. I barely manage to keep my bike moving forward. As I near the finish, a friend's teenage daughter spots me, and a look of alarm spreads over her face.

I leave something behind on those hills. I can't keep going this hard, I think. I'm exhausted in more than a passing way. The core of my body is a dull, throbbing ache.

A few months later, I'm delivering a package I've been asked to take to a friend, and as I enter his house, I walk into a surprise party for my fortieth birthday. I'm completely taken off guard. Initially, I'm happy and excited, but as the party progresses my excitement begins to wear off. Earlier in the day, my wife's Suburban was sprayed by a solvent of some sort. I suspect the vandalism was the work of the bitter ex-wife of a friend I'm representing in a restraining order case, and I'm upset about it—more upset than a ruined paint job warrants. Something deep inside me has been triggered. On the backyard patio, after the initial excitement of the surprise wears off, I stand near the barbeque grill with fire leaping from the dripping grease and smoke billowing. I'm slumped in thought. *Why am I this unhappy? Why is my life turning out like this? It isn't supposed to be this way.*

Later the party moves inside. I'm momentarily revived as my friends sit in a semicircle around me and tell "Bob stories." Most of the stories are told by my old friends. And from the expression on the face of one of my newer friends, it seems that he is thinking, *I haven't seen that side of Bob.*

After the stories and laughter are over, I'm depressed and ill at ease again. *I'm not the same person they're talking about. I don't have as much fun as that guy did. What has happened to my life?*

At this middle point of my life, anger I've built up for years is beginning to spew out. Many of my hard-wired habits, beliefs, and personality traits, which have been loyal soldiers to me, are under siege. I've harbored grievances against my senior partner and my wife, going back years. He's in firm control of the law office, and I don't feel there is any air left in the building for me to breathe. She's firmly in charge of child-rearing and religion in ways that seem foreign to me, and I feel I'm on the verge of exploding.

And I'm incapable of acknowledging my own faults and clueless as to how to resolve my bottled-up grievances constructively. I haven't initiated any steps to improve either relationship, and I've passed up the few opportunities with each of them when they've seemed to open the door toward making things better. At some deep level, I'm incompatible with both of them—we don't see the world the same way.

My repressed anger erupts in numerous situations where I can express it with righteous indignation. I'm bounced from an overbooked flight from Phoenix to Gallup, after arriving at the terminal well before most of the other passengers, and it means that I'll have to miss my son Matt's basketball game the next morning, and I'm the coach. I seethe and glare while complaining to the woman at the gate.

My anger comes out in barbed comments. I become embroiled in a dispute with an out-of-town lawyer named Dick when I feel he has reneged on his word. I tell a friend, "When he was born his parents didn't give him a name, they made a prediction."

I feel like I've lost my bearings. On Sunday, when a new priest at church starts talking about statues in Italy that are crying blood and prophecies about what is going to happen to the world in two years, I don't know what to make of it. I feel untethered, adrift—should I be afraid or is this sermon just nonsense?

Pressures that have continuously been building in my life for fifteen years are now coming to a head. I've been chafing at the role of junior partner at work, and it seems to me that I will never be on an equal footing with my senior partner, no matter what I do or how hard I work.

I agree to represent two of the defendants in a federal court case and I refer additional defendants to a close friend from law school, Cliff, who is practicing in Albuquerque. Cliff has become an exceptional lawyer. During depositions he assumes a neutral facial expression and takes control of the room as he lets a witness know that every question he asks will be answered even if it means the witness will have to sit there for days. As the depositions continue, I daydream the image of Cliff slicing the belly of a fat, shiny, silver fish with a knife and pulling the guts out with his bare hands. In law school, Cliff seemed anxious, but now fifteen years later he is masterful in his profession while I feel like I'm plodding along.

I'm in a routine that's draining. Every day the bedside alarm goes off at 5 a.m. I get out of bed, slip on the sweatpants I laid out the night before, and drive to work in the dark. After a couple hours at work I drive home, get dressed, and help get the kids ready for school. I drop them off at school on the way back to work.

One afternoon, I get a call from a friend. "Hey," he says. "We're meeting at Rudy's house and going for a ride after work. Can you go?"

Although I desperately want to go, I say, "Not today, man. Thanks for calling. Give me a rain check." I drive home after work and begin helping around the house and shuttling kids to and from activities. Our nighttime routine begins, and I help get the kids bathed and read them bedtime stories. The next morning the alarm goes off again at 5.

I seize on a solution that I naively think will resolve everything that's bothering me: I'm tired of being treated as a junior partner—either I become a full partner in every sense, or I start my own practice. I catch my partners one at a time to discuss these matters, and we start going to lunch periodically. We go on short retreats. There's an edge in the air. I'm trying to talk in calm, measured tones—in ways I hope they can hear—although I don't really know how to do that. No matter how I try to stifle my stridency, I know my senior partner senses the bile of my indignation and feels the edge of my resolve. As my senior partner talks back to me—also in measured, cautious tones—it appears to me that he's thinking, *This guy is too much. He's never going to be happy no matter what I do.* Over the course of a year, tension builds and then finally breaks. It's time for me to leave.

The first step in setting up my new law practice is to see if my secretary, Brenda, will leave the firm and go with me. We have worked together for seven years, but as far as I know, she has no idea about my plans.

First thing in the morning, I ask Brenda to come into my office. I feel nervous—the way I feel before the start of a trial. This is crucial. If she doesn't come with me, I don't know how I'll do it. It would be too hard to start a new office without an experienced secretary.

Brenda sits with pen and pad in hand. As usual, she is neatly dressed. She has wavy shoulder-length hair and she is friendly, with a radiant girl-next-door smile. But as I begin telling her about the discussions that my partners and I have had over the last several months, she's all business. I know she must be aware of the tensions, but I suspect she has no idea how serious it's gotten. "We haven't been able to work through the problems," I say. "So, I'm going to start my own practice."

A look of alarm flashes across her face. *Oh no,* I think. *I'm in trouble.*

I ask her to come with me to help start my new practice and I talk about salary and plans for the new office. Brenda says she will join me, and her worry seems to subside.

"Is the split going to be ugly?" she asks. "I hope not."

I tell her I don't think so and that my partners and I have worked through most of the details. "That's good," she says, though a flicker of skepticism flashes across her face. But she nods, seeming to be willing herself to accept the statement.

The logistics of the move are all-consuming. My relationship with my former partner remains strained, and tensions flair at times as we separate assets and client files.

Two weeks later, Brenda and I meet at the office on a Saturday. We've planned to sort out files and work on a set of goals for our new office. Normally, we have short, clipped exchanges under the pressure of the workday, with additional communication conducted through cassette tapes and Post-its.

For the first time, as we sit in the conference room, we actually have the leisure to talk at length. *This is nice. I feel so different when I'm around her? Why?*

Two months after I open the new office and hire a second secretary, I ask Brenda to come on a drive with me during the middle of the day. During the transition and startup of my new office, the mutual attraction and tension between us has been unmistakable, exposing a burgeoning ease and intimacy from which there seems no escape. I need to talk with her about what's going on between us.

We drive out onto the Navajo Nation toward Window Rock, Arizona, on my favorite cycling loop, which returns to Gallup through a twenty-mile canyon with sandstone cliffs and mesas on either side, and we just talk. I tell Brenda that I remember the minute details of my first sight of her ten years ago. Two months ago, we'd never had a real conversation; today I'm sharing personal secrets with her that I've never revealed to anyone. I don't say the words, "I love you," but I say everything else. Brenda listens, absorbing what I say and then shares the story of her life with me.

The next day, Brenda comes into my office mid-morning and sits in front of my desk. She begins talking, but she's struggling with her words.

After several starts and stops, she says, "You know how you said you feel about me yesterday. That's how I feel about you."

We talk and I extend my hand across the desk. She extends hers and our hands touch lightly. I've never felt anything like this. I pull back my hand and shake my head as if in a fog. I feel dazed. Euphoric. Frightened to the core of my being.

Full catastrophe living ensues for several months, and I ride waves of euphoria and crushing depression. At one point, it all becomes so painful, I consider whether I can continue—ultimately only my love for my children is what pulls me back from the edge of the cliff.

Brenda decides to leave and take a job at city hall. One thing is clear; we can't work together anymore.

My wife and I try joint marital counseling that ultimately fails. I move out of my big home on the hill to a small rental house not far from the railroad tracks, where every other week I'm able to spend time alone with my children. I cherish the time with them, and it pulls me back from waves of depression.

During their days with me, all four kids sleep in one room together for the only time in their lives. Before going to bed, they all lie on the carpeted floor from oldest to youngest with legs extended like a human xylophone and I massage their feet and legs before we read bedtime stories. We have a small safe shelter from the swirling world outside.

I weather the unavoidable judgment and gossip of a small town. A rock shatters the glass entry way at my new office, and we replace the glass. I begin having long, deep conversations with a constant stream of people and I seek counseling. I leave the Catholic Church. My close Catholic friends and I mutually put distance between ourselves. I realize my rules-based, black-and-white thinking hasn't been working, but I'm not sure what to replace it with. I read everything about psychology, religion, and spirituality that I can get my hands on, and I plug away at my new law office. Surprisingly, most of my clients stick with me, I gain new clients, and a couple of other lawyers want to join my firm. I file for divorce.

November 15, 1995, becomes the fulcrum of my life. Twenty-six years after standing on top of the Gallup High stadium concourse, the gate to what seems like a different dimension again opens unexpectedly. Shortly before our divorce is to be finalized, I'm walking toward the front door of

Mark, Matt, Megan, Bob, and Amy (left to right) squeezed onto a backyard treehouse. *Courtesy of Bob Rosebrough*

my former house. I feel compelled to speak some words to my wife that I feel may lead to a reconciliation. I feel compelled to say the words and I have to do it *now*. It feels as if my heel will get caught in the mystical gate that's about to slam shut behind me if I don't act quickly. *Leap now! Go!*

After the conversation with my wife, which does not lead to a reconciliation, I walk back to my truck and sit behind the wheel. I've done what I was called on to do. As I sit, I am flooded with a sense of peace and an infusion of spirit—boundless, all-encompassing, and centered in my heart.

The next night I go to dinner on my 42nd birthday with my four kids at our favorite restaurant. For months, at times, they've been bundles of anxiety, particularly the two older kids. Matt has been withdrawn and pensive, and Mark has been agitated and angry. At dinner, we all sit at a round table, enjoying the moment. They say nothing to indicate that they recognize a difference, but there's no fighting, no bickering, no complaining, no tears. We sit and eat and talk in peace. Somehow the newfound peace in my heart has, at least for one evening, spilled into their lives as well.

PART
TWO

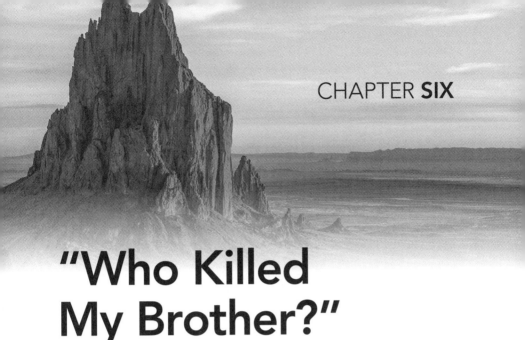

CHAPTER SIX

"Who Killed My Brother?"

Brenda and I are standing on a sandstone overlook on the south rim of Canyon de Chelly in January 1997 surrounded by a circle of forty friends and family members. Two years have passed since I left my old law firm, and it has been a year since my divorce was finalized. My bride is wearing a green, velvet, full-length dress. Her dark, curly hair frames her face, and we look at each other with relief and gratitude to be at this place and this point in our lives. Together, we've planned a simple marriage ceremony. My three older kids—Matt, Mark, and Megan handed out flowers to our guests as they arrived, and Amy, who is normally taking a nap at this time, is rubbing her eyes and yawning. Our friend and counselor Angie, who's standing in front of us, paid twenty-five dollars a few weeks ago to become a mail-order minister so that she can marry us.

The day after our wedding, we wake to tiny flakes of lightly falling snow. We bundle up and go for a walk on the canyon rim, following streams and rivulets of melting snow. The undulating slickrock is a labyrinth of still pools and gentle eddies. We follow the flow to the lip of the canyon and find an overhang beneath the canyon rim where we sit— warm, dry, silent, together. Married.

135

A January wedding at Canyon de Chelly during an interlude between two storms. *Courtesy of Lisa Rodriguez*

The bare, windswept trees on the top of the canyon are frosted with snow and melting water drips from the lip of the canyon just above us. Snowflakes fall against the backdrop of the red canyon walls. Ravens intermittently float by, riding the canyon gusts. An updraft near the canyon wall below us lifts the flakes until they flutter weightlessly around us before resuming their fall.

A couple months later, Brenda and I go to dinner at Genaro's restaurant, tucked away in Chihuahuita—the neighborhood where the lawsuits against Mexican coal miners culminated in an eviction that triggered the riot of 1935 in which Sheriff Carmichael and two coal miners were shot and killed. Genaro's decor highlights the mix of cultures and styles that epitomize Gallup. Velvet Mexican paintings hang near Navajo and Southwestern art on '70s wood paneling. The room is ringed with booths covered with puffy, '60s-style gold-specked vinyl. The jukebox offers a mix of modern, pop, country-western, and Mexican music. The center of the room is filled with fake-wood tables and black vinyl chairs.

When Brenda and I enter, we pause for a moment to chat with friends. When we turn toward the only empty booth, we see that our favorite waitress, anticipating our usual order, has already placed two waters and

A simple ceremony at a place of surreal beauty. *Courtesy of Lisa Rodriguez*

two Dr. Peppers on the table. A busboy brings a tray of tortilla chips and a small bowl of scorching salsa.

We are both in a reflective mood, and I tell her how it seems to me that midlife is a time when many of us face our mortality for the first time and seek deeper meaning in our lives. Brenda says that things she previously didn't understand have begun to make sense to her. She says she always knew she didn't want to have children of her own but didn't understand why. She talks about my four kids, who are now her spirited, high-maintenance stepchildren. "I know in my heart that I was meant to love them."

We finish our meal, feeling full and high on chili endorphins, and walk out among the small, clustered homes of Chihuahuita.

Our lives have been changing and growing. On a trip to Canyonlands in Utah earlier in the spring, I resumed meditating, a practice I'd started in college but drifted away from. After twenty-five years of athletics, my body and muscles were constantly sore and tight. A younger lawyer with a military crew cut who worked at my new office for a summer introduced me to yoga, and I feel as if I've been given a fresh start to my health.

When my son Mark plays an angel in *Godspell* and then Peter Cratchit in a community theater rendition of *A Christmas Carol*, it occurs to me that I'd like to be in a play, something I've never done. A few months later, when I see a flyer, I audition for the role of Frankenstein's monster, which I'm a natural for because of my height, in our local community theater production, and later I play Reverend Jeremiah Brown in *Inherit the Wind*. "I think I'm on the verge of being typecast," I tell Brenda. "Go on stage, throw a fit, and exit."

During my divorce, a female law-school classmate who became a top family lawyer in Albuquerque told me, "Nowadays you can still be a

A natural for the part—Bob as Frankenstein's monster. *Courtesy of Bob Rosebrough*

father after you divorce." And I find out she was right, that it's possible for a divorced father to deepen his relationship with his children—even on an every-other-week basis.

One night, the moment Megan slides under the blankets at bedtime, she says, "Tell us a story, Dad."

Amy chimes in, "Yeah, tell us a *stooory* from when you were a kid."

"Okay, I'll tell you a story. Once upon a time there was a little boy named Bobby and he was a sweet, innocent little boy, and . . ."

"Come on, *Daaad*, tell us a real story."

". . . And when his mom and dad would tell him it was time for bed, he'd do just exactly what they asked him to do, and he'd go to bed right away, and he wouldn't argue. How's that for a story?"

"*Daaad*. Come on, you know what we mean."

"Okay, let me think. Here it is: When I was in eighth grade, I really liked a girl named Margaret. She was really cute, but I was scared. I asked the girl who lived across the street from me, Vicki Sue, if Margaret would like me, and Vicki Sue said she didn't know. Well, Vicki Sue must have talked to Margaret because a couple days later at lunch break while we were outside, Margaret came over and asked if she could wear my jacket. I was with some friends and I got really nervous, and I told her no."

"Oh, Dad, what a dork you were. That's embarrassing."

Brenda comes in to kiss the girls goodnight. "You blew it, Bobby. You had your chance and you blew it big time. Good night girls."

Every Wednesday afternoon for a year, I grab the plump round knob of the door to Amy's preschool at three thirty.

I sign my name and time of arrival on a sheet next to Amy's name. Across a four-foot-high partition, two- and three-year-olds are in various stages of waking from an afternoon nap. One small boy approaches me and says, "My daddy is not the same tall as you." When I enter Amy's Pre-K building or "Vre-K," as she pronounces it. Amy, who is shy in group settings, looks up. Our eyes meet, and she quivers with joy and excitement. She catches herself instantly and freezes with self-conscious-ness. She casts furtive looks toward the other kids and her teachers as she walks stiffly toward me. Her walk is mechanical, but her face and eyes are aglow. I take her hand and we walk out to my truck.

During the summer, tension builds up noticeably with the kids. Brenda's been a taxi service each day, taking the kids from ceramics

Amy, Mark, and Megan while Matt is off at college. *Courtesy of Bob Rosebrough*

classes, swimming, doctor appointments, bowling, arts and crafts, and basketball camps. The TV is on too much and it's too loud. For the last month or so, Mark has seemed more distant and even agitated.

I have an idea. "When I get home tonight," I tell Brenda, "let me take the kids out on a picnic and give you a break."

We take the washboard road up Superman Canyon, past the spot where Christopher Reeve plucked Margot Kidder from the crevasse in the movie. We turn off the road onto a pair of tracks that wind to the top of a detached mesa. Less than a hundred yards later, the kids cry out, "Dad, there's a dead horse on the road." A herd of ten wild horses are milling around. As we slowly drive forward, a young colt bolts up and scampers off.

Megan's voice is filled with wonder and relief. "Oh, look—how cute. It wasn't dead, it was just resting."

We bounce and bump along to the top of the mesa to a rippled, undulating sandstone area, perhaps the size of three football fields, scat-

Winter on the rez. Bennett Peak halfway between Gallup and Farmington.
Courtesy of Bob Rosebrough

tered with piñons and cedars and a few mighty ponderosa pines. There are pools of rainwater here from the afternoon thunderstorms of the past two days.

Mark finds a benchlike area to eat our dinner and the girls approve. When we finish, he says, "Can we start a fire?"

I point out a spot near a dead tree.

Mark crumples a paper towel and starts building a small tepee with sticks around the paper. After he gets the fire started, he looks to me for advice. I tell him, "Once the fire gets to this point, I lay the sticks in a square grid rather than a tepee."

Several minutes later, he asks, "Should I put more wood on, Dad?"

"Whatever you want to do. You're doing a great job. It's your fire now."

Several miles behind us to the west of the hogback, a thick dark wall of rain—the kind the Navajos call a male rain—blackens the sky. In front of us are patches of blue sky tinged with pink and orange.

After Mark lays a row of sticks on the fire, he comes to sit by me. I shift and spread my legs wide and he sits in front of me and leans back, using me as a lawn chair. His arms rest on my knees and his head leans back onto my chest as we watch the fire while the clouds drift toward the edge of the cliff.

As my life with my family is growing and changing, Gallup itself seems to be undergoing a burst of creative energy. Margo Manaraze, a court reporter, starts taking "angel sighting" photos at various locations around town. She talks a lithe young woman with movie-star looks into wearing a wedding dress with wings and appearing at places in town where people are engaged in good works. Margo makes friends with Gary, a homeless Navajo man in his twenties who has fetal alcohol syndrome. When he is not intoxicated, Gary has a vulnerable yet noble demeanor. He frequently appears in Margo's photos with the angel, and they make a striking image. The unspoken message of the photos seems to be that there is an unseen protective presence, even in the lives of the most defenseless among us.

Channel 13 in Albuquerque covers the angel sightings with a TV segment, and the *Albuquerque Journal* runs a feature article on Margo and her photos in the Sunday edition with a large front-page photo. A reporter from the *Boston Globe* comes to town, and then *People* magazine does an article.

Gary and the Angel on Coal Avenue in downtown Gallup. *Courtesy of Margo Manaraze Waggoner*

And once again, the story of Emmett Garcia and Larry Casuse resurfaces, but this time with an unexpected twist. I receive a call from Gary Stuart, the author of *The Gallup 14*—a book about the murder trial that followed the 1935 coal riot in which Sheriff Carmichael and two coal miners were killed. Stuart grew up just yards from the alley where the riot took place but moved to Arizona where he became an acclaimed trial lawyer and taught both law and writing at the Arizona State University law school.

I had read *The Gallup 14* before receiving Stuart's call and was fascinated by the book but struggled with its format. Stuart was a meticulous researcher, but his book was written as a historical novel with fictitious characters commenting on a riot and murder trial involving real events and people.

Stuart calls me on the recommendation of one of his high school friends, the city attorney during Emmett Garcia's term as mayor. He is writing a book, also using the historical novel format. This book focuses on the Larry Casuse abduction of Garcia and is titled *AIM for the Mayor*. Stuart tells me that he's been rebuffed in his efforts to interview members of Larry Casuse's family and asks me if I know Larry's brother, Don Casuse. He wants me to contact Don to see if he will talk with me.

I know Don casually; he's good friends with Margo's younger brother, and I've run into him at times, not realizing the connection despite his name. It hadn't occurred to me that any of Larry Casuse's family members would still be in Gallup.

With the legitimacy conferred by Stuart's request, I'm eager to talk to Don.

I call Don and explain that Stuart asked me to interview him.

"No pressure," I say. "If you're not comfortable talking to me about this, I'll understand." Don agrees to talk to me.

A few days later, Don comes to my office well after dark, still in his work clothes, after a long day's work as a service tech. He's average height with a sturdy, athletic build and short black hair. The breast of his gray jacket bears a Pepsi logo, and he's wearing work boots. I invite Don to come in, and we sit at a small conference table in my office. I put a micro cassette in a small recorder and place it on the table as we begin talking.

I don't sense any hesitancy or nervousness in Don. He is matter-of-fact and he's not in a hurry, even after working a long day. I ask him to tell me how he and Larry grew up. Don seems comfortable talking about his brother.

"We were both born in Santa Rita, New Mexico," he says. "They have a big open-pit copper mine there. Matter of fact, the town doesn't exist no more. It's just a big hole in the ground."

When Larry was in second grade and Don, a year younger, was in first grade, the family moved to neighboring Bayard. Both Santa Rita and Bayard are small towns near Silver City, a town of about 10,000, in southwestern New Mexico, 250 miles south of Gallup.

Don says that he and Larry are the oldest of seven children.

Their father was Navajo from the Mexican Springs area twenty miles north of Gallup; his mother was Austrian. They met in Germany during WWII.

"She didn't speak English when she came over here, and she wasn't a citizen," he says. "He was fluent in Navajo. My English and my sisters' English isn't real fluent because they never taught us, because they didn't know it. We just kind of learned it at school."

Speaking at length like this is not something that comes naturally to Don. In my previous experiences with him, I've found him to be a man

(left) Larry Casuse's parents were an Austrian mother and Navajo father who met in Germany during WWII. (right) Don, Nizhoni, and Larry Casuse (left to right) in public housing near an open-pit copper mine in Bayard, New Mexico. *Courtesy of Ursula Casuse Carillo*

Larry Casuse's mother with four of the seven Casuse children. *Courtesy of Ursula Casuse Carillo*

of few words. Even so, I'm a little surprised. The majority of people I've interviewed tend to hold on to key facts they want to suppress or go the other direction and embellish. Don simply lays out the story without any hint of embellishment. He seems incapable of either exaggeration or guile.

In Bayard, Don and his family lived in public housing. "I guess you would say we were poor," he says. "It was the roughest part of town. There really was no minority. We didn't even know what a minority was. You know, we had a White mom and a Navajo dad and Spanish people all over the place. It was like we never knew nothing about prejudice."

"Looking back, I kind of see why we ended up in the projects," Don says. "I bet they had a lot of communication problems and stuff. We hardly ever saw our parents. My dad was always working shift work, and my mom was always working in Silver City. She was a waitress. I guess they were separated a lot back in Bayard at an early time, and we never knew it. Larry brought us up in a sense, you know, cause he was the older brother." When Don starts talking about Larry, there is a shift—it seems to me there is added respect and deference in his voice. His brow creases.

I ask Don to describe his relationship with Larry.

"We were buddies," he says. "I would say brothers—tight brothers."

"What did he enjoy doing?" I ask.

"Always reading," says Don. "I mean we'd be out getting a baseball game together and he'd be in there reading. Reading, reading, reading. And I'd say smart. I don't think he ever got a B ever, from the first day on. And, I always remember his books, books, books." Don's description of Larry confirms the impressions I had gathered from short conversations with a few of Larry's high school classmates. One of them, who became a bank officer, said, "He was a smart guy. He would have been president of the Navajo Nation, or something like that."

Don says Larry was bigger and heavier than most of the other kids in his class. In junior high he started playing football as a lineman and he went out for track and competed in field events.

I ask Don if any details about Larry stand out from their youth.

"I would say the whole family, not just me, going to him for answers," Don says. "If it was school, my mom and dad, financially, or anything. When he was just a kid, his advice was always correct. I envied him for being right all the time. You know, it seemed like he knew everything."

I ask Don if anything Larry said in those early days stands out in his memory.

"I remember one time he said he saw Jesus in a dream," Don says. "That was a real big deal. He was probably in the sixth grade, maybe seventh."

"What did he say?" I ask.

"He just said, 'Jesus talked to me,'" Don says. "He and my dad talked about it. It must have been a Saturday. I remember the next day we went to church, and he sat up front and he knelt all the way through mass and I always followed him. I did the same thing. I was just kind of a little tag-along."

I didn't see the story of Larry's dream coming, but Don is matter-of-fact about it, as am I. Our conversation takes place during a time when several people, for reasons I don't fully understand, have shared their personal, spiritual experiences with me without prompting.

Larry and Don were raised Catholic. Their mother was Catholic, and Larry and Don were altar boys. They went to mass every Sunday. Says Don, "It was part of us."

Don's father often talked about Navajo culture. "He had a little medicine box," says Don. "He would come in and bless us with eagle feathers, and he had stones, life stones, I guess you call them. He was always into the Native American Church. You know, the peyote. We never understood it. When my mom and him were having problems, he turned to religion quite heavy. But he never pushed it on us. He would do ceremonies for our protection."

When Larry was in junior high at Bayard, he won a spelling bee. "That was a big deal with the whole town," says Don. "They took him back to regionals in Las Cruces. I think that's where he got an idea that he was a little exceptional. The teachers knew it and they always wanted him to go higher and higher. And he did. They gave him a job in the library."

The Casuse family moved to Gallup in 1968 when Larry was 15 and Don 14. Larry was a sophomore and Don was a ninth grader so they were separated, with Larry going to Gallup High and Don going to junior high.

"Gallup was like a big city," says Don. "We moved to a big city and that's kind of where we got separated." For the first time in our conversation, pain and regret edge into Don's voice as he talks about the brothers' separation.

Don's classmates didn't realize he was Navajo. "Nobody ever knew I was Navajo until I picked up my tribal clothes one day," he says. "They always thought I was a Spanish guy. They knew Larry was a Navajo right away. He looked Navajo a lot more than anybody else."

"I remember the first year here," Don says. "People seemed like they didn't like Navajos." He describes walking down the school hallways—groups of Hispanic and white athletes would single out a Navajo, cluster around him and start pushing him around. "I remember that," he says. "That was kind of disturbing."

Don's description of the hazing strikes me viscerally. Bullying was the one thing that had put me physically in the face of tough kids in my otherwise conflict-averse youth. I can feel myself tense as he talks. And I'm struck by how different the experience he's describing is from the view of many Gallupians who like to think of the town as an idyllic melting pot.

Larry had Indian friends in high school, and the non-Indian kids respected them because they were big guys. But Larry also had white friends.

"He could talk to anybody," says Don. "He had a sense of humor where he could make you laugh and make you feel comfortable. It didn't matter if you were a peon or a millionaire; he could talk at that level. He always hung around with the smart kids. He wasn't a fancy dresser. His appearance didn't mean that much to him."

Both Larry and Don played football. Don says Larry was a guard on the Gallup High team, and though the team was terrible, Larry and his teammates stuck together and had fun. I think back to my first visit to Gallup when Farmington handily won the football game. I consider telling Don about the game, which Larry would have been playing in, but put it aside.

Besides athletics, Larry was a member of the chess team, and Don remembers him carving chess pieces and building chess sets. He also engaged in art, particularly graphic art. Don remembers one of Larry's artworks that featured a big fork, and another that included the equation $E=mc^2$. "He kind of dabbled in every kind of art," Don says. "It looked pretty nice.

"He really got involved in the Indian Club," Don says. "They'd get together for powwows. His junior and senior years was when he started going the Indian way. He really wanted to understand the Navajo way." Don says nothing to suggest that he had a similar interest.

Although Larry's friends, all big guys, were treated with respect, it bothered him that some of the other Indian kids were pushed around. "They were timid," says Don. "That kind of concerned Larry. He saw how people were treated. That's where he started changing, going the Native way."

After graduating from Gallup High, Larry went to the University of New Mexico in Albuquerque and became even more deeply involved in the Indian way. He lived with two or three Indian students and was always around Indian people.

"They were kind of rough guys," says Don. "They were educated; they were serious students. But you know, he always made me laugh. He was the guy you want to hang around with. It seemed like everybody wanted to do that. He had a sense of humor. You just wanted to be around him."

Larry joined the Kiva Club, the Native American student organization at UNM, and engaged in protests, one of which was aimed at Gallup's Inter-Tribal Indian Ceremonial. Says Don, "They said Ceremonial was exploiting Indians."

Life changed for Larry in the summer of 1972. That was when he ran over and killed the young Navajo woman in Gamerco, five miles north of Gallup.

"A girl ran out in front of him or he didn't see her, and he freaked out," says Don. "He said he knew a state cop that lived in Gamerco somewhere. So, he picked the girl up, put her in the front seat, and took her to the cop's house. She was snockered. I guess right away they jumped all over him for leaving the scene of a crime and evidence. I mean, he freaked out. He was an 18-year-old kid, or 19. All the law was completely against him. Whatever they had, they used it. They made him look like he was worthless. They were out to get him."

As Don talks I'm trying to sort out the new information about both the accident and prosecution in my mind. Some aspects of the accident and two trials seem clear to me; other aspects remain enigmas that I doubt I'll ever resolve.

Don's statement that Larry put the young woman in the front seat of his car rather than the trunk, as I've heard in different accounts, stands out, and I'm not sure what, if anything to make of it. According to every account of the event I've heard or read, the young woman's death was unavoidable. She was out on an unlit highway well after dark. I'm not sure it matters whether Larry put her body in the trunk or in the front seat. What was undisputed was that Larry left the scene of an accident that resulted in a death. The prosecutors seemed extraordinarily motivated—the successive retrials on short notice were unlike anything I have ever seen in the Gallup courts. Prosecutors, in my experience, never put that kind of energy and effort into a leaving-the-scene-of-an-accident case. And it was clear by all accounts that Larry felt overwhelming remorse and that he went through the ordeal without a meaningful family support system.

But there were several unknowns. Had the young woman been drinking? Had Larry been drinking? Was Larry trying to take her body to a state policeman's house or was he trying to hide and dispose of the body?

Larry was in jail for three or four weeks. "I called him up," Don says, "We talked two or three times until he said, 'I'm getting claustrophobia. I got to go.'"

I hadn't heard that Larry was jailed, and it surprises me. To my experience, most arrests for leaving the scene of a deadly accident don't result in extended pre-trial jailing.

When Larry got out of jail and went back to college, Don tells me that he got more serious and he started studying law. Don says that Larry wanted to fight the Gallup authorities the same way they were fighting him, by using the law."

Don continues by telling me about Larry's protest of the Navajo Inn. "He had pictures of the bar going towards Window Rock," he says. "I remember he had pictures of drunk Indians passed out on ant piles and just terrible stuff. I can see why he was mad." Don's voice and demeanor suggest that he never felt the desire to protest injustices like his brother.

Don says he had no idea that Larry was planning to abduct Emmett Garcia. At the time, Don was working at a grocery store a mile west of downtown Gallup. He was delivering meat near the chamber of commerce on Route 66 when he came upon the scene at the Stearns Sporting Goods store.

"I saw the body lying there," says Don, "and I didn't know who it was. At the time, there were people standing all around it. Cops were telling everybody to get the heck out of there." I'm amazed that Don would be anywhere nearby, but I don't want to interrupt the flow of his story. "People were running, sirens were going all over the place. I heard on the radio that the mayor was kidnapped, and I went back to work."

When Don returned to the grocery store, an Italian meatcutter said, "Your brother was shot." Don jumped back in his truck and went downtown—and it was all over. He couldn't get near 66. An ambulance passed him while he was trying to make his way there. Police cars were everywhere and there was a barricade, but it all seemed unorganized.

"It was something you see in the movies," says Don.

Don went to Rollie Mortuary, a block south of City Hall. "I guess I freaked out too," says Don. "I just started banging on the mortuary door saying, 'Who killed my brother?'"

A big garage door opened. Larry was lying on a slab. The chief of police, Manuel Gonzales, and the mortuary manager were there. Blood was everywhere.

Don says, "I started yelling 'Who killed my brother? Who killed my brother?' The police chief said, 'I don't know.' He wasn't a wise guy. He said, 'You can't be here.' He wasn't rude; he didn't start pushing me around. He was, like, freaked out too, I guess." The mortician showed Don out and shut the door. Don is somber as he tells of the encounter at the mortuary and seeing Larry dead, but it seems that enough years have passed so that he doesn't break down.

I'm relieved to hear that Chief Gonzales was not disrespectful to Don at a time when emotions were running wild. During my brief phone conversation with Gonzales several years earlier, I liked what he'd said about Larry: "He died for something he believed in." And I was impressed by the sincerity in his voice.

Before Larry's death, Don had quit high school; he left home at age sixteen and never went back. The mother of one of Don's friends took him in, and he lived with that family, but they pretty much left him alone. Don's girlfriend, whom he later married, was with him throughout the ordeal, and he feels he wouldn't have made it without her. Don doesn't say it, but according to the accounts of others I've spoken to, Don and Larry's parents, while going through their divorce, had left the children to fend for themselves.

Bad things kept happening. Don lost another friend. A little sister died. His parents finalized their divorce. Still, Don felt his life would have been different if it hadn't been for the abduction and Larry's death. "He always took care of me," says Don. "He would have been something big at the tribe or something." It's clear that Larry, more than his parents, was the primary source of support for his brothers and sisters.

To take care of his family, Don did bodywork on cars and became a Pepsi service tech, but he feels he could have been a lot better, a lot more, if Larry had survived.

The parent's divorce and Larry's death changed the Casuse family. Don saw one sister once in a while, and although he and one of his brothers talked sometimes, he told me that it was just like talking to an acquaintance.

People in town left Don alone for the most part after Larry's death. "To me, it seemed like they knew they did something wrong and they were ashamed," he says. I'm not sure what Don is suggesting. It's not clear to me whether he feels that Larry's prosecution was politically motivated or amounted to retaliation for his protest of the Navajo Inn and its overserving of alcohol to Indians, or that the standoff should have been de-escalated after Garcia broke free, or that the authorities made up the claim that Larry's death was self-inflicted—or all of the above.

After the shooting, many people Don didn't know and had never heard about suddenly claimed to be related to Larry. Don said his father noticed the same thing. "You never saw that before," his father said. "Now there's a bunch of Casuses all over the place."

Larry's Indian activist friends and Don were never close after Larry's death, and Don was suspicious of Larry's accomplice, Robert Nakaidinae. "All those guys are working for the tribe now," Don says of the activists Larry hung out with at UNM. "I'd always run into them out there [in Window Rock] and they were working for the tribe. It seemed like they kind of avoided me and I avoided them."

Don has strong opinions about Nakaidinae. "The word was," he says, "that he snitched or sold out. He didn't want to tell the truth. They told him not to tell the truth or something and they let him off." I assume the "they" Don is referring to is police or authorities in Gallup, but he doesn't say, and I don't press him to clarify the comment.

"Something happened," he says, "because he would never look me in the eye either, or any of my family. He knows a lot more than he ever let out. They slapped him on the wrist and let him go or something." Nakaidinae, I learned years after my interview with Don, faced two life sentences for his role in the kidnapping and shooting of Mayor Garcia, but a plea agreement was reached that, after parole, resulted in his serving only eight months in jail.

Don doesn't say it, but I assume that part of his dislike of the man is because Nakaidinae never spoke out publicly to refute the claim that Larry died of a self-inflicted gunshot, when more than anyone, he would have been in a position to know. "[Larry] was like a gentle giant," said Don. "He would let you pick on him and pick on him. Then right at the end when you knew he was mad—get the heck out of the way. No way he killed himself."

Don threw himself into his work, sometimes working twenty hours a day in an effort to become wealthy. His goal was to get rich, run for mayor, and expose the Gallup authorities. He wanted to reopen the investigation to prove Larry didn't shoot himself. As we talk, it strikes me as wildly unrealistic that Larry Casuse's brother could ever be elected mayor of Gallup, but it also seems to be completely understandable that Don would try to honor the brother that he loved.

About twenty years after Larry's death, the father of a baseball player Don was coaching told Don what he witnessed during the shootout on Route 66. Don had known the man for about fifteen years, when he approached Don during a baseball tournament and said he couldn't hold back the story anymore. The man told Don that he had been across the street, directly behind Gallup policemen. After Mayor Garcia escaped, the man said, a policeman shouted, "Kill him! Kill him!" The police opened fire and killed Larry without trying to de-escalate the confrontation or give Larry the chance to surrender. "It bothered him," Don says of the man who approached him. "He had to get it out. He's a tough old guy and I never expected it out of him."

After Don relates the conversation with the baseball player's father, we just sit in silence for a while. The claim that Larry committed suicide had never made sense to me. On the live radio broadcast of the event that I'd received from the high school teacher, I heard a prolonged fusillade immediately after Emmett Garcia burst through the glass door—that to me seemed inconsistent with a suicide. In addition, the *Independent* reporter I talked to said that several eyewitnesses disputed the claim that Larry's death was a suicide.

When we resume talking, Don tells me that the whole affair changed the way Navajos looked at Gallup. "I think it made Navajos not fear Gallup as much," says Don. "I think they were scared of the police. They were scared of the big officials. They realized, 'Hey, we're not as bad as they think we are. We're people too.' And maybe they started thinking too that's why Gallup's around here. It was eye-opening; the Navajos opened their eyes." I think Don is saying that Navajos began to understand that Gallup's economy—its existence really—was, in large part, dependent on their trade in town.

Don got a measure of peace from what Mayor Muñoz tried to do with Gallup's bars eight or nine years before Don and I sat down to talk. Don felt that Muñoz did exactly what Larry wanted to do. "It was Muñoz's fight," he says. "But it was the same fight."

Years after Larry's death, and in a roundabout way, Don became aware that the Gallup police were displaying a photo of Larry's body on the sidewalk, surrounded by police, as a trophy in the Fraternal Order of Police building. Don was out late at night with some friends from the Lion's Club, one of whom was a policeman. A couple of guys suggested going over to the FOP building where there was a bar and a pool table. They invited Don.

The policeman took off real fast and made a beeline to the FOP. His haste was evident, and several people wondered why he was in such a hurry. "I found out three or four weeks later that they had a picture in there of the cops standing over Larry when he was dead, and it was in the paper. It looked like they had their guns like they got a deer or something. It was a terrible-looking thing." The policeman had rushed to the FOP to hide it before Don arrived.

Don says that he thought some of the activists who knew Larry had heard about the photo and had done a "big walk or something" to protest its display by the police. Don didn't participate. I haven't heard about such a protest; Don doesn't say when it took place, and I don't press him for details. All he says is, "I ain't smart enough to go that way. You know, I ain't Larry."

Twenty-two years after Larry's death, Don went to a Catholic *cursillo*, a spiritual retreat. For all that time, the hate he stored after Larry's death and his relentless work and planning were getting to him.

"I was changing," he says. "I didn't know who I was."

Don knew a guy who did *cursillo* retreats and he went to his house one day.

At the *cursillo*, Don talked to the priest about Larry's death and prayed about it. Everything, he says, became clear. A lot of questions were answered, and he felt forgiveness. "It's a three-day retreat with Jesus and Jesus is there," says Don. "I never would have thought that in my whole life. But there's a presence of Jesus there."

"It healed me," he says. "Whatever happened was done."

Afterward, Don says he began to have a whole new perspective about life and people. He trusted God and he trusted his wife and family, but he still found it hard to trust other people, especially in Gallup. Don felt he was always going to be hesitant to trust Gallup people, but he thought his lack of trust might go away at some point. He never thought he'd come as far as he has.

"Larry's death lives with me forever," says Don. "It's easy to say, but it's simple. You know, hate is simple to defeat."

After Don leaves my office, I sit there, processing all that Don has told me. I had wondered whether Don was going to be angry as he talked about his brother's death, but his account of his *cursillo* experience came as a surprise to me. It seems to explain why he was able to talk about Larry without lashing out or breaking down.

It makes me think of a stream of similar stories—my own and those of others—involving a deep, spiritual sense of peace that I encountered in the months before my conversation with Don.

There was the Jewish lawyer from Albuquerque who had a branch office in Gallup; he was having problems with his partners, and he told me about a feeling on the left side of his chin, cheek, and brow. "I felt the palm of a hand," he said, "soft and warm, the way God's would be, turn my head to the right. And it dawned on me to start my own firm. The thought was not there until that moment."

A big, burly former FBI agent told me that he was on guard duty once in an open, exposed position while guarding a witness who refused normal protection. After reading Dietrich Bonhoeffer's *Cost of Discipleship* while guarding the witness, he felt as if he had gone through the vortex of a lens and everything was rearranged in every dimension. "It was an incredible time of peace and joy," he said. "And I'm not a joyous person. I'm a curmudgeon. It lasted for a long time, but there was no sense of time. I had no sense of myself. I was aware of what was going on around me, but it was as if I was in another dimension."

Margo, the court reporter, told me that after a bout of depression she woke in bed and sat upright. Several days before this I'd mentioned to her that I thought her angel-sighting project was touchingly respectful to the young Navajo man with fetal alcohol syndrome who was frequently included in the photos. Margo said that when she woke her spirit was above her body, suspended by guardians who communicated with her wordlessly. She saw three veils in shimmering colors that separated our world from theirs. The message they brought her was that she could leave her body if she wanted, or that she could do so later if she felt she needed to. "You know how you were telling me that I'm respectful?" she said to me. "That's how they feel about us. It's almost like we are heroes to them."

A high school teacher and football coach at Gallup High told me about his near-death experience. Years before, after a state playoff game, he hit a patch of ice while driving, skidded off the road, hit an embankment, and was thrown from his truck. He broke eight ribs and suffered lacerations that required six hundred stitches and was initially paralyzed from the neck down. He lay unconscious under his truck before EMTs arrived. "I could see the truck and me, pinned under it," he told me. "Someone was talking to me through telepathy or something—no mouths were moving. I could see a light. Something told me to stop. And then I heard, 'It's not your turn.' As soon as I heard that—I mean as *soon* as I heard that—they picked the truck off me and I could start feeling the pain. I kept yelling, 'You got to let me go back. I got to die.' Finally, my mother showed up at the hospital and she simply told me, 'Shut your mouth.'"

The day after my talk with Don, I ask my secretary to transcribe our conversation and I send a copy to Gary Stuart, the Arizona author. I have a few more conversations with him about his book by phone, but Stuart never gives me any feedback on my conversation with Don. The primary focus of his fictional history seems to be whether Larry Casuse was influenced by the American Indian Movement. That's much less interesting to me than how Larry Casuse was affected by what he saw in the hallways of Gallup High and the parking lot of the Navajo Inn.

CHAPTER **SEVEN**

The Earth Below Falling Away

It's six o'clock in the morning on the first Saturday in December 1999. It is pitch-black as Brenda and I wake to an alarm and begin rousting the kids out of bed and guiding them toward piles of boots, ski pants, heavy coats, and hats and gloves. Our goal is to get the whole crew to Red Rock State Park, just east of Gallup, by seven for the pilot briefing at the Red Rock Balloon Rally. Weather permitting, we hope to go up on a flight.

I've been living in Gallup for twenty years now, and I've come to a point where I want to live more fully here. I'm beginning to see how Gallup is missing an opportunity to grow by making our otherworldly landscape available to the public to hike, bike, climb, ride, and shoot. With some like-minded friends, I want to be part of making that happen. I have a deep need to make my mark and help shape Gallup for the better in some way despite the ever-present barriers. I feel that I not only have the ability now but also the history here that will enable me to help effect change.

The day before, while we were making plans for the rally, I found myself looking back and thinking of my first encounter with a Gallup hot-air balloon pilot. In 1979, shortly after I arrived in Gallup, Mike, a scruffy, long-haired balloon pilot dressed in Levi's and a flannel shirt was sitting in my office, asking me to help him form a non-profit corporation. Mike was one of my first clients. He was telling me that he and a group of his balloonist friends were starting a hot-air balloon rally just east of Gallup at Red Rock State Park and that they'd applied for Lodger's Tax money from the city to help promote and fund the event. But they ran into resistance.

"Councilor Hall said, 'I'm not going to pay for a party for a bunch of hippies,'" Mike told me. The balloonists were instructed that they needed to comply with some basic legal formalities if they were to have any hope of receiving funding from the city.

The idea of hot-air ballooning in the red rocks surprised me. With no experience in ballooning, I thought it was too dangerous a place to fly. There are places around Gallup where the landscape reaches out, grabs you by the chest, and won't let you look away—and Red Rock Park is one of those places.

On a geologic map, Gallup is sandwiched between two large elevated ovals formed eons ago—the Zuni uplift to the east, and the Defiance uplift to the west. Over time, both uplifts have eroded, leaving mountainous areas covered with ponderosa pines and high mesas and buttes dotted with junipers, cedars, and piñon trees. The channel of the Rio Puerco begins about twenty miles east of Gallup near the Continental Divide and carves its way west through both uplifts, first cutting into Gallup and then beyond, to Querino Canyon in Arizona.

Two features in this landscape are otherworldly. The Nutria monocline (or hogback) guards the eastern flank of Gallup. Multicolored layers of sandstone protrude at angles of between forty-five and eighty degrees. The hogback, thirty-two miles long from north to south, appears almost vertical when viewed head-on from the ground; it is steep and abrupt in comparison to the other edges of the Zuni uplift. From high in the air, the hogback looks like two sinuous, parallel Great Walls of China.

Erosion has revealed a second feature—a stunning row of red-rock cliffs that extends more than twenty miles east from Gallup. Near the Continental Divide, the red rocks tower straight and vertical. As they approach Gallup, they form bulwarks and ramparts before transforming into a rust-red maze of rounded, lithe canyons, capped in the background by Pyramid

The sinuous Nutria Monocline, or hogback. A gap in the hogback on the east side of Gallup allows for transcontinental travel to cross the otherwise rugged topography. *Courtesy of Chris Dahl-Bredine*

Church Rock. When the wind is coming out of the southwest, balloonists compete to fly between the spires. *Courtesy Palace of the Governors (MNM/ DCA), Neg. No. 015769*

Rock and the twin spires of Church Rock. And this, Mike told me, is where the balloonists began flying in the late '70s and where they were planning to stage their rally.

Twenty years later, Brenda and I now have the kids up and dressed. We drive out to Red Rocks Park, as we do every year on the first weekend of December. There, at a pilot's briefing at sunrise, we meet Eric, a gregarious balloon pilot from Rio Rancho with a quick smile and a deep laugh whom we sponsor each year. We exchange hugs with Eric and his crew. Up on a portable stage, rally organizers are releasing helium test balloons at intervals to gauge the speed and direction of the wind.

The rally has grown over the years to the point where it now hosts up to two hundred balloons on an invitation-only basis and is the second largest balloon rally in the United States, trailing only Albuquerque's International Balloon Fiesta. *Balloon Life* magazine has named the rally the Best in the West and Michael Crichton included a scene from the rally in his best-selling novel *Timeline*.

Mike was one of a group of young pilots who were mentored by the original Gallup balloonist Alan Wilson. Mike moved away from the area not long after he helped start the rally, but the rest of the group Wilson introduced to ballooning have stayed in Gallup and thrived. They are the people up on the portable stage in colorful parkas who are looking at sheets of paper, greeting friends, and glancing up at the sky.

Wilson—a big, muscled, adventurous man with luxurious white hair, a generous smile, and a quick wit—was one of Gallup's larger-than-life figures. He was born and raised in Gallup, played football for the University of Southern California, transferred to Harvard where he graduated summa cum laude, traveled the world, and developed an amazing array of talents and interests. After working for U.S. intelligence agencies as a Russian interpreter during the Cold War, Wilson returned to Gallup late in life. He taught French, Spanish, German, Serbo-Croatian, Russian, and Navajo, and studied Arabic, Indonesian, Yiddish, and Hebrew. He wrote twelve books, six of which centered on the Navajo language.

Wilson started a tradition of linguistic humor that the younger Gallup balloonists continued. Once, Wilson's balloon envelope was perilously draped on power lines, which were strictly off limits. One of Wilson's crew members spotted a plump employee from the Federal Aviation Agency that regulates ballooning, monitoring his accident.

"What are you going to do about the Fed?" Wilson's crew member asked.

"You mean overfed, don't you?" Wilson replied.

Until the late '70s, no one flew balloons among the red rocks; the terrain was forbidding, and, if there was an emergency, help was far away. "The sphincter factor was off the charts," a balloonist would later tell me. But interest in flying in such a setting was inevitable.

The early Gallup balloonists pushed the boundaries of suitable weather, and survived epic high-speed landings, crumpled chase trucks, landings in deep arroyos, long distance portages, and adventures that generated place names like Broken Basket Canyon, Calamity Cliff, Fiasco Land, the Erroneous Zone, and Lionel's Leap.

In time the balloonists became more selective about weather conditions, and they began seeking the sublime beauty of the red rocks more than an adrenalin rush; they eventually developed a sense of comfort

The envelope of a hot air balloon at the Red Rock Balloon Rally fills up with hot air prior to takeoff. *Courtesy of Bob Rosebrough*

there. What balloonists want most is the ability to fly in a variety of directions. On many days the red rocks—with myriad big canyons, little canyons, canyons that start big and get small, sunny canyon walls, and shady canyon walls—create conditions that allow for the variety of motion pilots crave.

Up on the portable stage, on the periphery of the park campground, one of the organizers looks at his watch and raises a portable microphone. Brenda, the kids, and I are drinking hot chocolate and stepping from side to side trying to stay warm as we chat with Eric and his crew. The lead announcer reads off some data about wind speed and elevations.

Eric beams. "Conditions are ideal," he says. A gentle wind is coming from the east that, until it is overtaken by the prevailing southwesterly wind later in the morning, will carry balloons gently west where the balloonists can drop in and out of a row of red rock canyons: Outlaw Canyon, Arena, Dune, Padre and two canyons that, from the air, look like utensils: Spork and Foon.

About every third year, the rally is weathered out. The two previous times we have flown, the winds were stronger. One year we were quickly carried north past Pyramid Rock and Church Rock to a landing spot a mile west of Kit Carson Cave; a couple of years later, we flew even farther north and west to the upper reaches of Superman Canyon. We've never flown into the canyons directly west of the park campground, and the prospect of doing so is beyond thrilling.

My son Mark, now 13, and a friend get the first ride. They take off from the northern launch field with views up canyon toward Church Rock, twin sandstone spires jutting above the ridge north of the red rocks. The launch field is cradled between two red-rock ridges that end abruptly in bulwarks. The ridge west of the launch field is partially covered by a steeply angled sand dune. Spectators who have climbed up the dune are now standing on top of the western ridge, profiled against the sky, and are looking *down* on the balloons as they lift off in waves.

A field marshal gestures toward Eric and says, "You're clear to go." Eric fires his burner and those of us in the crew outside the wicker basket release our weight from its rim and the balloon gently floats up to join the array of vivid colors and varied shapes filling the basin above the launch field. As the balloons lift off, they spread, each taking a slightly different course.

Thirty minutes later, Eric touches down in a small V-shaped canyon

Skirting cliffs at Red Rock Park with a light wind from the east. *Courtesy of Bob Rosebrough*

just east of Arena Canyon, and Brenda and I, who have followed the chase truck, trade places with Mark and his friend. Mark is animated and excited; his buddy is wide-eyed and seems almost stunned.

After Brenda and I get settled, Eric fires his burners and the basket begins to lift off the sand floor of the canyon. It feels as if we are stationary, and that the earth below is falling away from us. As we rise higher, we float toward a large canyon wall and the rising sun casts the complete shadow of our balloon and basket against a canyon wall to the west. We wave to ourselves.

Everything is completely calm and still. We feel no wind, because we're moving *with* the wind. As we rise, the massive bulk of Pyramid Rock looms into sight with a couple of hikers at the top. We float west into a large canyon with a Navajo homesite. Four balloons have landed within a hundred feet of the home and members of the family are helping one of the chase crews gather the envelope of the balloon before stuffing it in a large bag.

Over the years, the balloonists have developed friendships with the Navajo families who live in and near the red-rock canyons. A year or two earlier, one of the rally organizers told me of landing near another Navajo home. A Kinaalda, a coming-of-age ceremony for a young Navajo girl, was taking place, and the pilot scrambled to take off again—not wanting to interrupt the ceremony. But a grandmother came over to the balloon and said, "Please stay. We were praying that something special would happen today." The pilot tethered the balloon and took up about thirty people for short rides. The ceremony was on its fourth day and the Navajos dug a cake out of an earthen oven and shared it with the balloonists.

Above us balloons are moving faster than us, drifting west. Below us in the shelter of the canyon, several balloons hover motionless. A couple of motionless balloons are partially tucked away in alcoves of the canyon walls. After an hour of bliss, we land in the next to last canyon to the west and walk our still-inflated balloon to the mouth of the canyon where our chase crew is waiting to help us pack up before heading into town for a late breakfast. There, we tell stories of the day and make plans to reconnect next year.

I admire the Gallup balloonists. They've brought something completely new to Gallup that the community, after some initial resistance, embraces and points to with pride, and I haven't seen that happen in Gallup before. I also envy the connection they've developed with the Navajos who live near Red Rock Park.

In 2001, I make my first deep connection with a Navajo couple, Benson and Gladys Silversmith. Benson is a traditional Navajo man, and the couple live twenty-four miles north of Gallup in Tohatchi, six or seven miles north of Mexican Springs where Larry Casuse's father was from. One night as Benson was driving into Gallup to pick up Gladys, he hit an elderly Navajo woman dressed in dark clothing who walked out onto the highway after dark. The woman died. The accident happened in the Twin Lakes area, about ten miles north of Gamerco, where Larry Casuse hit and killed the young Navajo woman in 1972.

But Benson, unlike Casuse, isn't prosecuted or even threatened with criminal charges. Instead, a man who claims to be the common-law husband of the dead woman files a civil suit against Benson in Navajo Tribal Court, seeking money, and Benson's insurance company hires me to defend him.

I meet Benson in the conference room of my office. We shake hands Navajo style—with a light touch—and sit. Benson speaks English, but Navajo is his first language and he is a man of few words in both languages. He answers most of my questions with one or two words and sometimes only with a nod. At times he appears anguished, but he never cries; he just stoically bottles everything up inside. Benson's bubbly, extroverted wife does almost all the talking.

Toward the end of our conference, Gladys says, "We're having a healing ceremony for Benson in two weeks and we would like you and your wife to come if you can."

The plaintiff's lawyer is relentlessly aggressive in seeking what he hopes will be a big insurance payoff. The case drags on and as it does, the healing ceremonies continue, including three overnight ceremonies. One of the ceremonies takes place on the weekend after the September 11 attack on the World Trade Center towers. Through the night, Brenda and I are seated around a fire with Benson's family and friends. Prayers are offered for "our country." The prayers seem to assume that a war is now inevitable. One woman prays, "Our men have volunteered to serve in all wars, as they will in the war which will now be coming. Please protect and guide them in this war."

I feel a collateral benefit from supporting Benson and Gladys in their healing ceremonies. It seems to me that the ceremonies are helping me continue healing both from my divorce and law office breakup.

On the morning of the first day of the trial, Benson gives me a two-and-a-half-inch long arrowhead with strings attached that he asks me to wear underneath my tie. "It will protect you," he says, "And me." Benson and Gladys teach me that if you have a real interest in Navajo people and are openhearted with them and receptive to their customs, they will embrace you and open their lives to you. And the experience with the Silversmiths gives me a real sense of the anguish and trauma created by an accident that causes death, particularly to Navajos whose creation story teaches them to fear looking at the dead and who by custom abandon a home if a death occurs in it. Benson's trial concludes with the judge's ruling in Benson's favor.

Unexpectedly, not long after Benson's trial, Larry Casuse's story pops into my life again. After I finish explaining an estate plan to an elderly Slavic widow one afternoon, we visit casually for a while and she starts telling me about the time she served on jury duty in Gallup many years ago. As she talks it's apparent to me that she's referring to Casuse's second trial, the one that ended with a hung jury. I ask her who else was on the jury. "I don't remember, but I think there were six of us from town and six Navajos," she says.

I ask what she does remember, and she says, "I just remember beating up on those poor Navajos." She sounds remorseful. "We just kept pushing them to vote guilty. There was one Navajo woman who wouldn't change her vote. We finally gave up. The judge declared a hung jury."

I ask her about the details of the prosecution's case, but she can't remember the who, what, when, where, and why of the evidence. She just recalls the factions that formed in the jury room, the racially divided debate, and how all the Navajos but one gave in to the townspeople. She doesn't remember whether the jury knew of Casuse's history of protest in Gallup while they were deliberating, or whether that played a role in the push by the non-Navajo jurors to convict. I assume at least one of the non-Navajo jurors must have been aware of those protests, given the way information flows in Gallup. I find myself wishing I could read a transcript of the trial, but I assume that a transcript is not available this long after the trial, particularly in a case that wasn't appealed to a higher court.

Just before I meet Benson Silversmith, a young doctor comes to Gallup to work at Gallup Indian Medical Center after finishing his schooling. Peter Tempest, who is nine years younger than I, was born on the Navajo Nation in Tuba City, Arizona, where his father worked as a doctor at that city's Indian Hospital before the family moved to Gallup. Peter graduated from Gallup High and went to medical school at the University of California at Los Angeles before returning to Gallup. I quickly develop the sense that Peter is a kindred spirit.

On a group road-bike ride, as our cycling group is heading east near the red rocks, Peter steadily moves up to the front of the pack, incrementally pushing the pace. Furtive glances in the pack silently communicate, *This guy is strong.* Peter and I quickly develop a friendship based on cycling, skiing, and exploring the rugged landscape around Gallup. At times, I find

Bob and Peter Tempest at the base of Lizard Head in the San Juan Mountains. *Courtesy of Peter Tempest*

myself wishing that he had moved back years earlier when my level of fitness would have allowed me to push him as much as he is pushing me.

Before Peter came back to Gallup, I'd been scouting hiking and biking loops on Pyramid Rock, the White Cliffs, the hogback, and near the overlook on Gallup's north side, when I wasn't heading north to the canyons of southeast Utah or mountaineering in the San Juans. And I developed climbing routes and bouldering areas near the hogback and in Superman Canyon.

I didn't fully appreciate the terrain I'd been exploring, in part because only a handful of other people have any interest in the area, and in part because the land hasn't been treated well. It's overgrazed in places and covered with ammunition casings and broken bottles at target-shooting sites. There are no maintained trails or designated-user areas. My favorite bouldering area is littered with illegal dumping. The prevailing mindset seems to be that the land is there to be mined, built on, grazed on, or dumped on. Even the red rocks, for all their beauty, lie behind a refinery and a transmission line. No one other than the balloonists seem to consider using the land for public recreation—and they float above the disarray.

While volunteering in the late '80s as an assistant editor for *Summit*, a small mountaineering magazine, I had come across an article written by Yvon Chouinard, one of the leading climbers of the golden age of climbing in Yosemite, and the founder of Patagonia, the outdoor clothing company. As a teenager, Chouinard escaped the suburbs of southern California by hopping a ride, hobo-style, on a freight train that passes through Gallup. On his way home, Chouinard looked out from his perch on the train and was mesmerized by the red rocks. He said the view inspired him to spend his life exploring the outdoors and seeking adventure. Ten years after my stint with *Summit*, I reread the story about Chouinard. And looking at Gallup's landscape through Chouinard's eyes, I begin to rethink the potential of outdoor recreation where I live. At a deeper level, I think we can't fully live healthy lives if we don't treat the land around us well.

By the time Peter returns to Gallup, I'm burned-out following my disastrous Tour of the Gila race, and mountain biking is moving from a fringe fad to a major sport. Peter, who had been introduced to mountain biking in California, is ahead of the game. I'm just starting to ride a mountain bike and it's not going well. I'm flogging myself on every ride. I'm on and off the bike constantly. Either my clip-in pedals don't work, or I don't know how to use them. Maybe my center of gravity is just too high? On an exploratory ride on top of the red rocks, I stall out on a sharp turn and do a slow-motion fall into a cactus. I fall multiple times on each ride, sometimes going over the handlebars. Just when I'm about to give up, I at last get a feel for my bike.

Peter and I talk regularly and compare ideas on where to develop trails. I connect a couple of two-track roads northeast of town in Superman Canyon by clearing a mile and a half of single track. Peter connects two-track roads on Gallup's north side with some difficult single-track segments to create an eight-mile mountain-bike loop that locals quickly dub Pete's Wicked Trail. Together, we establish a trail on top of the red rocks.

On a fall weekend trip to Telluride, Colorado, Peter and I get ready for a big ride over a high mountain pass. He hands me a guidebook for Telluride cycling, titled *Tellurides*, and says, "There are enough good rides in Gallup to do a guide."

"If we include hiking, road biking, rock climbing, and cross-country skiing," I say, "there's more than enough to do a guide."

Back in Gallup, Peter and I meet for lunch and talk through the format of the book and divide up the work. I'm excited about the guide, but I'm not sure how I'm going to make the time to do my part.

Less than a month later, without further discussion about the guidebook, Peter arrives at my office unannounced and sets a stack of papers on my desk and says, "Here you go." His part of the manuscript is largely done—and I haven't even started. Peter's work shames me into starting to write, and once I do, I get rolling and finish my part. I use the project as an excuse to take my kids out and take photos of them on the trails. I talk Brenda, who's not a cyclist, into going out with me on the difficult Pete's Wicked Trail, where we walk our bikes up several sections until we reach a high point. Although she's tired and irritated by my choice of trails, I ask her to walk her bike over the high point and then ride back toward me and the camera. As she is riding down, I cajole her by saying, "And try to look happy!" She laughs and smiles as she rolls over the hill and I snap a photo. "If you use this photo," she says, "you'll ruin any credibility that your book would have had." We both laugh.

The last page of *The Gallup Guide: Outdoor Routes in Red Rock Country* is headed "About the Authors" and reads, in part, "Bob Rosebrough and Peter Tempest are longtime residents of Gallup. Both are avid outdoorsmen who have traveled to far corners of the earth only to conclude that everything they were looking for is in their own backyard."

While it's true that there are great, even world-class venues and routes

Brenda riding a rare gentle section on Pete's Wicked Trail with the hogback in the background. *Courtesy of Bob Rosebrough*

Peter Tempest on the High Desert Trail's Third Mesa. *Courtesy of Chuck Van Drunen*

for outdoor activities in Gallup, one big problem remains. Aside from two Forest Service trails more that twenty-five miles apart in the Zuni Mountains, all of the routes in our guidebook, although not fenced or posted for trespassing, lack legal, public access. The problem is not unique to Gallup. Such western communities as Durango, Moab, and Sedona, which don't have some of Gallup's socials problems, are far out in front on public recreation. But in most Mountain West communities, social trails developed from repeated use by local enthusiasts are

Bob with Megan and Amy below Lizard Head. *Courtesy of Bob Rosebrough*

evolving into maintained, legally designated trails—a difficult and at times exhausting process.

A year after *The Gallup Guide* is published, I get a call and then a visit from a consultant with the Northwest New Mexico Council of Governments, the COG. The COG was the fiscal agent for the Fighting Back Initiative when I was cochairman of the planning task force. Since then, I've made peace with Patty Lundstrom, the executive director with whom I battled ten years earlier during the Fighting Back Initiative. She now also represents Gallup in the state legislature.

"The COG recently held an annual forum soliciting ideas for economic development," the consultant says, "and Ron Berg suggested that Gallup focus on developing outdoor recreation to boost tourism."

My sense is that most people in town are anxious about the future, worrying that Gallup is slowly deteriorating. Early in its history, Gallup experienced explosive growth, and later it saw bursts of prolonged prosperity, but times have been tougher lately. The frenetic years of coal mining were followed by a post–World War II boom of self-made business successes in the '50s and '60s that were fueled by the extension of credit to Navajos, traffic coming to town on Route 66, and the filming of a slew of Hollywood westerns. The Ford and GMC dealerships in Gallup sold more pickup trucks, the vehicle of choice for Navajos, than any other truck dealers in the country. In the late '60s and early '70s, it seemed as though most rock stars and movie stars were wearing turquoise Indian jewelry, much of which originated in, or flowed through, Gallup. Indian jewelry continued to be a key part of Gallup's economy, but in the late '70s sales declined to a steady level, well below that of the boom years.

Now the market for Indian jewelry is being threatened by foreign knockoffs that are driving prices down. And Gallup no longer has an exclusive franchise on the trade. One local businessman tells me, "We don't have a lock on the Navajo business anymore. It's just not like it used to be. They've been to the big cities now, and there are things there that we don't have. Many Navajos are comfortable driving all the way to Albuquerque and Phoenix now."

And although few in town talk about it, it seems to me that the Navajo's willingness to drive farther to trade probably has something to do with Gallup's pawnshops and payday lenders who buy low and sell high, package liquor stores that carry fortified wines, and a plasma center where public inebriants sit in a chair and take a needle in the vein every three days to get money to buy more alcohol.

The consultant continues, "We'd like to know if you and Peter Tempest would be willing to help us."

Both Peter and I sign on to the adventure tourism initiative, as do many others. Quality of life for Gallup residents is the primary motivation for Peter and me. We think the town can't be a healthy, vibrant place if people don't have the ability to enjoy the sublime landscape that surrounds us. If it's necessary to package outdoor recreation as a way to boost economic development through tourism to get policy makers to buy in, we're fine with that too.

Adventure Gallup, a non-profit corporation, is formed, and the first order of business is to obtain legal, public access to trails. That won't happen, though, without the cooperation of Gamerco Associates, the fractious, family partnership in which my former boss Tim used to own a small interest. Gamerco Associates owns forty square miles of land around Gallup, a virtual private land monopoly.

Initially, a talk with one of the four Gamerco general partners, the only one who still lives in Gallup, goes well—almost too well. He seems to say that we can pick any property we want to develop trails on, but he rushes through the meeting and it isn't clear whether he has conferred with the other three general partners. There is no indication that he understands the importance of this effort to the health as a community, our self-image, and the image we present to the world. We tell him that we're primarily interested in the property north of Gallup, the area where Pete's Wicked Trail is located and that's close to an interstate exit that would be convenient for tourists.

The prospects of a quick deal with Gamerco fall apart when a cowboy who holds a grazing lease with Gamerco to the property gets wind of what's in the works. The cowboy is frenetic and obsessive; although he pays minimum annual rental payments, he acts as if the north-side property is his birthright. He begins lying in wait on weekends to ambush mountain bikers on Pete's Wicked Trail and aggressively evicts bikers from the land by tailgating them on horseback.

The cowboy's deceased father was married late in life to one of the Gamerco heirs, and because the land is used for grazing, Gamerco receives a reduced property tax rate that it doesn't want to lose. We explain to the cowboy and the Gamerco general partner that the property can be used jointly for both grazing and mountain biking so that the property tax exemption can be maintained, and we tell them that the trails are on the ridges and rough, rocky areas where the cows never go, but the cowboy will hear none of it. He lobbies the Gamerco partners incessantly. Because the city would have to accept an easement, he contacts all the city councilors with offers to take them on horseback rides on the property while exaggerating the dangers of the area.

He frames everything through the lens of a battle between born-and-raised Gallupians and out-of-towners; when talking to city councilors, he starts by saying, "I was born and raised in Gallup, like you." In one city council meeting he talks about coal-mine fires, sink holes, and how he fears for the safety of pregnant women hikers who are exposed to such hazards. He offers to take city councilors out to the land to show them the burned skeleton of one of his cows.

There's no groundswell of support for Adventure Gallup from old-time Gallupians. The mayor and city councilors, all of whom were born and raised in Gallup, don't evince any enthusiasm for the project. They don't see the potential in our landscape. I think they take it for granted and don't realize how special it is. I cite Gallup's history of moviemaking, of western films in particular, to persuade them to look at the land differently. Almost everyone born and raised in Gallup has a story about a movie star. Phil at the title company has told me that his father, a staunch Democrat, had a drink with Ronald Reagan in the 49er Lounge at the El Rancho Hotel while Reagan was filming *Knute Rockne, All American*. A Gallup north-sider told me that he remembers Kirk Douglas hanging out after hours at Kauzlarich's bar on the north-side during the filming of *Ace in the Hole*. "There's a reason so many westerns were filmed in and around Gallup," I tell the councilors. "Our landscape is special."

The Gamerco general partner who lives in Gallup tells us that he'll agree to grant the trail easement if we can get the approval of the cowboy, but it's a cop-out. He knows there's no way the cowboy is going to agree unless the partner tells him he *has* to. At times during the discussions, I want to say to the general partner, "Why don't you just be a man and tell us straight up that you aren't going to do the deal and stop wasting our time telling us to get an approval you know we'll never get. And besides, you own this property, not him." But I don't; it would kill any chance of ever coming to an agreement.

One of many westerns filmed in the Red Rocks. As I said to Adventure Gallup skeptics, "Our landscape is special." *Courtesy of Octavia Fellin Public Library, Gallup, New Mexico*

I go to Albuquerque to meet with one of the other general partners and spend the afternoon talking and negotiating with him. He gets the cowboy on the phone and we go back and forth for more than an hour. Then, after talking alone to the cowboy for about fifteen minutes, he joins me again, holds out his hand to shake, and says, "We have a deal."

When I get back to Gallup, a message is waiting for me that the general partner who lives in Gallup has already killed the deal.

A few months later, Gamerco Associates negotiates with an out-of-town company to build a power plant northwest of Gallup, and the city offers Gamerco a 99-year lease of all of its excess treated effluent water to cool the proposed plant. I lobby the mayor and the city councilors, asking them to condition the deal on Gamerco granting public access to the north-side property in exchange for the water rights, but the mayor and councilors aren't open to the idea of a tradeoff, and they seem stubborn in not understanding how public recreation will benefit the community.

During the depths of this depressing time, Peter and I take off for a weekend to Colorado, to Durango, our neighbor three hours to the north—to check out the National Mountain Bike Championships being held there. Here in Durango are all the trails and outdoor access that I wish we had in Gallup, and the entire community seems on board. I'm frustrated and deeply disappointed by the roadblocks we've experienced and throughout the weekend the question lingers: *Why don't I just move here?*

Before the weekend is over, I have a clear answer: I want this. But I want it where I live, and I want to be part of making it happen, no matter how frustrating it is or how long it takes. And I really don't want to live in a wealthy, Anglo-dominated community. I just want the town I otherwise love living in to share its landscape with its people. To give up and move to enjoy this elsewhere will be a cop-out I can't live with.

Not long after I get back to Gallup, the 99-year water lease is set to be approved by the city council, and I attend the meeting. It's the first time I've been back to a city council meeting since I blew up and stormed out of a meeting ten years before, during my struggle with Mayor Ed Muñoz. One councilor who was at the meeting back then eyes me warily as he enters the council chambers. But I say my piece in an entirely different way this time. I tell the mayor that I think the price for the city's water is too low and the term of the lease is too long. There isn't an alternative use for the water at this point, I say, but it may have value and other uses in the coming years, with new technology. "Ninety-nine years," I say, "is a long time."

I also say that the residents of Gallup would benefit if the council would require Gamerco to provide some corresponding benefit to the quality of life of the community to offset the industrial effects of a proposed power plant. The mayor interrupts me and talks about how much the town would benefit from a power plant. I remain calm and say, "I respectfully disagree with the structure of this deal." I pause after the word *respectfully* and then yield the podium and take a seat.

The council votes unanimously to approve the 99-year water lease (but for reasons unknown to me the power plant is never built). None of our elected officials seem to see the benefits of public outdoor recreation and its potential to improve tourism, enhance our quality of life, and just help us be whole and healthy. But those of us who have been working on Adventure Gallup for over a year, without any success, see it so clearly that we aren't going to give up on it. And that means that at some point, if we are ever going to bring our dream to life, we will need to have someone inside city hall.

CHAPTER **EIGHT**

"They're Worried About You"

Nine months have passed since the failure to secure trail easements from Gamerco Associates, and during that time one of my law partners, Dolph, and I purchased and remodeled a new office building in downtown Gallup. The two of us, with a younger lawyer, are now located next door to the office where I started practicing law twenty-three years earlier.

While my grand scheme to promote and elevate the natural beauty of this part of the world has tanked, we're doing our own small part, at least, to beautify Gallup. Our new office is spiffy, with a wooden viga over the entrance, large wood framed exterior windows, Spanish-style lathed-wood doors throughout, a lobby with a brick floor, and hardwood floors in each of the offices. In the gravel strip outside the office bordering First Street, we haul in sandstone boulders, and a local welder cuts and drills holes to install steel figures of hikers, a rock climber, and mountain bikers among the boulders.

One day in February 2002, Dolph comes into my office looking puzzled. He tells me that he talked earlier in the day with Sheriff Frank Gonzales, the younger brother of Manuel Gonzales, the former police chief. Dolph seems both intrigued and unsettled by the conversation they had.

"He suggested that I run for mayor," Dolph says. "Frank wants to run for city council, and he said that he and I should run together with another one of his friends. He thought that it wouldn't take too much time if we shared the responsibilities of being mayor."

Dolph shrugs his shoulders slightly and slows his words, the way he does when he's skeptical. He tells me that he can't imagine how a mayor-by-committee system would work, and neither can I, but he does think the mayor's race will be wide open. He's also skeptical of any kind of partnership with old-school Gallup politicians such as Frank Gonzales, and I agree that such a partnership would be a challenge. Still, it's a fascinating idea. Are the winds of change blowing through town?

With the next municipal election fourteen months away, the current mayor, John Peña, has decided not to run again, and no one else has yet announced a run for office. Dolph, who ran a good race for attorney general of New Mexico but lost before joining my law practice, still has political aspirations, but he tells me he doesn't feel it's the right time for him to run. He's immersed in his children's activities at the moment, so he won't put his hat in the ring.

As I listen to Dolph describe his conversation with Frank Gonzales about taking over the mayoralty, something builds inside me. During a pause in our conversation, I blurt out, "I want to run." It is a moment of utter clarity.

That night I talk to Brenda. Seven years have passed since I started my new law practice and shortly thereafter separated from my first wife. It has been five years since Brenda and I married. In this time Brenda,

"In what may well be a trend for the night . . . " was the call by KGAK news reporter, John McBreen. Making the rounds at city hall on election night.
Courtesy of Lisa Rodriguez

after leaving her position at my office, has worked as the secretary for the city manager before going back to school and becoming a speech therapist for the Gallup schools. She knows what the mayor's job is all about, both the good and the bad. She's cautious and apprehensive, but she says

Brenda graduating from the University of New Mexico as a speech therapist.
Courtesy of Bob Rosebrough

unequivocally, "If it's what you really feel you want to do, I will support you completely."

After I make the decision, I'm energized, efficient, and focused in a way I've never quite felt before, almost as if a force or energy is acting through me. It feels like an out-of-body experience. The next day at the office I list the names and phone numbers of fifty people and I start making calls. I begin by saying, "I want to share something with you that I don't want you to hear secondhand."

It occurs to me that, as a first-time candidate, I should get some advice. I reach out to a group of people, including Mayor Peña, with whom I differed openly but respectfully during the power plant water giveaway. Although I have no intention of bringing it up, I assume that one of the reasons he's decided not to run for reelection is that he and the publisher of the *Gallup Independent* were combatants in a wrestling match in the lobby of City Hall two years earlier—an on-the-floor tussle that didn't end until the police were called.

Mayor Peña welcomes me into his office. It's the same sunny room where thirteen years earlier I met briefly with Mayor Muñoz to cut a deal on our downtown package-liquor zoning ordinance. Spacious and designed for work, not show, the office contains a varnished maple desk, a conference table, and filing cabinets. Entering, I feel comfortable, almost at home.

A collection of large, framed photographs of an extravagantly diverse group of Gallupians decorates the walls. A dignified, white-haired woman proudly wears her Slavic gown as she stands looking out a window, a cat by her side. A Muslim businessman in a headdress made of eagle feathers kneels in prayer. A short Italian grandmother with a massive, spiraling beehive hairdo smiles pleasantly. A Japanese woman and her daughter glow in each other's presence. A short, round Croatian businessman with an intense glint in his eyes holds a rolled-up set of blueprints and stands in front of otherworldly red rock formations. An elderly Mexican woman kneels in prayer with lace draped over her head, bathed in light—she is calm and seems intensely present.

Mayor Peña confirms that he's not running again and says, preemptively, that he doesn't intend to endorse anyone. Midway through the conversation, he says, "You haven't mentioned any plans to listen to people. That's important, you know." After half an hour, I thank him, shake hands, and leave.

With each Gallup politician I talk to, I pick up an idea that I wouldn't have thought of otherwise. And each time someone comes to me with a question such as, "What are you going to do about all the broken glass bottles that litter our open spaces?" I think of my conversation with Mayor Peña and say, "I have some ideas, but this must be important to you. What do you think?" I find that many people just want to be heard on a problem or issue they care about. I also get some good ideas that would never have occurred to me, ideas I jot down in a small notebook.

Another Gallup politician tells me, "It's important to ask people for their support and for their vote. It's important for you to ask for that." After a few trial runs, I develop my own version of the "ask." I tell people, "I would like your support. Your support does not have to be public. Gallup's a small town and I'm not asking you to support me in a way that will cause you grief, but in any way that's comfortable to you."

After a couple months of planning and information gathering, I spring into action. A full year before the election, before anyone else has announced, I call a reporter at the *Independent* and set up an interview to make my formal announcement.

I set up an account and lend my campaign $2,000, highlight names on a list of registered voters, and send out five hundred letters asking for financial support and commitments to place campaign signs. I include a return card and stamped return envelope with each letter.

I'm advised that I should pick a campaign theme from my heart, and I do: A New Day for Gallup. I have the slogan translated into Spanish ("Un Nuevo Día para Gallup") and Navajo (Nahat'á 'ániidii bá ha' íí' á Na' nízhóózhígi) and pick a greenish turquoise and a rusty shade of maroon for my campaign colors. The colors are separated on my cards and yard signs by the skyline of Pyramid Rock and Church Rock above Red Rock Park. I begin writing eight open letters on various topics to the citizens of Gallup. I plan to run them once a week in the *Independent*, during the two-month period between the official filing date and the election, still many months away.

I start going to city council meetings held every other Tuesday evening. I call the mayor and the city councilors in advance as a courtesy, and I say, "I'm going to start attending council meetings regularly. I'm not trying to start any trouble, and I doubt that I'll ask to speak. I just want to be up-to-speed on the issues." For the most part, the council

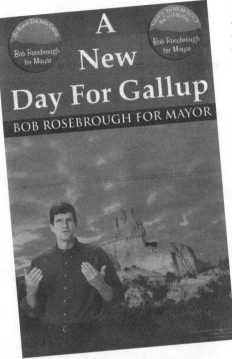

A campaign pamphlet with a series of open letters to the citizens of Gallup. *Courtesy of Chuck Van Drunen*

meetings have items for open, public discussions. I make appointments with city staff to request copies of the city budget, revenue projections, the city charter, and organizational charts, and I ask basic questions about how the city functions.

I feel that Gallup is ready for a burst of change. I know I am. The town has an incredibly diverse population and is surrounded by a gorgeous landscape, yet the community is fraught with social tensions and poverty, and the landscape, while beautiful from afar, is an inaccessible mess up close. I tell people how I see our challenge as a community, "Gallup has a higher, greater potential than most communities, and the barriers that impede that potential are also greater. Let's find a way to push through the barriers."

Although I'm the first candidate to announce, the field eventually grows to six, including a former mayor, Frank Colaianni. He was the operating partner in the Navajo Inn at the time Larry Casuse began to oppose Emmett Garcia's appointment to the UNM Board of Regents. Back in 1977, Colaianni was elected to the city council, four years after Garcia was abducted by Casuse. He somehow managed to avoid the controversy that derailed Garcia's once-promising political career. Colaianni is friendly and lighthearted on the surface, but in his business and political dealings he is reputed to be as hard and inflexible as a coal miner's drill bit.

In 1983, ten years after Garcia's abduction, Colaianni was elected mayor for a two-year term; he was defeated in his bid for reelection when a prominent retired banker ran against him. Colaianni owns or is a partner in three Gallup liquor licenses. Several people have told me that he's an astute and disciplined investor, a skill he uses to secure not only his security but the financial future of his grandchildren.

Colaianni recently built a huge, white, Tuscan-style home that stands alone on top of a large hill in the wealthy part of town, a half mile from where I live. A long concrete driveway bordered by a wrought-iron fence curves up the hill to the house. I overhear one of the Baptist ministers in town referring to Colaianni's home as "the house that liquor built."

Charlie Chavez, a sitting city councilor who has served for twelve straight years, also joins the race. Chavez, a friendly, well-liked man who owns a restaurant and lounge on the west end of town, is from a large, politically active family. One of his brothers is the Gallup Fire Chief and another manages the city's senior centers. The city manager and utilities director are extended relatives. The publisher of the *Independent* has recently been sarcastically referring to Gallup as Chavezville, and Charlie seems to relish bickering back and forth with him.

The other three candidates are Billy Armijo, a charismatic, high-energy retired fire fighter who finished a close second in the race with Mayor Peña; Joe Darak, an out-of-town schoolteacher; and Ralph Rains, an iconic figure in Gallup. Raines is a bushy-haired, heavily bearded man and bounces from job to job as a painter in splattered work clothes. He runs for mayor every four years on a platform of planting more trees and has a small but devoted, none-of-the-above contingent of supporters.

I have a couple of things working against me. Almost all of Gallup's modern mayors have been born and raised here. Even after twenty-three years of living, practicing law, and raising kids in Gallup, I'm still considered an outsider to many in the community—and always will be. My grandfathers didn't mine for coal underground, cut timber in the Zuni Mountains, work on the railroad, or operate a trading post. And it's been just seven years since I split away from my old law partners under strained circumstances, left the Catholic Church, and divorced and remarried while being, for a time, the talk of the town—circumstances that collectively would be disqualifying in most small towns.

But Gallup is different. For years, I've been telling people, "It's hard to be pretentious and live in Gallup." Because it's so raw and real here, paradoxically, my personal problems might actually make me more electable in Gallup than if I were still just an out-of-town white guy who'd never suffered a setback. And although I'm divorced, my wife Brenda is a friendly, extroverted woman with a bright smile who was born and raised here and seems to know everyone in town.

It seems to me that three of the other five candidates would have run whether or not I chose to, but I suspect that two of the five, Colaianni and Darak, both late entrants, are running at least in part to block me from winning once they have seen my campaign gain traction.

A year or two earlier, I represented a woman who had ended her personal relationship with Darak; she was concerned about getting some of her property back. It appears to me that he might be trying to settle a personal score with me. His campaign platform is suspiciously similar to mine, and friends tell me he is campaigning around town saying that we do need a change but that I'm not electable because of my divorce. I meet and talk with each of the candidates, and when I meet with Darak, he beams with pleasure as he makes a point of telling me I can't win because of my divorce.

In the case of Colaianni, although I generally want to stay out of the political fray in the year leading up to the election, I have gotten into one controversial matter that I suspect has caught his attention. A local businessman bought a liquor license far out in the county, where Sunday sales are permitted, and proposed to transfer the license less than 100 yards from Gallup's northern boundary. Effectively, the transfer would reopen Sunday sales in Gallup, which the city voters had banned in a referendum. The transfer requires approval from the county commission, and I start gathering evidence and witnesses to testify. The transfer is successfully blocked at the county hearing. Not long thereafter, I hear that Colaianni is entering the race.

On most weekends over the course of the year, I pick up a pack of my campaign cards and start walking door-to-door with the daunting goal of covering the entire city. Gallup spreads out over eleven miles on either side of Interstate 40, and its neighborhoods are separated by cliffs, canyons, and mesas. The city easily covers three times more area, in a random, irregular sprawl, than most cities with a population of only 20,000.

Billy Armijo is the only other candidate I encounter while canvassing. On a sunny winter day, I run into him and his campaign manager, up on the north side of Gallup, the older, poorer part of town. Billy is friendly, but he seems puzzled and says, "What are you doing over here?" I think he assumes I would only canvass the more prosperous areas of town.

The other political issue I take part in during the run up to the mayoral election has to do with water. A month or two before the filing date, Patty Lundstrom, the director of the Northwest New Mexico Council of Governments, suggests that I attend a public meeting on the Navajo-Gallup Water Supply Project at which U.S. Senator Pete Domenici is to preside. The project is the only possible source of renewable water for the New Mexico side of the Navajo Nation—and for Gallup. The futures of both communities hinge on the pipeline.

"I'm hoping that Domenici will use the meeting to announce that he's going to introduce legislation to authorize the project," Lundstrom tells me. She's been working on this project more than twenty years—her entire professional career—and she knows that the project will never happen without strong public support from the senator.

Patty Lundstrom, NWNMCoG director, and Pete Domenici, US Senator and chairman of the Natural Resources committee, each devoted years of work to the Navajo-Gallup Water Supply Project. *Courtesy of Patty Lundstrom*

Senator Domenici is wearing a bolo tie and a vest featuring a Navajo design on the front and he's in a pissy mood. He's sitting in Mayor Peña's chair in the council chambers flanked by members of his staff.

The senator is an icon in New Mexico politics, having served the state in Washington, DC, for thirty years. He first gained a national reputation when he was named chairman of the powerful Budget Committee after Ronald Reagan's victory over Jimmy Carter in 1980. He also now chairs the Senate Natural Resources Committee that will have to initiate the authorization process for the pipeline project. Born Pietro Vichi Domenici, the youngest of six children of northern Italian immigrants who ran a successful grocery business in Albuquerque, Domenici is widely called Saint Pete by many in New Mexico—particularly among Gallup's Italian community, where he has deep, lifelong friendships. Now in his golden years, Domenici is rumored to be in the early stages of a progressive disease of some sort. Throughout the state, there isn't a new public building being built that local politicians aren't considering naming after him.

The water supply project, or NGWSP, is dependent on the Navajo Nation's settling its water rights claims in the San Juan River with New Mexico's Interstate Stream Commission, and the word is that the Navajos and the state are getting close to a settlement. There's a palpable buzz about the project, but the excitement clearly hasn't found its way to Domenici. During the meeting, he continually complains that there's no money in Washington and he nitpicks technical aspects of the project.

I'm sitting in the back row of the council chambers, taking notes and watching the body language in the room. Domenici has picked out a lateral pipeline on the project to carp about, one that will provide water for the eastern section of the Navajo reservation.

"We don't have the money for this," says Domenici. "How did this get into the project? Why haven't I heard about this before?"

His staff is looking down, avoiding eye contact and shuffling papers. The audience of engineers, local elected officials, Navajo Water Resources staff, and Gallup businesspeople seem stunned. I make eye contact with Lundstrom and she grimaces. A couple of rows in front of me a Navajo man in his early fifties dressed in Levi's and a plain, collared shirt is shifting in his chair. He stands and sets a binder on the seat next to him. Domenici doesn't appear to have noticed him stand. When there is a pause in the senator's complaints about the lateral pipeline, the man says in a firm, authoritative voice, "Senator, there are Navajo people who need that water."

A stunned silence descends.

"Who said that?" Domenici looks around the council chambers and then focuses on the man who stood. Everyone present wonders how this is going to play out. The Navajo man and Domenici have an exchange about whether or not the senator's staff was given project material describing the lateral pipeline in advance of the meeting. One of the senator's staff, who looks like a cowering puppy, confirms that the material was received some time ago.

During the exchange, Domenici appears puzzled and somewhat curious about the Navajo man addressing him. Neither Domenici nor the Navajo man seems angry. They both speak with self-assurance and authority, as coequals. The Navajo man sits, and the dynamic in the room has changed. Domenici shifts from airing grievances to discussing solutions. He begins talking about the legislative process and what it will take to get a bill authorizing the project through the Senate, but he stops short of saying that he will introduce legislation to seek congressional authorization. I look again at Lundstrom, who shrugs with a relieved look that says, *Maybe we're back on track.*

As the audience is filing out of the council chambers, I sidle up to the city's water department director.

"Who was that guy?" I ask. I don't need to explain the question.

"Michael Benson," he says. "He works for the Navajo Water Resources Department. He used to be a radical."

In January, shortly after the pipeline meeting, the official mayoral campaign starts on filing day, two months before the election. That evening I hold a campaign kickoff event that opens with a Hispanic band and closes with a Christian praise and worship ensemble. The pastor from the First Baptist Church has a big, booming Texan voice and is dressed in cowboy garb. He twirls a lasso and shouts that he is "rounding up votes for Bob" as people arrive. A racially diverse group of friends stand at a mic and give brief, personal endorsements of my candidacy. The weekend after filing day, a group of my mountain-biking buddies, armed with rebar drivers, wire, yard signs, and list of addresses, put up three hundred yard signs within a couple of hours. The campaign is on.

My opponents match my energy. Frank Colaianni throws his own campaign kickoff event, and old-time Gallup comes out in full force. Charlie Chavez works his large network of supporters. Billy Armijo, like me, is out every weekend going door-to-door all over town.

A full schedule of debates and forums are scheduled, and at every forum all the candidates show up with energy and a list of proposals, projects, and ideas. Armijo is dynamic and energetic; he speaks from his heart. Chavez, with his personal knowledge of every issue gained from his long tenure on the city council, speaks as the voice of experience and practicality. Colaianni presents himself as the smart, successful business-man that he is. Darak's sole purpose in life seems to be to steal my thun-der. Rains, whose only issue is trees, is seldom seen.

At the third forum, Colaianni starts saying that people need to be wary of candidates who have grand visions for the city when they haven't been able to manage their own family life. Several people look at me to see how I am going to react. I don't.

At the fourth and final campaign event—a televised set of short speeches on the local TV station where we each go into a room by our-selves and speak to a fixed camera—there's an edge in the air before the speeches start that I haven't noticed before. The candidates speak in alphabetical order. Chavez talks at length about his marriage and chil-dren. Colaianni also gives special emphasis to his marriage and family life at the beginning of his speech. I'm the last to speak and I begin by saying, "I'm a divorced man. I've remarried and I'm an active father with four children," and then I go on to the issues.

After I finish my speech, I mingle with the other candidates, and something is different. The tension seems to be broken, and it seems to me that the fact that I've openly acknowledged my divorce has something to do with it. For the first time in these forums, the other guys, except Darak, who appears to be even more agitated, seem relaxed and calm.

Each week between filing day and the election, I run a quarter-page ad in the *Independent* on a different topic. These "open letters" address the city's water future, quality-of-life projects, downtown revitalization, and the development of a more business-friendly environment in the city's Public Works and Planning and Zoning departments.

Not long after my open letter on the topic, the city water staff hold an informational meeting on the Gallup's water future in the council chambers, the same space where Michael Benson spoke to Senator Domenici a couple of months earlier. The meeting is well attended, and most of the mayoral candidates are present, as well as a contingent of community leaders and activists. The Navajo-Gallup Water Supply Project is one of several items on the agenda, and several Navajo Nation representatives are present, including Benson.

A couple of the candidates ask pointed questions that are calculated to solicit answers from the city water staff that will contradict positions or statements in my letter. The staff don't take the bait; they seem wise to the questions and give guarded, politically neutral answers. I take notes but don't speak.

In my open letter on water, I had written, "Here's the bottom line: NGWSP [the Navajo-Gallup Water Supply Project] will only be achieved with a committed effort from our congressional delegation. We, as residents, need to know whether our congressional delegation can make the pipeline a reality."

As the water future meeting ends and I start to leave, Michael Benson approaches me.

"Bob Rosebrough, I didn't like your letter on water," he says. "I think you sounded like a petulant child." Somehow, he says this in a way that doesn't draw my ire. In fact, I've been looking for a chance to meet him since the meeting with Domenici.

"Hi, Michael," I say, extending my hand. Benson seems surprised that I know who he is. "If you have a minute, let's go out in the lobby and talk." I know what I'm going to say to him. We find a seat in a corner of the lobby, under photos of Mayor Peña and the four city councilors.

Michael Benson at Wellesley College in the early 1970s.
Courtesy of Michael Benson

"It's interesting to me that you didn't like my letter," I say. "When I was writing, I was actually trying to follow your lead. I was in the room when you talked to Senator Domenici. I saw you pressure him, and that's what I'm trying to do as well. Are you the only person who has the right to pressure him?"

As Benson and I talk, it feels almost as if we're fencing, but with prop swords rather than sharp blades. Benson clearly likes to test people in authority, and I actually feel flattered to have been selected as one of his targets. I don't think he would waste his time with a candidate he didn't view as being viable. Several Navajo water representatives gather apprehensively a discreet distance from us, trying to gauge how the conversation is going.

As we continue to talk, I'm thinking, *I wonder if I'll be able to work with this guy?* I suspect Benson is thinking the same thing. I tell him I'd like to talk to him again when we have more time. He says he'd like that as well. We part, and I remind myself not to get too far ahead of events. I've still got a lot of campaigning to do.

The last three of my open letters are titled "Alcohol," "Our Land," and "Our People."

My letter on alcohol says, "We need to have a blunt talk about alcohol. Alcohol abuse has been the biggest single factor in preventing our community from realizing its potential." I talk about the days when it seemed hopeless in Gallup and how all we heard for decades was, "It will never change." And I talk about the changes that flowed from Mayor Muñoz's Walk to Santa Fe—the imposition of an alcohol excise tax, the banning of drive-up windows, and the securing of funds for the Nanizhoozhigi Center that extended the first step in intervention from 12 hours to 72 hours. I describe the downtown zoning ordinance we passed that encouraged three bars to move away from downtown, and the responsible server training program that our downtown development group sponsored that's now mandated statewide.

I urge a middle course between prohibition and the unfettered abuses of the past, and I propose further zoning measures, nuisance suits, state legislation to grant extended local control of alcohol sales, and strict enforcement of existing ordinances. The letter concludes, "We've found our path as a community. Let's finish the journey."

After the letter is published, I get a call from a friend who's an accountant. "I liked your alcohol letter," he says. "That was well done." Later he'll change his tune at an inopportune time. But for now, his vote of confidence is a victory.

In "Our Land" I describe having recently taken my son Matt to college in Iowa. "I spent over 40 hours driving on the interstate. Leaving Gallup, I took a southern route. Coming back, I took a northern route. Both ways, I looked at the scenery with fresh eyes, to see if there was any place as beautiful as Gallup. Only one place came close: Colorado Springs. Yet even Colorado Springs with Pike's Peak and the Garden of the Gods couldn't quite match Gallup. It lacked the captivating immediacy of our sheer red rock cliffs, rugged mesas, and sandstone uplifts.

"I want us to consider the potential for outdoor recreation, open space, and the resultant opportunities for economic development through adventure tourism. Possibility is all around us. Take a look with me."

My series ends with "Our People." "The diversity of the people of Gallup is our most wonderful asset. Many of us who have been drawn to Gallup are here because of the multi-cultural nature of the community. But the blending of our cultures has not been peaceful. The truth is that part of what has brought us together has been forceful conquest. There is a need to recognize, acknowledge, and seek reconciliation for past injustices. Before we move forward together, we need to be honest about the past and acknowledge the injustices that continue to separate us.

"Our diversity, if given the honor and respect it so richly deserves, will be catalytic. It will draw tourists, but it will do something much more important than that. It will transform us. It will enrich each of our lives and help us grow strong, principled, open-hearted children."

While the campaign is generally going well, there are distinct moments of resistance. I walk in a Martin Luther King Jr. Day parade and the next day a photo of me appears on the front page of the *Independent*. The photo was taken when a young man, with whom I had no connection, was briefly by my side, carrying a sign protesting the Iraq war that said, "Get the U.S. out of Iraq!" The next day several people tell me that some of Gallup's old-timers are calling me Baghdad Bob.

A few weeks before the election, I visit a local radio station to record an interview with the energetic station owner, a wealthy man who moved to Gallup late in life from San Francisco after working as a lawyer in telecommunications. The station owner is close friends with Frank

Colaianni, and Colaianni's son-in-law is the station manager.

The owner has been taping interviews with each of the candidates, and during the course of my interview I say all the things I've said in my open letters. Before I leave, the station manager cautions me. "I don't think you know what you're getting into Bob," he says. "You can't say things like acknowledging past injustices and filing nuisance suits against problem bars. They're going to come at you from every direction and try to tear you apart."

I tell him that I appreciate the advice, but that I've been in Gallup now for almost twenty-five years and I've made friends and helped many people. "If I'm attacked over the positions I'm taking, my friends will stick up for me."

He gives me a look that says, *Don't say I didn't tell you so.*

A few days later, I have a conversation with the son of State Senator Lidio Rainaldi, a champion of Gallup's political old guard. The senator's son questions me aggressively about my desire to reach out to Navajos. A friend of mine runs into him later and reports that the senator's son said, "I think Bob is turning his back on the people who built the town." My friend says, "He seemed adamant about it."

I'm startled by this mindset. To me, it's pretty simple. We live within what was the Navajos' homeland, and the economy of our city relies, in large part, on business trade with the Navajos. Why shouldn't we be reaching out to them? Why is such an effort cast as an either/or proposition? Why isn't what's good for them good for us too?

The senator's son isn't the only person I encounter who has what seems to me to be irrational fears about Navajos. A Hispanic life insurance salesman regularly pops into my office unannounced, trying to sell me a policy and talk politics. Almost every other time he shows up he says in an apocalyptic tone, "The Navajos are going to take over Gallup!" And after I give him an *are-you-really-serious* look he follows up with, "You know it's true."

What my campaign has shown me, however, is that the insurance salesman doesn't have anything to worry about. Navajos, though they make up about a third of the population of Gallup, are not part of its political fabric. They don't contribute to political campaigns in Gallup and often don't vote. Many, if not most, retain their county voting registration so they can vote in Navajo Nation elections.

But the final days of the campaign are winding down, and I can't dwell on old-timers' attitudes about my Navajo outreach proposal right now. It's hard to tell how the race is going to shake out. None of us have done any polling; Gallup is just too small for that. Chavez, Armijo, and Colaianni all have solid bases of support, and the talk around town is that any of the four of us can win.

With election day looming, I think about the campaign and feel that we've done all we can do. Regardless of the result, I'll have no regrets about missed opportunities or things undone. I've loved the campaign despite some bumps. I'm an introvert by nature, and what I treasure is that I've been forced by the campaign to get to know hundreds of new people that I would never otherwise have met, some in heartfelt ways.

One new friend, Chuck, who sought me out after I announced my candidacy, is an example. He is twenty years younger than me and unfailingly upbeat, with an infectious laugh, a positive outlook, and a flood of ideas for the campaign and for Gallup. Chuck tells me that in college he ran an underground newspaper and that eventually he'd like to start an alternative monthly magazine in Gallup. I give him a list of names and addresses of some of my supporters, and he comes back with testimonials and photos that he combines with my open letters into a newspaper-like campaign publication. On the weekend before the election, a team of volunteers divvies up the town's neighborhood and delivers the publication across the city.

On the night of the election, an hour after the polls close, I drive to my office just fifty yards or so from the entrance to City Hall, with Brenda and the kids. I'm excited and nervous as I open the door and start turning on lights and tuning the radio to KYVA at 1230 on the AM dial.

My family trails into the office behind me. We listen together as veteran news reporter John McBreen runs down the list of the candidates for mayor and city council to kill time as he waits for the first election results.

We hear the sound of rustling paper, and the McBreen says, "We have the first precinct reporting. In what may well be the trend for the night, the small downtown precinct 38 at the Rex Museum reports 4 votes for Frank Colaianni, 20 votes for Bob Rosebrough, 6 votes for Billy Armijo, 1 vote for Joe Darak, no votes for Ralph Rains, and 2 votes for Charlie Chavez."

McBreen is predicting I'm going to win. Only about 30 votes are in and he's predicting I'm going to win.

Results are soon rolling in from throughout the city, and it appears that McBreen is right; it looks like I'm going to win. And win big. My family and I walk over to City Hall, and as I enter the council chambers, outgoing Mayor Peña, the city clerk, and her staff are behind the platform; the clerk is posting numbers on a huge white board with columns for all the voting precincts in town.

I glance at the board, and then, I'm surprised when the packed room bursts into applause—the first and only time that will happen in my life, I suspect. Billy Armijo and Joe Darak are sitting in the audience. Billy seems shell-shocked and disappointed; Darak's expression is blank, indecipherable. My family finds seats and I work the room, acknowledging Armijo and Darak, accepting congratulations, thanking supporters, and telling city employees I'm looking forward to working with them. The acting city manager, an extended relative of Charlie Chavez's, looks resigned. He invites me to a ground-breaking ceremony for a new clinic at the Gallup Indian Medical Center in the morning.

A photographer wants to get pictures of Mayor Peña and me out in the lobby. Before we go out, I look at the final results on the tally board:

Frank Colaianni	585
Bob Rosebrough	2,297
William Armijo	866
Joseph Darak	168
Ralph Rains	59
Charlie Chavez	480

Although I felt I had a good chance of winning, I'm shocked and surprised by the margin. After the photographer is done and my family and I gather to leave the building, Frank Colaianni and his nephew come in. We stop to talk. Colaianni is cordial and gracious. I tell him that I'll give him a call to see if we can have lunch in the next week or two; he tells me that he'll look forward to it.

The next morning, Brenda, the kids, and I are still excited. I attend the ground-breaking ceremony at the medical center. Portable chairs are set out and the crowd, which comprises Indian Health Service administrators, doctors, the acting city manager, an incumbent city councilor, and fifty or so Navajo people, few of whom I know, mingles. Late in the event, almost as an afterthought, the master of ceremonies recognizes the city manager, who in turn introduces the councilor and then me, saying, "Bob won the election for mayor last night." Heads turn our way and there is a low but clearly audible murmur that seems to signal approval from the Navajos.

A few days later I see Billy Armijo and we talk for a while. He's gracious and encouraging. Of all my opponents, he's the one I felt most connected to as we canvassed the streets of Gallup. Before we part, Billy tells me that he ran into Frank Colaianni recently.

"And?"

"They're worried about you," he says. "They're afraid of what you're going to do about alcohol."

CHAPTER NINE

"How Many Heart Attacks?"

Two days after the election, I enter Gallup's Sacred Heart Cathedral with the city clerk for a meeting with the bishop of the Diocese of Gallup. I'm apprehensive and preoccupied as I think about how to make my pitch to him. After leaving the Catholic Church eight years before, I've only been back to the cathedral a couple of times for funerals.

The cathedral is constructed of brick and huge, high-arching wood beams. Globelike lights hang from the high ceiling. On either side of the church and to the left and right of the altar are a series of arched alcoves formed from brick, each consisting of a series of precise, indented arches. Vertical swaths of blood-red cloth frame the figure of Jesus on the cross on a soaring wall of intricate brick work. For a moment, the beauty of the place draws me out of my unease.

The city clerk, a pianist for the cathedral, leads me to a small office where the bishop and a priest are waiting. The bishop, a small, friendly man in his late fifties with salt-and-pepper hair is wearing a black suit with a white collar. To my relief, he's eager, even excited to see me, and he congratulates me on the campaign. After we settle in, he tells us that he likes my idea—an interfaith ceremony called Many Cultures, Many Faiths, One

Day one, March 11, 2003. *Courtesy of Lisa Rodriguez*

Gallup—to take place after the swearing in of the new city officials.

"You can hold the ceremony here," he says. "We would be glad to host it." He authorizes the priest to help the city clerk and me with the details.

A few days later, I'm standing in the city council chambers with my right hand raised. Brenda is standing by my side with Mark, Megan, and Amy—now 16, 13, and 8—who are excited but subdued as they try to figure out their new roles. What does it mean to be the child of the mayor? What does it really mean to be mayor?

Two new city councilors are also sworn in. Frank Gonzales, the former police chief and sheriff in his mid-sixties represents Gallup's west side. A mid-forties Hispanic woman, who moved to Gallup from Las Vegas, New Mexico, to manage a radio station, represents Gallup's east side. There are two incumbent councilors. A mercurial Anglo, also in his mid-forties, who co-owns a print shop with his brother, represents Gallup's wealthy south side. And an Italian man in his late-fifties with a quick, easy laugh who works at his brother's full-service gas station represents the north side. The manager of the radio station and the co-owner of the print shop seem to form an instant kinship, and Frank Gonzales and the north-side councilor are life-long buddies who grew up on the same block in Chihuahuita.

These are the people I'll be governing with for the next four years. I wonder how well we're going to work together. I'm cordial with all four of the councilors, but to be honest, I don't feel a real connection or sense of common mission with any of them. Historically, there has been tension and, at times, open conflict between Gallup mayors and city councilors. The mayors have tended to have ambitious agendas, and the councilors have been prone to protecting their turf and the status quo, and less interested in proposing policy or projects. But that's not to say the city councilors don't want to make their mark; they've just been predisposed to do it by publicly putting mayors in their place.

The only person I know I can count on is Brenda, who has been fiercely and unconditionally loyal and supportive at every step and turn of this journey. But she doesn't have a vote.

After the swearing in, we go to the interfaith gathering at the cathedral, where comments and prayers are offered by representatives of nine faiths or traditions: Catholic, Hindu, nondenominational Christian, Baptist, Native American Church, Islam, Latter Day Saints, traditional

What will it be like to be a child or wife of a Gallup mayor? *Courtesy of Lisa Rodriguez*

Zuni, and traditional Navajo. Near the end of the gathering, the Native American Church representative, raising feathers aloft in one hand, asks everyone to come up to the altar for a blessing. The Hindu representative hangs a large flowered garland around my neck, and a short Zuni woman in a purple, flowered dress and a turquoise necklace approaches me to talk. I take a knee and we talk eye-to-eye as we clasp hands. A color photo of the scene appears the next day in the *Independent*—it looks almost like I'm proposing to her, but for the fact that she's talking and I'm listening.

In the days immediately after the election, I get my first taste of being in the eye of the press. The *Independent* article the day after the election says that I stepped out of character on election night in my victory speech to a crowd of excited supporters. "Breaking his usual calm, measured demeanor," the article says, "Gallup's new mayor, after thanking his supporters and asking for their continued help, broke into a full-blooded yell: 'Tomorrow in Gallup is a new day!'" The "full-blooded yell" strikes me as a bit of an overstatement—but I note that I should regulate my public comments.

My hometown newspaper, the *Farmington Daily Times,* finds the election newsworthy and sends a reporter to Gallup to do an article titled "Farmington Native Is Mayor of Gallup." The *Daily Times* summarizes the election results, talks about my continuing connection to Farmington through family and friends, and emphasizes Gallup's racial diversity as extending beyond New Mexico's tricultural English, Hispanic, and Indian heritage. "Gallup is an ethnically and racially mixed society," the *Daily Times* reports, "consisting of strong Arab, Asian, and East Asian communities." The article quotes a Muslim man who says something about me that strikes me as a stretch: "He is good, strong, gutsy, brave—all of the above."

Gallup Life magazine, I think, comes closest to hitting the mark, in an article summarizing Mayor Pena's accomplishments and the results and themes of the campaign. The article concludes by saying, "Whatever happens in the next four years, Gallup residents can be assured that a Rosebrough administration will be anything but routine." I like that, and I hope to prove it true.

At City Hall, I settle into the mayor's office, a place where I've always felt comfortable during earlier visits. I bring in some family photos for my desk and check out the filing system. All the drawers work but one.

It's locked. My secretary in City Hall doesn't have a key or know what's in the drawer. I have plenty of space for files and storage without the locked drawer and, eventually, I give up trying to open it.

Soon after the election, I'm invited to speak to classes at two elementary schools and a middle school. At two of the three schools, the kids ask, "How much money do you make?" When I say that the mayor's salary is $21,000, the response, in unison, is, "Woooo." The kids think I'm rich.

A second-grade boy follows up with: "Do you live in the white house on top of the hill?" He is referring to Frank Colaianni's house.

"No, that's not my house," I tell him. "I live about a half-mile south of that house. My house is a lot smaller."

The second day after I'm sworn in, I look out the window of my office and see a stream of clear water gushing down Second Street toward Route 66. A city water main has broken, and just after the turbulent stream of water passes an alley, it curves and flows into a sporting goods store owned by Rudy Radosevich, one of my best friends. The next day a large front-page photo in the *Independent* shows a two-foot wall of water flowing out the front door of Rudy's store, with the campaign sign, "A New Day for Gallup: Bob Rosebrough for Mayor," still in the window.

The day after the water-main break, my partner Dolph comes to my home in the evening, mixed drink in hand—something he's never done before—and tells me that his wife is filing for a divorce and he's moving to Albuquerque to follow her and his children. At the office the next day, the firm's junior attorney announces he too is going to leave to start his own practice. Within days of my election, I'm on my own, as a part-time lawyer, with a financial overhead well beyond my ability to meet.

During the campaign I felt as if an unfamiliar force or energy was working through me. And although events after the election are already beginning to spell trouble, it seems to me that the force or energy is enduring, that it will always be with me. Being fully immersed in government and my law practice, I don't have time to worry about things that would normally consume me; I wake up every morning and throw myself into the day.

At the moment, my plan is to build momentum and excitement in the community, as well as a real sense of progress. I want to do this before tackling Gallup's perpetual alcohol and public intoxication problems. A few days after the election, I announce four 100-day initiatives, each with citizen task forces and staff support: Native American Relationships, Neighborhood Cleanups, Water, and Quality of Life.

I try a different approach in my effort to reach out to Gallup's Navajo neighbors that stems from a conversation I had with an elderly Navajo politician during the campaign. He told me that Gallup mayors seem to think they're equal to Navajo Nation presidents, but they aren't. He said that Navajo Nation presidents see themselves as being more equal in status with U.S. senators and governors than border-town mayors.

"Mayor Muñoz was always upset when the president didn't want to meet with him," he said, "but he should have been trying to work with the Eastern Navajo Agency or the chapter house presidents around Gallup, not trying to go directly to the president." Keeping that conversation in mind during the first 100-day initiatives, I visit six Navajo chapter houses near Gallup, seats of local governance that also provide social meeting places on the Navajo reservation. None of the city councilors express any interest in joining me.

At each meeting I introduce myself and say I would just like to talk. Before going to the chapter houses, I ask a friend who is married to a Navajo how I should introduce myself to the people I'll meet. He says that Navajos introduce themselves by saying what clan they are from, beginning with the maternal side of their family and then the paternal side.

When it's my turn to speak at a chapter house, I say, "My name is Bob Rosebrough. My mother's father was German, and her mother was English. They lived in Florida, where my grandfather had an orange orchard. They moved to Jal, in southeast New Mexico, where my grandfather had a ranch when my mother was young. The eastern boundary of my grandfather's ranch was the state line with Texas. My mother was a rodeo queen at Eastern New Mexico University. My father's parents were either English, Irish, Welsh, or Scottish. I'm not sure. If you look at a map of Great Britain up on the right side just below the Scottish boundary, there is a place called Rosebrough Farm. That may be where my father's family came from. My father's father was a deer hunter during the Great Depression in Datil, down near Pie Town. He lost the lower part of his arm in a cotton gin when he was a young man. When he was hunting, he rested the barrel of his rifle on the stump of his forearm when he took aim. I was born at the nearest hospital to my grandfather's ranch in Jal and when I was three, we moved to Farmington. I moved to Gallup in 1979 after I graduated from law school."

This introduction seems to break the ice; the Navajo men seem to like the description of my one-armed deer-hunting grandfather. Although unwieldy, the introduction seems to set a comfortable personal foundation for the rest of the conversations.

At some chapter houses, I speak during the course of a formal meeting and address the officers while standing; in others we sit in a circle and talk. Every meeting is cordial and productive. Beyond introduction, the meetings seem to build a foundation for future collaboration, and hopefully they will set the stage for a relationship with the Navajo Nation president. At the Pinedale chapter near the end of my visits, as I am waiting my turn to speak, I scan an agenda and stop on a line that reads, "Visit by Our Mayor." I feel great pleasure at the idea that they see me as theirs.

Near the end of the first 100 days, I make a call to Navajo Nation President Joe Shirley Jr.'s office and ask for an appointment with him; I'm relieved to get a quick call back from Shirley's staff giving me a date and time to meet in Window Rock. I doubt I would have been granted a meeting without undertaking the chapter house visits first.

Opinion in town is divided about my Navajo outreach. Many people are excited and congratulatory, but one campaign supporter, says, "I'm concerned about some of what I'm hearing in town. One guy told me, 'I didn't know we elected an Indian lover.'"

The 100-day neighborhood cleanup initiative is less controversial. On nine Saturday mornings throughout the summer, city crews and volunteers meet in different neighborhoods with the support of Youth Conservation Corp kids, the summer youth work program. We spend the morning picking up trash and debris, and then we have lunch at an elementary school or senior center in the neighborhood with a local band performing. In six of the neighborhoods, we begin taking steps to form neighborhood associations. Two of the city councilors are excited about the associations and dive in to take responsibility for the associations in their respective districts. Two don't.

The initiative on water comes together with the involvement of the owner of a dry-cleaning business in Gallup. She serves on the board of New Mexico First—a group formed by New Mexico's two U.S. senators that holds an annual statewide town hall designed to build consensus on issues of public policy—and persuades the group to hold its first local town hall in Gallup. A Water Town Hall is held that exceeds expectations.

Eighty people including Michael Benson, who is one of ten Navajo Nation representatives, receive an extensive white paper and spend a Saturday at Gallup's branch of the University of New Mexico in group sessions that lead to a plenary session where recommendations for a comprehensive water plan for Gallup are approved by consensus. None of the councilors have signed up for the town hall, but the east-side councilor drops by briefly; then she leaves after making the rounds and shaking hands.

There is a steady rain all day during the town hall, which is rare in Gallup. I see the rain as a good sign and say so.

The chairman of the Navajo Nation Tribal Council Resources committee, George Arthur, and I, with the help of our water staffs, make mutually supporting proposals regarding the integration of one of the city's well projects into the Navajo-Gallup Water Supply Project. We hope that integration will benefit both the Navajo Nation and Gallup. Arthur and I address the group together; he presents his half of the proposal first. Then, I add Gallup's half. The proposal is unanimously approved by the town hall. It seems like a breakthrough moment, in what we know will be a prolonged effort to pursue the only hope of a renewable water supply for either the Navajo Nation or Gallup.

The Water Town Hall is a soaring success that, for me, is personally marred late in the day. Brenda has been urging water conservation measures, and several participants who were in her breakout group propose that she spearhead a water conservation campaign as Gallup's first lady. A friend of my ex-wife objects, and it appears personal. A concerted effort to get her to back off fails, and the proposal dies for lack of consensus, which is required by the rules of the town hall. A hushed pall falls over the room. Within the span of two minutes, I am elated and then disappointed and emasculated—powerless to protect the woman I love who unfailingly and fiercely protects me.

The Quality of Life Task Force, with guidance from our new city manager and finance director, identifies ways to fund a slate of new quality-of-life projects. The finance director proposes a $6.7 million general obligation bond election to replace expiring bonds, thus maintaining, but not raising, property tax rates. The city's last general obligation bond

According to a *Gallup Life* article, "Gallup residents can be assured that a Rosebrough administration will be anything but routine." *Courtesy of Brian Leddy*

election in Gallup went down to a resounding defeat several years earlier.

I privately reach out to the other mayoral candidates and ask them to publicly endorse the bond election as a show of community unity, and with the lone exception of Billy Armijo, they decline or simply don't return my call. Billy agrees but seems lukewarm about it. I ask an out-of-town consultant how to frame the election and he says, "Investment. The public needs to understand that this is an investment in the community." We come up with a theme for the bond election, and we put up signs that read, "Invest in Gallup's Future: Vote YES on August 12." The bonds are approved with slightly over 60 percent of the votes.

The task force also recommends shifting some of the city's lodger's tax revenue away from advertising and into tangible tourism-related amenities and community events—in other words, shifting money from I-40 billboards and TV commercials to brick and mortar tourism-related projects. All four councilors are eager to join in the selection of new projects, particularly projects for their districts.

I start my term as mayor with a small but excited, energetic professional staff. Before I took office, the old city manager resigned to take a job with the state offered by our new governor, Bill Richardson, a former congressman, U.N. ambassador, and secretary of energy who is reported to be planning to run for president. The city attorney's position has been vacant for years, and we don't have a utilities director. After advertising widely, we set out to hire a manager and an attorney.

City managers in Gallup have typically been hired on the basis of personal relationships. The mayor who preceded John Peña made no secret that he hired his city manager because the man owed him money—the hire was the best way to ensure that the mayor was repaid. I try a different approach.

After asking Council of Government's director for advice, my office sets up a two-day selection process with three panels: technical experts, citizens, and the council. We receive more than thirty applications for the job and select finalists. Eric Honeyfield, an experienced city manager from Raton, New Mexico, with an engineering background, stands out from the other applicants.

"I'm an engineer," Honeyfield says. And though he says there may be more collateral damage than we have stomach for, "If you give me a clear goal, I'll get there."

For years the party line in city government has been that it isn't possible to hire a full-time city attorney, but that turns out to be a canard fostered, I suspect, by people who didn't want a lawyer telling them what they shouldn't do. To my surprise, one of Gallup's best lawyers applies for the job.

At my suggestion, we create a citizen's advocate position to help guide locals through the city bureaucracy. We form a Development Commission with appointees from the business community, a carryover idea from Mayor Peña's administration, and hire a director for that commission as well as a new utilities director.

"It may have been the most productive period of time in the city's history, with a number of changes that have set Gallup off in new directions," reads the *Independent*'s article summarizing the accomplishments of the first 100 days of my mayoralty. Again, the newspaper's characterization strikes me as a stretch. While it might appear to be the most productive period in the reporter's limited experience, my tenure so far can't really be compared with Gallup's explosive early growth or the boom times of the '50s, '60s or early '70s. I have the uneasy feeling that the paper is building me up so that I can later be torn down.

With our new city manager and city attorney on board, joining an exceptional finance director who stayed on from Mayor Peña's administration, we don't slow down after the first 100 days. I've come into office wanting to jolt the community and inspire growth. The money from the GO bond election alone is not enough to do that. The city manager tells me we need another $14 million to make a real impact. We need to cut recurring costs to generate money, to pay for revenue bonds.

At a training for newly elected municipal officials in Albuquerque, I compare the number of employees in each city in New Mexico with its population, do the math, and see that Gallup has significantly more employees per capita than other New Mexico cities. Our city manager confirms that we are overstaffed and that we are generally underpaying our workers. We implement a reduction-in-force plan through attrition from resignations and retirements, and a limited hiring freeze that in time trims thirty-one employees. Frank Gonzales pushes for a comprehensive pay plan to assure comparable pay for comparable work, a rare and complementary policy initiative by a city councilor. We now have fewer employees, pay them better, and reduce overall labor costs.

Honeyfield identifies other areas where we can cut costs. He introduces safety incentives that reduce worker's compensation premiums by $170,000 annually and recommends a plan to privatize management of the city's Red Rock Park to reduce a huge annual deficit there.

Our finance director wants to retain the savings, but with Honeyfield's encouragement, I'm pushing to use the newly freed-up money to issue revenue bonds—which don't require an election—to build the financial pot. Combined with the GO bonds this will give us $20 million. The finance director resists, and the councilors who want the new projects but don't want to buck the director are wide-eyed on the sidelines.

Honeyfield is telling me, "Keep pushing, mayor. This will have a real impact and we'll still be solid financially." At an all-day planning retreat with the councilors, Honeyfield, and the finance director, we all get on the same page and approve $14.7 million in revenue bonds, a number the finance director can live with. The revenue bonds, combined with the GO bonds approved by the voters, allow us to fund a slate of new projects, including a new aquatic center, artificial turf for four multiuse sports fields, upgrades to neighborhood parks, renovation of Gallup's historic El Morro Theatre, completion of our courthouse plaza, and eight historic

"Gallup needs a face-lift." Bob and Brenda Rosebrough attend a downtown mural dedication in the city hall courtyard. *Courtesy of Lisa Rodriguez*

murals for the downtown. "This town is poised to explode," Honeyfield tells a reporter. I trust he means in a good way.

Based on a town hall recommendation, a Water Board is created that proposes increases in our water rates. This generates a revenue stream that pays for nine new water-line projects, including boring a space for a new water line beneath I-40 and completing a retention dam project started during Mayor Peña's term that will prevent flooding in the downtown.

It's apparent, too, that Gallup needs a face-lift. We set aside some of our revenue bond money to condemn and demolish dilapidated motels on Route 66, but before we file expensive, lengthy foreclosure lawsuits, Honeyfield issues a do-not-extinguish order to our fire department for the three worst motels. Shortly after the order is issued, one of the motel owners comes to see Honeyfield and asks, "You mean to tell me if that building catches fire the city won't put it out?" His motel burns to the ground that night.

Another dilapidated motel on the list has a dozen or so detached structures, and shortly after issue of the do-not-extinguish order, all the structures at that motel also catch fire simultaneously. The city manager says, "I suspect it was spontaneous financial combustion from that insurance policy rubbing up against that mortgage deed." All three motels on the do-not-extinguish list are demolished quickly with minimum expense to the city.

Our city attorney begins a push to require upgrades of the hangars at Gallup's airport, and Honeyfield proposes a new architectural-standards ordinance that eventually results in removal of thirty billboards and the upgrade of twenty commercial signs.

To my delight, Adventure Gallup is on its way to become a reality. Representative Lundstrom secures state funding for the city to acquire a 40-acre rock-climbing area on a row of sandstone cliffs west of town, and she negotiates an easement with Gamerco Associates for an area northwest of town, where we start designing a 24-mile single-track trail system for mountain biking and hiking. We also begin developing a motocross and off-highway-vehicle park, acquire a lease for a 100-acre target-shooting range, and improve our existing archery range so that we can begin establishing separate user areas. The goal is to give everyone a piece of turf and to move beyond the era when motorcycle riders, target shooters, and mountain bikers were bumping chests.

On weekends several of my mountain biking buddies and I, under the guidance of our local bike mechanic, start walking the large tract of land northwest of Gallup that Lundstrom negotiated with Gamerco for hiking and biking trails. We flag a stacked loop trail system with three loops—First Mesa, Second Mesa, and Third Mesa, patterning the nomenclature on that of the Hopi reservation mesas. The whole system will come to be named the High Desert Trail.

On a calm, cloudless Sunday afternoon, a mountain biking buddy and I start out from the trailhead to see how much of the area we can ride. There are several tracks ahead of us that create flowing, undulating lines in the soft soil. After an hour or so we catch a group of our friends at the Second Mesa overlook as the sun is starting to dip; we sit on the high mesa looking west at the other half of the trail system, the more difficult half, which is also flagged but has no bike trail yet. After several years of utter frustration, we literally see our dream coming true.

While the push for quality-of-life and infrastructure projects is generally popular among Gallupians, there is a small but potent undercurrent of resistance. Where does this come from?

I'm sitting at lunch in downtown Gallup with Honeyfield, one of his friends from Raton, and a Council of Governments employee. The walls are covered with old photos of the working men and women of Gallup.

Honeyfield's friend asks him, "How many heart attacks do you need?" she says.

"A few more than in Raton," he says.

The COG employee and I look on, not understanding. Honeyfield and his friend laugh, and she explains their private joke: Every small town has some old-timers who think they run the place. They're usually politically influential or wealthy, or both, and they pitch a fit over every new proposal. The black humor is that five or six well-placed heart attacks among such people would open the doors to progress in any small town.

The COG employee and I start naming names in Gallup and we are quickly up to double digits. Some of the wealthy, powerful old men of Gallup seem to take their obstructionism to another level. I'm told that a Slavic businessman who owns a second home near Durango and who has tastefully renovated several downtown properties in Gallup gets in a heated argument over the landscaping requirements for the new professional building he's building in Gallup, so he digs up sagebrush from the outskirts of town and plants the sagebrush at the building, technically complying with the requirements. Predictably, the bushes die and are not replaced. A semi-retired Gallup lawyer spends weekends at his home in a golf-course community in Rio Rancho and his Tuesday evenings in Gallup at our city council meetings, at which he protests plans to raise water rates and generate a revenue stream to replace aging water lines. The wealthy owner of a radio station has a second home in Sedona, yet objects to plans for hiking trails near his home below the hogback on Gallup's east side.

These people send a consistent message: Don't mess with the formula. Gallup is a place to extract wealth, nothing more. Leave Gallup alone and don't try to spruce it up. We don't care if Gallup suffers, we can afford to go somewhere else to enjoy our money.

Occasionally, my responsibilities as mayor allow me to escape and experience different worlds—a saving grace that takes me beyond the black cloud of small-town politics and old ideas. One weekday, I'm invited to the convention hall at Red Rock Park for a ceremony in which a group of Navajo Code Talkers will be awarded Congressional Silver Medals. During the early years of World War II, when they were young men, the Code Talkers developed a code that they used in battle in the Pacific to help defeat the Japanese.

For many years the Navajo Code Talkers were a common sight in Gallup.
Courtesy of Jeff Jones

The Code Talkers are now in their late seventies or early eighties; they are dressed in their Code Talker Association uniform of garrison caps with yellow trim, khaki pants, and long-sleeved shirts in various shades of yellow, from pale-butter to vibrant goldenrod. They sit alert, listening to federal, state, and military dignitaries speak. I'm the only representative of the city and I'm not scheduled to speak. The Code Talkers wear strands of turquoise around their necks or silver bolo ties. A few of them also wear conchos, broad black leather belts decorated with oval or round silver disks. They all seem at ease, comfortable with each other and the setting.

The Code Talkers are a common sight in Gallup. Their association meets regularly at the Chamber of Commerce, and for years they've marched in parades; now, though, as they've gotten older, they often ride in the back of a large vintage pickup truck. Two years earlier, in 2001, a group of Code Talkers were invited to the White House to receive Congressional Gold Medals, and in 2002 a Hollywood movie very loosely based on the Code Talkers called *Windtalkers* was released, but most of us in Gallup are so used to the Code Talkers' presence that we tend to take them for granted.

Navajo Code Talker Day, honoring men who used their language on behalf of a nation that years before had attempted to eradicate that same language through its educational system. *Courtesy of Brian Leddy*

As I listen to the dignitaries speak, I hear platitudes that raise more questions than answers. I don't understand why the 2001 group received a gold medal in the White House and these men are receiving silver medals at a city park just east of Gallup. How was the code developed? How were these men selected? How effective was the code, and how did it really work in the field? My understanding about the Code Talkers and their history is only superficial and I'm not learning anything from the speakers that adds to my knowledge.

There doesn't seem to be a set length of time to the ceremony, and even after many speeches, the formal awarding of the medals, and the departure of many of the dignitaries, there is no end in sight and no suggestion as to what may come next or when the festivities will break up. A different sense of time seems to prevail. In a way that is out of character for me, I just sit back, soak it in, and observe. The president of the Code Talkers Association, Albert Smith, walks by and nods but doesn't speak. Several other Code Talkers make eye contact from a distance, but don't approach. I just continue to sit and observe; there is a flow and a cadence to the men's interaction that is foreign but interesting to me.

Eventually an emissary approaches me, an Anglo man from Gallup who worked for the Navajo Nation years ago and helped the Code Talkers form an association when the government lifted the seal of secrecy on their mission. "The Code Talkers are telling me they appreciate your presence here," he says. "They're used to bigwigs coming to these events—making a quick speech and then rushing off." He's describing what I normally do. I don't really know why I've been lingering, but I think it's because, for the first time, I want to know who these men are and what their mission was all about. I want to talk to them, but before I do, I want to know much more about them.

One of the first things I learn when I begin to study the Code Talkers' history takes me by surprise; Navajos were not the first American Indians to serve as code talkers. In WWI, the American military used both Cherokee and Choctaw code speakers to develop codes. The shift to a Navajo code in WWII made sense for several reasons.

Adolf Hitler, I learn, knew about the use of Native code talkers in WWI and before WWII he sent thirty German anthropologists to the United States to study Native languages. The Germans reportedly never made it to the Navajo Nation. Besides that, the choice of Navajo to design a code was made in part because the Navajo language was almost completely unintelligible to most other Native Americans. At the time, Navajo was still a mostly unwritten language; there was a decidedly limited pool of non-Navajo speakers of the language, and those few were generally not fluent. Non-Navajo speakers typically spoke only a limited "trading" version of the language.

That the American government would want to use Navajos to develop a code was ironic in several ways. Navajos were being asked to play a critical role in the defense of a nation that had starved their ancestors into surrender and then imprisoned them, seventy-eight years earlier. And while Navajos and other Native Americans had been granted citizenship in 1924, and therefore the right to vote, they were blocked from voting for decades by state and local laws. But the most ironic aspect of the whole project was that Navajos were being asked to use their language as a tool of war by a nation that had attempted to eradicate that language by means of its educational system. Most of the Code Talkers, who attended Indian boarding schools in their youth, told stories of how they were punished for speaking the Navajo language. The irony was not a revelation to me; several Navajos

my own age had shared stories with me over the years about being physically beaten for speaking Navajo, most often in private religious boarding
schools, and their feelings of resentment.

I wondered how the Navajos would fit into the military, and what
the selection criteria were to work on the code for the Marines. I discover
that the Navajos had no problem meeting the physical requirements of
military service. Most of the Code Talker recruits were closely tied to
the land and physically fit. They had grown up herding sheep, horses,
goats, and cattle. Many lived a semi-nomadic lifestyle. They were used to
walking twenty miles to a trading post or following a herd for days. The
enlistment ages for new recruits to the Marines at the time ranged from
18 to 32, but Navajo men within that range generally didn't have birth
certificates at that time, and some who were younger than 18 gave an
older age when they signed up. All the Navajo Code Talker recruits had
to be fluent in *both* Navajo and English; speaking Navajo alone wasn't
enough.

After boot camp, the original 29 Code Talkers, who were the ones
who received Congressional Gold Medals in 2001, eagerly looked forward to a ten-day leave, but while their non-Navajo pals went home to
their families, the Navajos were told that their mission was critical and
that there was no time to spare.

These 29 recruits had been told that they were part of a special service, but even by the end of boot camp they still hadn't been told what
their mission was going to be. The first day after boot camp, a Marine
officer took the 29 into a room and gave them simple, direct instructions.
He stressed that their work was to be kept secret. They were not to tell
their mothers, fathers, wives, or even fellow Marines. As a group, they
were to use the Navajo language to create an unbreakable code to be
used in military communications. They were told to begin by selecting
a Navajo word for each letter of the English language. After giving his
instructions, the officer wished them luck and left the room, closing the
door behind him. At first, many of the 29 wondered if this was just a test
of some sort, but they soon accepted the task as being real and settled
down to work. One of the 29, Gene Crawford, had been in the reserves
and worked with codes, so he helped direct the discussion.

Navajo Code Talker Carl Gorman tracks enemy movements on the island of Saipan in the Marianas, June 27, 1944. *US National Archives (127-MN-83734)*

Navajo Code Talkers George Kirk and John Goodluck at a camp on Guam Island. Code Talkers were required to be fluent in both English and Navajo. *US National Archives (127-MN-94236)*

The method used to create the code is fascinating. Several things were important. Each word chosen needed to be distinctly different from the other words that were chosen. Each word had to have a clear pronunciation. The group started by picking an English word—typically the name of an animal, a plant, a mineral, or some common object—for each letter of the English alphabet; the English word chosen was then translated into Navajo. The Navajo word would represent the English letter of the alphabet. As an example, if a Code Talker wanted to communicate the word *book,* he would have said *shush* (bear), *ne-ahs-ah* (owl), *tlo-chin* (onion), *ba-ah-ne-di-tinin* (key), which were the Navajo translations of the English words representing the letters b, o, o, k. For some words—particularly military terms that would have to be used frequently—the letter-by-letter coded translation was dispensed with and one English word was given an equivalent Navajo code word. A squad, for example, was *dibeh-li-zini,* which is Navajo for "black sheep." The code thus mixed letter-by-letter translations with word-for-word translations. A listener could be fluent in Navajo but without knowledge of the code he would hear a random series of Navajo words—mostly nouns, with an occasional verb thrown into the mix—that made no sense. The coded radio transmissions wouldn't contain any sentences or even phrases that would be intelligible to someone without training in the code.

The Navajo language, because it is unique, made the code unbreakable. But because of differences in local pronunciations, the code was also a challenge for the talkers themselves. These differences had to be worked through and resolved; the words chosen by the first 29 Code Talkers had to be pronounced by all of them the same way.

Navajo incorporates four levels of tone—high, low, rising, and falling—that can completely change the meaning of a word. It also includes glottal stops and aspirated stops. As a result, many of the distinguishing sounds of Navajo are extremely difficult for non-Navajos to pick up.

I wondered how the code was used on the battlefield and I learned that the task of the Code Talkers was to receive a message written in English, perform an on-the-spot encryption into Navajo code, verbally transmit the encryption by radio to another Code Talker, who would then decode the message and write it down. Extensive practice with the code and repeated memorization were essential. The Code Talkers were particularly adept at memorization because Navajo at the time, wasn't

Navajo Code Talker Wilfred E. Billey. While being discharged, Code Talkers were told not to talk about their mission, even with family members.
Courtesy of Brian Leddy

written. Navajo songs, prayers, and stories had all been memorized and handed down from generation to generation.

The Japanese tried to jam the Code Talkers' radio transmissions by shouting, cursing, singing, and banging pots. The Marines countered by using dummy Morse code, forcing the Japanese to spend time decoding meaningless messages.

Once the code was used in battle, its accuracy and speed led to a call for two hundred more recruits. Messages that military decoding machines took 30 minutes to decipher could be transmitted by Code Talkers in less than a minute. By the end of the war, there were more than four hundred Code Talkers. In battle, the Code Talkers, like the Marines they served with, faced an enemy that employed mass attacks in the Pacific islands where it rained continually and snakes, lizards, and insects were pervasive. And even on their own side of the battle lines there were dangers. Frequently, Navajo Code Talkers were suspected of being Japanese soldiers in disguise and were taken at gunpoint to sergeants, lieutenants, and colonels who then saved them from their fellow Marines.

I came across a story in several sources that amazed me. By December 1944, the Japanese knew that the code used by the Marines in the Pacific was based on the Navajo language and they also knew that they held a

Navajo prisoner of war—Joe Keiyoomia from Shiprock, New Mexico—who had been captured in the Philippines in 1942. Keiyoomia had been tortured by the Japanese, who initially thought he was Japanese and therefore a traitor. He survived the Bataan Death March and was then placed in a prisoner-of-war camp in Japan. Once the Japanese figured out that the American code was based on Navajo, they questioned and tortured Keiyoomia again, but he didn't know anything about the code or the Code Talkers. He only understood bits and pieces of what the Japanese wanted him to decode, and he told them that it sounded like nonsense to him. The Japanese stripped Keiyoomia naked and made him stand for hours in deep snow. His feet froze, and when a guard shoved him, the soles of his feet were torn because they had frozen to the parade ground where he stood. After Keiyoomia's release from the camp, he underwent four years of medical treatment before returning to Shiprock. Years later Keiyoomia would say about hearing the Navajo language while a prisoner, "It gave me hope. It told me that American forces were getting close."

The more I read, the big question that forms in my mind is: How important were the Code Talkers to the success of the American forces in the Pacific theater? I find no evidence of how any one particular code transmission was pivotal in the outcome of the war or a battle. Rather, the Navajo code was an essential everyday component of the American war effort that allowed Marines in the Pacific to communicate securely and quickly in extreme conditions. On Iwo Jima, for example, six Code Talkers worked around the clock during the first two days of the five-week battle. They sent and received eight hundred messages without error. The Code Talkers provided a means to communicate and coordinate amid the fog of war that wouldn't have existed otherwise. I read that Major Howard Connor, a signal officer said, "Were it not for the Navajos, the Marines never would have taken Iwo Jima."

A few weeks after the Code Talker medal presentation at Red Rock Park, I'm invited to attend a "welcome home the troops" ceremony for a transportation company made up of Gallup-area men and women who have just come back from Iraq after a 15-month deployment. The ceremony is held at the armory in Gallup, a no-frills, metal-walled building with folding chairs set up on a concrete floor.

The company arrived in Iraq two weeks *after* President Bush landed a jet on an aircraft carrier lying off the coast of California and declared an end to "major combat operations" in Iraq. "That's when the urban warfare started," the captain of the company, tells me. He is a member of the Campos family from Chihuahuita. I ask him how the war is going and whether he thinks it's getting better or worse. He pauses and takes a deep breath.

"It's a civil engineering nightmare. It's a petroleum engineering nightmare," he says and pauses again. "There is a generation from 18 to 40 in age that grew up under Saddam that is brainwashed. They've been taught to hate the West. That's all they know. The kids under 13 seem open to Americans. Maybe there is hope with them." The tone of his voice suggests otherwise.

Of the thirteen members of the company at the ceremony, all are Navajo except the Captain. Ten men and three women. Five are missing from the ceremony, and they are all Navajo too, except for one white man who is married to a Navajo woman. I ask Captain Campos, "What kind of soldiers do the Navajos make?" I have the impression that Navajos, in the tradition of the Code Talkers, continue to be exceptional soldiers.

"They're great," he answers quickly. "They're proud of the history of Navajo service. They volunteer more than anyone else. When you brief the troops and tell them this is a dangerous mission and ask for volunteers, they are going to jump in."

Later in the day in my office at City Hall, with the six-month anniversary of my election approaching, I reflect on the progress we've made. It has exceeded my expectations; many things have fallen into place that I didn't see coming. But I have a self-imposed deadline approaching. I intend to tackle Gallup's chronic problems with the overservice of alcohol, and I feel dread in the pit of my stomach. A battle is looming over Gallup's alcohol problem that I wish I didn't need to fight but won't be able to live with myself if I don't. How can the battle not be fought, when public drunkenness has stigmatized Gallup for decades and stifled its potential as a community? How can it not be fought, considering the human toll? To me, the problem reflects an absence of heart in the heart of Indian Country. The easy part of being mayor in Gallup is over. It's time for the other part.

CHAPTER TEN

A Dream About a "Thwart"

I'm standing on the floor of the council chambers facing a room of crossed arms and stern faces. Almost all of Gallup's liquor license owners are present among the capacity crowd, with two notable exceptions. Neither of Emmett Garcia's two former partners in the Navajo Inn, Frank Colaianni and Reed Ferrari, is anywhere to be seen.

Everyone is tense, including me. I know the license holders don't want to hear what I have to say, and though I'd rather be doing something else myself, I feel an obligation to talk to them directly before proposing policies that will affect their livelihoods. The liquor guys—almost all of them are men—are huddled, talking to each other in low tones with arms crossed. Colaianni's daughter is one of the few women in the room. On the floor with me are the director of the State Alcohol and Gaming Division, Gary Tomada, and Bernard Ellis, a nationally recognized alcohol epidemiologist who has tracked Gallup alcohol statistics since Eddie Muñoz's days.

The east-side councilor is sitting silently in the back row of the Council chambers; the south-side councilor, listening from an adjoining conference room with the door open, is out of view. They are like moths drawn toward the flame, but they don't want to get burned. The other two councilors haven't joined us.

Since I've been mayor, I hear citizen complaints during Open Door Friday sessions, every day on the street, and especially during meetings of neighborhood associations. Alcohol-related complaints are far and away the most frequent I receive. No other issue even comes close. People complain about aggressive panhandling, property damage, defecation in public places, and fields of broken bottles, as well as deaths from exposure.

During my first month in office, I drafted a "Survey on Alcohol-Related Issues" and sent it out with the city's utility bills. I got back 1,879 responses. The stack of returned survey forms is two feet high. Among the respondents, 9 percent don't want the city to change anything, 91 percent want the city to either prohibit the sale of alcohol (20.4 percent) or begin limiting hours of sale or restricting the sale of beers and wines designed to appeal to alcohol-dependent people (70.7 percent), and 84 percent favor nuisance suits against the package liquor stores with the highest incidence of alcohol-related offenses in their immediate vicinity.

It has taken me some time to sort out my thoughts and feelings about the problems that have earned Gallup the name Drunk City. A turning point came when I was president of the Gallup Downtown Development Group and proposed the zoning ban on daytime sales of package liquor in the downtown business district. I was sitting in front of a Gallup banker's desk. A stack of loan files sat on the corner of the desk to the banker's right. The banker, a garrulous man who spoke a couple of decibels above the norm, and I were talking about two problem bars in the downtown.

"I think both the Commercial Club and Club Mexico regularly serve their customers well past the point of intoxication," I said.

The banker nodded in agreement. "That's a successful business model in Gallup," he said in matter-of-fact tone.

I couldn't say those words in that tone, I thought. *I couldn't say those words without some trace of the anger I feel coming out.* And the paradox struck me. The banker, who was normally effusive and opinionated, spoke in a flat, nonjudgmental voice. While I, typically soft-spoken and deferential, had to strain to keep the lid on my anger.

Many aspects of Gallup's alcohol problem didn't bother me that much. I saw public intoxication, panhandling, and littering as not much more than bothersome. But overservice to alcohol-dependent people provoked me viscerally. Each time someone tried to justify or downplay the practice by saying things like, "Well, it's a business," I felt resentment rise. Most of my anger arose from the inhumanity of contributing to an impaired person's greater suffering, but part of it also was the toll the practice had taken on Gallup's reputation and spirit over the decades. And when I was in a position of public responsibility in Gallup, although I knew it would be convenient to not care, I didn't seem to have a choice.

I start the meeting with the liquor license holders by reviewing the results of the alcohol survey and I tell them about the alcohol-related complaints I hear every day as mayor. Then Tomada, the State Alcohol director, talks about the alcohol-server training program that began in Gallup with his help that has now been adopted statewide. Ellis, the epidemiologist, talks statistics.

"We don't have any bigger problems here than in other cities, do we?" says one licensee defensively. Ellis is momentarily taken aback by the question, but he gathers himself and replies that Gallup has a much bigger problem. Statistically, he says, Gallup has "epidemic levels" of alcohol-related problems. McKinley County has the highest level of alcohol-related deaths in New Mexico, he explains, and New Mexico has the worst statistics of any state in the nation.

With the stage set, it's time for me to say what I really want to say.

"I have three main concerns," I tell the group in the calmest, most matter-of-fact voice I can muster. "First, I have a real problem with any sale of alcohol to people who are already intoxicated. We have a law against that, but it's my perception that the Sales to Intoxicated Persons statute is not effectively enforced, and I think it should be. Second, I have a problem with licensees who choose to cater specifically to alcohol-dependent people by selling products like fortified wines and malt liquors with high alcohol content. Third, I have a problem with all the broken glass we have in the community from alcohol containers. It looks bad and it's dangerous."

Before I finish, I toss out what I think they will view as good news, my attempt at a peace offering. I note that the surveys show that a small majority favor permitting the sale of alcohol in restaurants on Sundays, which is currently banned. I tell them I'm open to the idea.

I yield the floor and the floodgates open. A heavyset bar owner complains that he's been unfairly "targeted."

I tell him that's news to me because we haven't done anything yet except to put out a survey and set up this meeting.

"Who came up with these questions?" says another licensee. He can't believe the option of prohibition was included; he is genuinely aghast. I tell him I wrote the questions for the survey.

I come back to the issue of broken glass. I suggest that the licensees, as a group, contribute $20,000 for a community clean-up to pick up glass.

Without responding to my suggestion, Charlie Chavez, one of my mayoral opponents who owns a bar on Route 66, speaks and says he doesn't care if Sunday sales by the drink are permitted. He says he works six days a week and doesn't want to work another day, too. All the comments and questions came from local liquor license owners. The representatives of corporate owners like Albertsons, Walmart, and Giant, though present, take in the show without comment. They seem to be more curious than agitated, and many are taking notes and looking around the room as if to gauge reactions to the discussion.

None of the licensees respond to my stated concerns or express any interest in working on solutions cooperatively. I tell them I'm going to propose some voluntary actions—no sales before 9 a.m. and restriction of malt liquors in 44-ounce glass containers and fortified wines—for their consideration. I tell them that if we can't get unanimous voluntary compliance, I'll seek legislative action. The meeting ends, and I move to stand by the door.

As the liquor licensees file out, all but a few avoid eye contact with me and only two or three shake my hand. One of the liquor dealers, who is avoiding eye contact, says, "Can you believe he wants *each of us* to put in $20,000?" in a loud raised voice.

Here we go again. I've seen this before, when Eddie Muñoz was mayor. The alcohol industry has a well-rehearsed drama drill, and they're telling me that it's about to start up again. Step one is to fudge the facts and paint proposed reform, no matter how moderate it may be, as extremism. That's what the license holder is doing now by saying I want $20,000 in clean-up money from *each* of them rather than the group as a whole. Personal attacks will follow, casting me, as well as anyone who sides with me, as a zealot and insisting that our real goal is prohibition. Then they'll make predictions of imminent doom, like, "Gallup will dry up and blow away without alcohol" and "This is going to bring back all the negative publicity and we don't need that right now." And, they'll bring in their lawyers and lobbyists and start calling in favors, particularly among our area legislators.

I had hoped that after the conflict of Muñoz's era we might have advanced beyond the manufactured drama. I had talked myself into believing we were at a point where we could find a pragmatic, middle course.

The liquor dealer's words hit their mark because I know that the drama drill works. I know the survey numbers I shared with the liquor dealers will not withstand the onslaught. When the licensees feel threatened, as they do now, I've seen them generate a pack-like mentality of relentless frenzy. And while Gallup is enamored with change in the abstract, the average citizen abhors the conflict, negative publicity, and divisiveness that accompany alcohol-related change as much or maybe more than the underlying problem itself. By the time the drill ran its course with Muñoz, the community was exhausted. Muñoz barely escaped recall and, shortly thereafter, lost a bid to be elected to the legislature in a race against Colaianni's nephew.

A couple of weeks after my meeting with the liquor licensees, Hank Stokes, a wiry, red-haired minister from Georgia comes to see me. Hank started a non-denominational Christian church in town, and we have met and talked frequently, sometimes while sitting on high vantage points around Gallup while taking a break on mountain bike rides.

Hank sometimes shares prophetic dreams and premonitions with me. When I decided to run for mayor and told Hank a couple of days thereafter, he said, "I know. I've known since I first met you."

After we narrowed the city manager applicants to three and the *Independent* ran their names in the paper, Hank told me, "I have a feeling you're going to choose the man named Honeyfield from Raton."

I know Hank doesn't know any of the city manager applicants or anything about them. I ask him why and he says, "I just had a deep-rooted feeling when I read his name in the paper. I don't know the reasons why. I just know." As it turns out, it was not a close call. After the evaluation process, Honeyfield stood head and shoulders above the other applicants.

Hank is normally an exuberantly optimistic guy, but he's had a dream about me that has shaken him. He tells me that, in his dream, my efforts to take on Gallup's alcohol industry have aroused a giant, dark, metallic creature called a Thwart that he describes as being malevolent, unrelenting, and that crushes all that stands in its path.

"It's a powerful, powerful force of some kind that is trying to keep this community suppressed," he says, "I think you need to be careful Bob.

I think you've stirred up something very powerful." He's dead serious.

I don't know what to say. I'm not going to be deterred by a dream, even if it's the dream of a friend and minister whom I really like and trust. "I appreciate you sharing this with me," I say, and then change the subject. Although I try to put it out of my mind, the concept of a Thwart is one that will stick.

Although my administration has created momentum and raised expectations over the first six months of my term, there's only a limited opportunity of time to effect any change on alcohol issues during this honeymoon phase. And another problem is looming.

Bob Zollinger, the publisher of the *Independent*—the newsman who once wrestled Mayor Peña in the lobby of City Hall—applies to the city for Industrial Revenue Bonds to help finance an addition to his building and a new state-of-the-art printing press. I don't think he really cares that much about whether the bonds are approved; I think that's secondary. It seems to me that he enjoys interjecting himself into the news rather than merely reporting it.

During the process of applying for the IRBs, Zollinger issues us, the city, a series of demands and ultimatums. He comes to my law office and to the mayor's office, enters without stopping at the reception desks, and strides around without taking a seat. While making random disjointed comments, he eyes me as if he is stalking prey, then says, "This meeting is over," and leaves without waiting for a response.

A series of meetings is held by the city to consider Zollinger's IRB request and adopt a policy that will apply to all future IRB applications. After one meeting in which things didn't go to his satisfaction, I'm told Zollinger got into an argument with his attorney and took off his jacket and threw it down in the street outside City Hall.

Eventually, a scaled down version of Zollinger's IRB request is approved; Zollinger then begins demanding that we pay part of *his* legal fees and reimburse him a fee for an electrical hookup to his building extension that he's already paid to the city. Then he comes to City Hall. As he is talking to a secretary, the city manager comes out to use the copy machine. Zollinger angrily makes his legal fee and electrical hookup demands. When Honeyfield tells him, in no uncertain terms, that the city is not going to pay, Zollinger leans in, and using a low threatening voice, curses the city manager and says, "I'm going to bill the city anyway, and I'm going to add some zeros to the final total." After about ten minutes during which he is repeatedly asked to leave, Zollinger finally departs.

After the encounter, the city manager suggests getting a restraining order against the publisher, and a couple days later when I go into the mayor's office, I find a stack of police reports about an inch and a half thick on my desk the city attorney has gathered for my review. Leafing through the reports, I read that Zollinger, when being escorted away from his wrestling match with Mayor Peña, mocked a Hispanic police lieutenant, calling him "boy."

The other police reports in the stack tell the same story: they describe the publisher berating a heavy-set female employee at City Hall and then saying, "Why don't you go back to your hole, and eat at the trough?" He tells a police officer responding to a call about a fight at the *Independent,* "Take your head out of your ass and get the hell off my property." Other reports chronicle conflicts with two other policemen, a female reporter, and a postal clerk.

Zollinger also has a good side. He's reputed to go out of the way to help some of his key employees with medical bills and travel leave when family members are battling medical emergencies. Zollinger's reporters say that he tells them to pursue news stories no matter where the facts lead them, even if it means that he loses a friend or a subscriber. As a result, people actually read the *Independent,* and Gallup hasn't become a news desert like cities where chain newspapers have taken over.

And although some Gallupians complain about it, Gallup benefits from Zollinger's policy of extending the paper's news coverage to include the Navajo Nation, thereby helping to solidify Gallup's status as a hub of commerce for Navajos. But Zollinger's good side isn't one that he tends to share with school superintendents, district attorneys, county commissioners, and especially mayors and city managers.

Between the battles looming with the liquor dealers and the publisher closing in, I'm feeling a sense of urgency about the regulation of alcohol.

After considering several options, I propose a strategy adopted in the state of Washington for "alcohol-impacted areas." The concept is to give local governments, which are normally required to defer to the state regarding alcohol regulation, the authority to regulate hours of sale and the right to ban the sale of products specifically designed to appeal to alcohol-dependent people.

The approach seems fitting in our circumstances; the Navajo Nation is dry, and Gallup is soaking wet. It seems to me that prohibiting early-morning sales of package liquor and the sale of fortified wines and high-alcohol-content malt liquor in 44-ounce bottles represent a reasonable middle ground between the two existing extremes. For the sake of marketing the concept to the council and the community, I propose that we use the words "local empowerment district" instead of "alcohol-impacted area."

The third partner in the old Navajo Inn, Reed Ferrari, poses a problem for the local empowerment district proposal. Ferrari, 77, is now an alcohol wholesaler in Gallup, and he bottles fortified wine in such large volumes that it's shipped into Gallup in railroad tank cars. A limitation on the sale of fortified wines would be a major hit to Ferrari's wholesale business, and he's a well-liked man in the community. Many people in Gallup affectionately call him "Reedie."

I propose that the retail liquor dealers comply with the proposed limitations voluntarily, and the ensuing negotiations that extend over several months are contentious and slow. Eventually, all but three of the retail licensees agree not to serve alcohol before 9 a.m. and not to sell malt liquor in 44-ounce containers and fortified wines. Of the three retail holdouts, two licenses are owned by Colaianni and one is owned by an Arab businessman.

My next step is to seek city council approval of a resolution asking the state to create a Local Empowerment District for Gallup that will give us the authority to regulate certain hours of sales and certain products locally. The city council votes unanimously in favor of the resolution, but I sense that council support is thin at best. Their hearts aren't in it. The east-side councilor seemed to be initially fully on board, but her enthusiasm waned when a local grocer pulled his advertising from her radio station, to protest her support of my alcohol agenda. The other three councilors don't let me know their positions prior to the vote and, although they vote for the resolution, they do it silently, without making supportive comments.

Gallup's citizens, who filled out a record number of anonymous survey forms and have been eager to complain privately, also seem to be observing a code of public silence. One Hispanic man in his late sixties, the son of a Gallup coal miner, takes me aside after critical comments I make about a Gallup bar owned by a prominent Italian family appear in the *Independent.* "I'm proud of you, Bob," he says. "I don't think anyone has ever taken them on before."

I suggest that he consider stating his opinion in a letter to the editor. He looks back at me wordlessly wide-eyed.

A young professional man from a prominent Italian family calls me when I start taking some blowback on our Local Empowerment District legislation and says, "It almost makes me embarrassed that my name ends in a vowel." Publicly, though, he remains silent.

A Croatian businessman pulls up to my house when I am getting my mail at the curb.

"Keep doing what you're doing," he says.

"I could really use your voice on this," I say.

"Keep doing what you're doing," he replies. Gesturing with his hand toward the big white house on the hill, he says, "When is enough, enough." Then for the third time he says, "Keep doing what you're doing," as he drives off.

Despite these clandestine words of encouragement, I sense that I've used up a ton of political capital.

After the vote on the Local Empowerment District resolution vote, a liquor licensee says in my presence, "We shouldn't be complaining just against the mayor. This wouldn't have passed if the councilors hadn't voted for it. They need to be accountable too." It's pretty clear to me that the councilors will fold quickly if they start having to take any real heat.

The fact remains that a New Mexico city can't regulate sales of alcohol. Our Local Empowerment District must be approved by the state legislature and the governor. I begin looking for an opportunity to make my pitch to Governor Bill Richardson, an immensely talented but complex, guarded, and volatile man.

I had tried to make a personal connection with Richardson nine months before I was elected by going to a private fundraiser for him in Albuquerque. At one point, we were alone together on an outdoor deck waiting for a meal to be served, and I began asking him for advice on politics. He answered only a few of my questions before leaning back in his chair, lighting a cigar, and silently putting up a rock-solid wall between us, signaling he was done.

When Richardson was elected, his top legislative priority was DWI penalties and prevention, which makes me think we might have a shot at winning his support for our Local Empowerment District legislation. Without his support, we have no chance. The 2004 legislative session will last thirty days, and to be on the agenda this year, we need Richardson to put our proposal on the governor's call.

But beyond placing us on his call, we need Richardson to put his political clout behind the legislation. When Ed Muñoz was mayor, a major media push aided his alcohol agenda, with the support of the hospital and a grassroots Navajo movement. We have none of that. And although I think the Navajo legislators will help us, they don't have near enough political clout to push through legislation by themselves. I lobby New Mexico representative Lundstrom, but she is lukewarm at best. It seems to me that Lundstrom, having seen firsthand the blowback from the liquor industry that Muñoz generated, doesn't want to tell me no, but that she also doesn't want to put her weight behind or express public support for our legislation either.

Our state senator from Gallup, Lidio Rainaldi Sr., is a lost cause. Several weeks before the start of the legislative session, Frank Gonzales, the west-side councilor, accompanies the senator, 76 at the time, to the mayor's office to see me. Senator Rainaldi has a deep, gravelly voice, a thin gray comb-over, dark bags under his eyes, and bushy black eyebrows. He carries a zippered folder that I never see him open, and he's wearing a bolo tie and sporting a large turquoise ring. He's spraying vitriol like a high-pressure garden hose that's slipped from someone's grasp.

I try to explain the concept of the legislation, but the senator is not in a listening mood. He lectures me aggressively about how important alcohol is to Gallup's economy and how the publicity that will be generated by our proposal will make Gallup look bad. I glance out of the corner of my eye at Frank, and he seems to be shaking his head in frustration at the senator, but I know he'll never take him on. That's my job. Senator Rainaldi tells me that he'll fight me all the way and make sure the legislation never gets out of the state senate.

I've had enough. "If you want a fight," I say, "I'll give you a fight."

A couple weeks later, having decided to piggyback my pitch to Richardson onto a meeting set up by Lundstrom on the Navajo-Gallup Water Supply Project, I take the stack of alcohol surveys and the summary of the results with me to Santa Fe.

The wood-paneled cabinet room we gather in contains a huge circular wooden table. A wooden replica of the Seal of New Mexico dominates the eastern wall over the chair where the governor sits. The seal features two eagles, a smaller Mexican eagle perched on a cactus with a snake dangling from its beak, and a larger American eagle standing erect with its wings spread, clutching three arrows in its talons. The seal is said to symbolize the change in New Mexico's sovereignty when it became a state and America's dominant but protective role in preserving the state's heritage and culture.

I tell Lundstrom that I'm going to bring up the Local Empowerment District legislation at the end of the meeting, and though she gives me a mildly disapproving look, she doesn't tell me not to.

At the end of the NGWSP meeting I show Richardson the alcohol surveys, describe the results, and explain the Local Empowerment District concept. I ask that he support us by adding our proposal to the governor's call. Richardson agrees quickly, saying, "It's the right thing to do." He answers so quickly that I feel I need to caution him.

"We've been working to try to get voluntary compliance from the liquor licensees," I tell him. "There are still some hold-outs, and you should know there'll be some strong opposition from some of the licensees."

"It's the right thing to do," Richardson repeats. He gives me the name of an aide, tells me how to reach the man, and says he will instruct the aide to help us get legislation drafted through the Legislative Counsel Service. I want to feel euphoric but I don't. It seems too easy—too quick.

After the meeting with Richardson, we gather resolutions of support from the Navajo Nation president, the Navajo Nation Council, and the chairman and council of the Pueblo of Zuni.

As the legislative session approaches, Richardson's aide is distressingly non-responsive to my calls and emails, and on the occasions when I reach him, he seems ambivalent and evasive about our proposal. Shortly before the session begins, my secretary at City Hall calls me out of a morning meeting in the council conference room, saying I have an urgent call from John McBreen, the local radio news reporter.

"The governor's call came out and your Local Empowerment District legislation is not on the list," he says. I'm stunned and my heart sinks. I make a series of calls and I'm told that Rainaldi went to Santa Fe with a couple of the liquor guys and that they changed the governor's mind. I call McBreen, who has talked to the governor after we talked, and he says,

"The governor told me, 'I don't know what you are talking about. Your mayor never talked to me about that.'"

I don't bother to call the governor's aide. Instead, I call Richardson's deputy chief of staff. "I'm coming to Santa Fe in the morning," I say, "and I have a lot to talk about." I'm furious, my voice loud and threatening. As I speak, I'm wondering how much of this the councilors and staff in the adjoining room can hear.

"It's your choice," I say. "I can either talk to the governor or I can talk to the TV stations. I'll let you make that decision."

Then I call a couple of close friends who, though they're not on Richardson's staff, work regularly with him, and I ask them for a favor. I ask them to get a message to Richardson: I'm angry, but I'm a reasonable guy, and even though he has just screwed me, he can still work something out with me.

I tell them I need Richardson to get the message today. Then I call Gallup's lobbyist in Santa Fe and tell him I am driving there, and I need him to get me an appointment with Richardson in the morning, a near-impossible task.

The next morning, as I'm sitting outside Richardson's office with our lobbyist, the deputy chief of staff comes out, greets us, and eyes me warily. Having gotten the anger out of my system yesterday, I'm composed, and I thank him for setting up the meeting. He starts to guide us in, but pauses and says, "Let me give you some advice. It won't serve you well to be angry in there." It doesn't seem like he's trying to bully me; it seems like he is trying to help me. I nod, and he jokes with the lobbyist bemoaning the fact that this period, the days just before the legislative session starts, is rutting season in Santa Fe. He holds up his fists and butts them together in front of his chest.

Inside, Richardson is sitting uncomfortably in a leather chair and he's squirming. But it doesn't appear that he's uncomfortable with my presence; it seems he's just not comfortable in his own skin this early in the morning. Our lobbyist takes the lead and asks Richardson to add us to the legislative call list. Richardson's deputy chief of staff says the deadline for the call has passed and all they can offer at this point is a "memorial," which will call for study of our proposal during the interim period between sessions and introduction of the proposal to be made in the sixty-day session in 2005. It's essentially a face-saving measure.

"I can tell you one thing. Your legislators don't support this." Governor Bill Richardson speaks at a rally for Local Empowerment District legislation at the New Mexico capital, with Navajo Nation President Joe Shirley Jr. to his right and Zuni Pueblo Governor Arlen Quetawki to his left. *Courtesy of Peter Procopio*

Richardson offers no apology and makes no admissions nor accusations. He eyes me cautiously, and jokes with our lobbyist to try to lighten the mood. Then just before we leave, he imparts something I already know: "I can tell you one thing. Your legislators don't support this."

Although we no longer have any hope for passage of our proposal in this legislative session, we hold a rally, along with Navajo Nation President Joe Shirley Jr. and Zuni Pueblo Governor Arlen Quetawki, on the steps of the state capital to demand that the power to curb alcohol sales be given to communities. The rally draws hundreds. Governor Richardson attends and pledges to provide funding for liquor inspectors to work in the Gallup area, and to launch more special operations to target liquor vendors who break the law by selling to intoxicated persons.

"Let me say that I have heard your pleas. I'm with you," Richardson says. I'm standing two feet behind him and to the right, and the statement he's reading appears to have been written by an assistant, not spoken from his heart.

The press reaction to our initiative could not be more split. The *Albuquerque Journal* runs an editorial titled "Santa Fe Should Allow Gallup

Governor Bill Richardson, an immensely talented but complex, guarded, and volatile man. *Courtesy of Peter Procopio*

Liquor Law." It begins, "Gallup has a problem: too many alcoholics and too many establishments that seem to cater to their addiction." After expressing a general preference for statewide uniformity of laws, the editorial concludes that, "The problem is so acute in Gallup" that "letting Gallup experiment with local-option regulation could point the way for the rest of the state."

A wildly different tack is taken by an over-the-top, hard-to-follow *Gallup Independent* editorial, the first of many to come. It says that our push for local alcohol options is "racist" and then builds to a crazed crescendo and adopts the moniker that arose in my campaign, "Read this, Baghdad Bob, who wants to trample the needy and do away with the poor. Shakespeare is right: First do away with the lawyers." For good measure, the *Independent*'s publisher also adopts the anthem of his fellow Gallup millionaires: Stop spending money on quality-of-life projects. Don't mess with the formula.

It's ten months into my four-year term, and I feel as though a complete reversal has occurred since the days of my campaign, when everything that could go my way did. Now, because I've taken on alcohol, roadblocks are popping up all over. I could skate and fold, but really, I can't do that anymore than I can move to Durango and ride its trails daily. Gallup is my home and I want the best for it. I'm just going to have to slog through this for better or worse.

Without any real chance of help from Santa Fe for the time being, we Gallup officials are left to fend for ourselves and do what we can locally. The city manager presses our police chief to start enforcing the sales-to-intoxicated-persons ordinance. When his informal requests are ignored, he tells me, "I gave the chief a memo saying that there won't be any raises for the professional staff of the police department until active enforcement of the sales-to-intoxicated ordinance is implemented." Within a couple of weeks, enforcement is underway. And not long after, two problem bars, Cowboys, located on the north side across the street from the *Independent*, and The Other Place on the south side, near a bowling alley, decide to sell out, one to an incoming Applebee's and one to a hotel developer.

Our city attorney tells us that while we don't have the legal authority to regulate alcoholic beverages, we do have the authority to prescribe limits on the size of glass bottles. He proposes to ban glass bottles 18 ounces or larger. Several liquor licensees attend the hearing on the ordinance and vocally oppose the move. The council goes through a series of amendments over the details and eventually amends the ordinance to ban glass bottles 23 ounces or larger. It appears to me that the councilors are shifting. Initially they supported my alcohol initiatives publicly, but they expressed private reservations. Then, on issue like the Local Empowerment District resolution, they were silent both publicly and privately. Now, they seem to be trying to find a middle ground between my positions and those of the liquor licensees. But I fear that it's inevitable that they'll eventually publicly oppose me and any further reforms on alcohol, as most Gallup city councilors have done in the past.

The size limitation on glass containers, combined with a bounty of five cents a pound for glass, turns out to be a real success. Within a couple of months, the fields of broken glass in Gallup's open spaces are gone, and they don't come back. I'm elated to see even one tangible, visible change for the better, but I'm afraid the council has gone as far as they are going to go.

CHAPTER ELEVEN

"When You Go to War, You Let Your Hair Down"

After several rushed exchanges during and after water meetings, Michael Benson, the former radical who stood up to question Senator Domenici at the Navajo-Gallup Water Supply Project meeting when I was running for mayor, drops by my law office after hours and we make time for the conversation we talked about having during the campaign.

There are 700,000 homes in the United States that don't have running water—150,000 of them are on Navajo land. Gallup's problem is different; everyone in the city has running water, for now. But Gallup's water comes from wells whose water level is dropping steadily. Eventually, the wells are going to run dry.

The proposed solution for both Gallup and the Navajo Nation is the NGWSP, but the project's life has depended on the forging of alliances between groups of people who were historic enemies. In addition, if the project is to come to life, factions opposed to establishing by law a specific quantity of water that the Navajo Nation is permitted to divert from the San Juan River will have to be overcome politically.

Water Is Life—a recurring message in Navajoland graffiti. *Courtesy of Brenda Rosebrough*

Ultimately, for an Indian tribe in the Colorado River basin to actually have water come out of a spigot requires both a settlement with the Interstate Streams Commission, which quantifies the tribe's water rights, and then a congressional authorization and appropriation of money over a period of years to build a water system. The Navajo-Gallup Water Supply Project was first discussed on the congressional record in the early 1950s. During my campaign for mayor, several people with knowledge of the project took me aside and whispered, "The settlement talks with the Navajo Nation are going well. This might come together during your term if you're elected."

When Michael arrives at my office, I show him into a small conference room with a large, framed color photo on the wall of an elderly Navajo Code Talker surrounded by a group of four- and five-year-old Navajo girls in traditional dress at a powwow during the Gallup Inter-Tribal Indian Ceremonial.

I've never encountered anyone who speaks like Michael. He says things that would cause most people to take offense, but though he says them assertively, he does so in a matter-of-fact way, without anger or emotional drama. He leaves room for people to hear him without taking offense. And he speaks precisely and gets right to the point.

From the time I saw Michael confront Senator Domenici, I've been wanting to have a private, unhurried conversation like this with him.

Some critical public hearings on the water project are coming up, and it seems to me that Michael has been crucial to advancing the Navajo Nation's settlement of water rights in the San Juan to the point where the goal line is now in sight.

Aside from wanting to hear about his history with the NGWSP, I'm eager to talk with Michael about what drew him into activism as a young man and whether he ever crossed paths with Larry Casuse in those years. I've often wondered what Casuse's life would have been like if he'd survived his activism, and I wonder whether there are any parallels in Michael's life story that might offer insights. It seems to me that Michael represents what Larry Casuse could have been if he'd survived the turmoil of the early '70s and the bullets on Route 66.

I ask Michael where he grew up, and he tells me that his family lived sixty miles north of Gallup in the Two Grey Hills area just east of the Chuska Mountains. The Chuskas are a ten-mile-wide swath of mountains that stretch fifty miles to the northwest from the southernmost point in the range. They average about 9,000 feet in elevation—about 4,000 feet above the plains below. Two Grey Hills is known for a distinct pattern of Navajo rugs that features a dark border, four matching corner designs, and a large central diamond shape woven in a variety of earth tones.

Whatever need Michael and I felt to joust in our earlier interactions is gone by now. He tells me that he was born to a single mother who later gave birth to two daughters; he grew up in his grandparents' home nearby. "It was one of those Navajo settings where my mother had our home over here," he says, and my grandparents' home was about a quarter mile away."

Unlike Casuse, Michael was immersed in the Navajo way of life from birth, and that cultural grounding, and the family support inherent in Navajo culture, seem to me to be a significant reason why Michael survived his activist years and Casuse did not. Michael's family lived on land next to a major canal that Michael says was originally built by the Ancestral Puebloans (formerly known as the Anasazi), centuries before Navajos settled in the area.

Michael tells me that his grandmother, Ethel Denetclarence, was a "Navajo nationalist" who lived in poverty. She had come from a wealthy, prestigious family that lost most of their livestock, the source of their wealth, in the forced stock reduction imposed by the U.S. government

Transmission line and scar (far right and distant) on the Chuska Mountains. "It left a big scar, and it just hurt her, and she complained about it," said Michael Benson of his grandmother, Ethel Denetclarence. *Courtesy of Bob Rosebrough*

during the Great Depression. The forced slaughter of livestock, designed to help preserve eroding grazing areas, was a financial gut punch to many Navajo families of that era.

"She made me feel real Navajo and to feel like we were under siege," says Michael. "She didn't like airplanes flying over; she didn't like those jet trails. When the Tucson Gas and Power transmission lines went over the Chuskas, it left a big scar, and it just hurt her, and she complained about it. When we came to the Ceremonial in Gallup, she came with us, but she would always point out that it was horrible the way they treated the Navajo religion. It bothered her that Ceremonial would have pieces of the Night Way ceremony—what people usually call Yei-bi-chei—in the summer when it's a winter ceremony."

Some of Michael's earliest memories were of working with his grandfather and his younger sister to irrigate and plant seeds in their fields. Michael's grandfather was an irritable man who was always working. Michael was small and couldn't keep up, causing his grandfather to grumble. Michael's little sister was just three years old. Her job was to put seeds in the ground after her grandfather plowed. Every now and then she would forget her job and sit down and play.

"When the corn came up, you could see that a baby did it," says Michael. "In one place there would be just one stalk; in other places, there would be too many. There would be spaces in between and I remember when my grandpa saw that, even he just laughed."

Michael grew up speaking Navajo until he went to a boarding school.

"We'd be speaking Navajo—that's all we really knew," he says. "I remember playing outside and those dorm attendants would walk around and tell us, 'Speak English!' I remember the kids making fun of my pronunciation, my accent, and that's when I told my sisters, 'Let's just speak English,' so we started doing that and we became more proficient."

Michael's grandmother knew some English words, but she pretended she didn't. Michael would try to trick her by inserting an English word like *sugar* into a sentence that was otherwise Navajo. When she would pass the sugar, Michael would tease her.

"I would say, 'Grandma knows English!' and she would say, 'No, don't say that!' and 'I don't know any of that stuff!' That was her attitude. Oh, she was beautiful!" says Michael. His voice rises and he shifts upright in this chair as he talks about her.

I ask Michael what his impressions of Gallup were when he was a kid.

"I used to like coming to Gallup," he says. "The neat thing was, there was a bus every day in the morning coming and then going back in the evening. I remember the Ceremonial was fun. We'd camp up there in the cliffs. We would watch Ceremonial from over there. You would hear stories in Two Grey Hills about how so-and-so got robbed by Mexicans in Gallup. And I hate to say this, but there's a prejudice we Navajos have against Mexicans. Are you aware of that?"

"I have heard that," I say. I think back to my campaign when an elderly Navajo man told me, "If you get elected you may have a chance of getting the pipeline through. It'll never happen when there is a Mexican mayor in Gallup." I don't mention that conversation to Michael. Instead, I ask him about where he went to high school.

Michael says that in the ninth grade, he was faced with a pivotal decision. At the time, he was going to a private Catholic school near Window Rock. One of the nuns asked him to fill out an application for a scholarship at Lenox Prep School in Massachusetts. In the spring, when school was to end, the nun told Michael, "You got it!"

Michael's decision was agonizing. "I was hoping my mom would say

'Stay' or 'Go,'" he says, "but mom left it completely to me."

Michael decided to go to Massachusetts and doesn't say why. While at school there, he met people who were fascinated with, and respectful to, Indian people, and that was new to him.

I ask Michael what led him to become an activist.

"Going east was what helped radicalize me," he says. "An organization called United Scholarship Services helped to support a lot of the Indian kids that went to prep schools and colleges in the East. At school, I was elected president of the Organization of Native American Students, and I headed that organization for four years. There was some noise against me by the other kids, the other tribes, so at one point I stepped down to be executive director, but I took all the power with me. They elected a young Choctaw boy and he was just glad that I was doing the work," says Michael.

After graduating from Lenox Prep in 1969, Michael went to Wesleyan University in Connecticut where he continued his activism. When the American Indian Movement took over Alcatraz Island in 1969, Michael conceived the idea of taking over Ellis Island. The attempt failed when the battery gave out on the boat that was ferrying Michael and his fellow activists to the island.

Eventually, Michael grew depressed by the Indian activist scene in the East. He felt that many of the activists from eastern tribes had lost any real connection with their culture. Michael tells me about one man who looked black but said he was Catawba, a tribe from South Carolina that lived along the Catawba River. The man said that he was the last person to know the Catawba language and that he was working with a university to write down as much of it as he could.

"I could see where some day we'd have Navajos saying, 'I'm Navajo' but culturally we wouldn't be Navajo," Michael says. "We'd be grasping at things."

"They'd do this stupid ceremony," Michael says. He describes a gathering in which little Sterno cups were lit and men took names like The Great Medicine Man. It seemed contrived to Michael, but the people in the ceremony were serious about it.

"They were claiming to be this tribe and that tribe," Michael tells me, "when you could see nothing of that in them. In my young mind, they were half-assed. It made me sad, utterly sad. It worked on me."

Dispirited at Wesleyan, Michael caught a rash. His hair started falling out and his face puffed up. He tells me there are Navajo ceremonies for problems that arise from contact with non-Indians. His grandmother told him that that was what the problem was. "In a way, she was right," Michael says. "My body was probably weak from all that depression and seeing Indians like that. I can't stress enough how that affected me—seeing those remnants of tribes in the East. And I was forgetting my language being in school out there for five years."

During Michael's second year at Wesleyan, in 1970, the students went on strike against the Vietnam War and to protest the shootings at Kent State.

The Wesleyan professors joined the students in protest, and the university was shut down. Michael left school and returned to New Mexico, where he went to work in Gallup at the Indian Center as a community developer. The Indian Center was in a rundown building just across the railroad tracks from Gallup's downtown, just north of where Larry Casuse's body was later dragged out onto the sidewalk. If was one of just five centers across the country that was funded by a federal grant.

At the time, Emmett Garcia was the newly elected mayor of Gallup and Larry Casuse was about to start his freshman year at UNM. Michael felt his job at the Indian Center was to wake up young Indian people. He got ideas from reading about other activists.

"One thing that really shook up people was our demonstrations at Ike Merry's house," Michael says, referring to the founder and longtime director of the Gallup Inter-Tribal Indian Ceremonial. "People can be

The all-white, all-male Gallup Inter-Tribal Indian Ceremonial Directors.
Courtesy of Octavia Fellin Public Library, Gallup, New Mexico

impersonal at their offices, but when you go to their house—and we did it on a Sunday—it got a lot of attention."

Michael wrote a leaflet at the time called, *When Our Grandfathers Carried Guns,* and when he and fellow activists started passing out copies around at the Ceremonial, they were banned from the event. The Ceremonial officials said they were inciting people. The activists fought the ban in court but lost. They then went to area high schools to help organize protests. There were walkouts by Indian students at Gallup High, Tohatchi, and Chinle. "We were real proud of that," says Michael. It occurs to me that our two- or three-year age difference was significant for Michael and me. I was just behind the curve of the student activism of the late '60s and early '70s, while Michael was right in the midst of it. And besides that, I grew up in the conservative bastion of Farmington.

Michael wanted the protests to be peaceful, but a lot of young people were talking about violence. "I pushed AIM away because we didn't want to be violent, and in my mind, we were superior," he says. "We were culturally a tribal people, and a lot of the AIM people were urban people that somehow woke up to being Indian all of a sudden."

Michael's group at the Indian Center had a newsletter that Mayor Garcia took offense to and then tried to control politically. "There was a story almost every day in the newspaper about stuff we were doing," Michael says. "I remember this young guy saying, 'We didn't make the paper today! Come on, let's do something!'"

Michael says that a common political tactic of establishment political leaders is to place a member of an oppressed group of people on an organization's board who is sympathetic to the establishment, thereby undercutting activism. He says that Mayor Garcia and his political allies put a Navajo man, John Pinto, on the board of the Indian Center and then nominated him to be its chairman. There was a meeting at which Mayor Garcia moved to put an activist chairman of the Gallup Indian Center on leave.

"It was a major power grab," says Michael. "John Pinto just sat there, and finally he said, 'No, I can't. It's my people.'" Garcia didn't know what to do. A Navajo woman got up and started talking about unfair treatment.

"So finally, the mayor said, 'Well, I guess we can't do anything,' and they left," says Michael.

During the summer of 1972, Michael went to Washington to work there for the summer, and during that time, students from the Kiva Club at UNM began to help the Indian Center agitate against the city and the Ceremonial.

I ask Michael if he knew Larry Casuse.

Michael nods yes and seems reflective. "During that time that I was away, Larry Casuse came in and started being active around here," he says. It seems to me that Michael doesn't have an already formed answer to my question and that he's trying to sort out his thoughts about Casuse.

"When I went away," he says, "I guess there was a spokesman vacuum, so he came to the fore. I remember just meeting him, but I didn't really know him or get to talk to him. I felt uneasy about him. It could have just been jealousy; he took some of my role when I went away that summer, so it could have been that. He had that AIM presence—wearing a headband, whereas we didn't. The activists that I recruited, we didn't dress like AIM."

Michael tells me that Casuse focused on Mayor Garcia as a symbol of the problem since he owned a bar (the Navajo Inn), made money off Indians, presided over police who were unfair to Indian people, and supported the Ceremonial, which many Navajos believed degraded native religions.

"Larry pinpointed him," said Michael. "He owned the Navajo Inn and it was terrible. I remember a friend of mine calling it The Beach, because the Navajos would get drunk and just lie around and there wasn't much shade or anything, and it looked really pitiful."

I ask Michael if he was around on the day Larry Casuse died.

Michael nods yes and says, "I remember James Blackgoat—he was one of the people who worked at the Indian Center—saying, 'They shot Larry Casuse!'"

Michael walked over to Route 66 where the police were already keeping people away.

"Larry's action and his death really changed a lot of minds around here," says Michael. "I could see it when they had a visitation. He was in a morgue here, and we were shocked. There were like hundreds of people in line to pay their respects, so I knew then that a lot of people had been touched."

Michael says that before Casuse kidnapped Mayor Garcia, Michael and his fellow activists were criticized by other Navajos. Some Navajo people in St. Michaels, a community west of Window Rock, wrote a letter to the paper objecting to their protests. There was a feeling that a lot of Navajos didn't like what the activists were doing. A lot of the older people had been critical of the Indian Center protests when they started. But when Casuse was killed, it seemed to be a turning point.

"In the Navajo way when you go to war you let your hair down," says Michael. "And I remember the old ladies doing that, and they looked scary with their hair down just loose like that. It was really neat for me to see."

After Casuse's death, Michael helped get a permit for a memorial march. "I think it was the biggest Native American protest—it was a memorial—in modern times, or maybe ever," says Michael. "It was wonderful to see. It started off at the Ceremonial grounds, and people filled the street entirely, and it went on for a mile or two. But the town, I think, was in fear."

As the marches continued, one night someone threw a bucket into an electrical transformer. The lights went out and marchers rioted. A lot of windows were broken along Front Street.

Shortly after the abduction and shooting, Mayor Garcia lost his bid for reelection. "I think he lost primarily because of the marches," says Michael.

In the fall after the marches, Michael went to school at Stanford for several years. He then worked for the Navajo Nation for five years before he quit and started *Maazo Magazine.*

"It means 'marble,'" says Michael. "Running that magazine was a hard life, but there was a lot of prestige." While publishing *Maazo*, Michael met several Gallup businesspeople who supported the magazine through advertising. At times their financial support made the difference between the magazine surviving or folding. The support from Gallup businesspeople softened Michael's views about the town.

Michael tells me that in 1992, after publishing his magazine for ten years, he took a job as a public information officer for the Navajo Nation Department of Water Resources, explaining water basins, and then began to work on the Navajo-Gallup Water Supply Project.

Michael worked under the tutelage of John Leeper, an Anglo who grew up in southern California. Leeper received a PhD in civil engineering at Colorado State University where his dissertation topic was on water

"It started off at the Ceremonial grounds, and people filled the street entirely, and it went on for a mile or two," noted Michael Benson of the 1973
protest march. *Courtesy of the* Gallup Independent

development on the Navajo Nation. Before my conversation with Michael,
I had spoken at some length with Leeper and Patty Lundstrom, the Council
of Governments director and state representative, about the NGWSP, and
Michael's role in building support for the project on the Navajo Nation.

While there was still stiff opposition to the project in Farmington and
San Juan County, there was an air of optimism on the Navajo Nation side
of the project. It appeared that Navajo support was now solid, and Leeper
and Michael, among others, played a major role in making that happen.

Leeper was a rare engineer in that his disposition was well suited to
the political challenges of the water project. "We had four or five great
engineers before John Leeper, but they couldn't deal with Navajo politics," Lundstrom told me. "And that was a gift that Leeper had. He's a
PhD engineer and he could teach at any Ivy League school he wanted to,
but he chose to dedicate many years of his life to this project. He could
work with the politics of the Navajo, which is almost impossible for an
outsider. But he did it, because he's an even-keel guy, and he always kept
the big picture in mind as being the most important thing to look at, as
opposed to the petty politics."

"The town, I think, was in fear. I think he (Garcia) lost primarily because of the marches," said Michael Benson. *Courtesy of the* Gallup Independent

Michael represented the Navajo Nation in many meetings on water in the region and he trusted Leeper and looked to him for technical and policy advice.

"When I would go to meetings like the Colorado River Water Users Association," Michael says, "John knew I was going, and he would give me messages, and I just did what I was told. When I was going to a meeting where I was told to make a speech on something, I would ask John, 'What should I say?' And he was always on the mark. You know, he would just give me a few pointers, and then I would follow it and flesh it out. And almost every time, it would cause a big stir."

"He had a lot of faith in me," says Michael. "I would tell him, 'I'm just lucky.' And he would say, 'You make your own luck,' which a lot of people say."

Leeper also ran cover for Michael. "I had a low position forever, but I was lucky that I was allowed to go to big meetings with Domenici and others," Michael says. "Sometimes I would represent the Navajo Nation, because nobody else was there. And John knew that, and there were people that didn't appreciate my outspokenness, and I had to have protection. John protected me from, like, the department director."

While Leeper provided policy direction and counsel, Michael was politically indispensable because of the role he played with Navajo politicians and grassroots Navajo groups during ninety Navajo chapter meetings that were held to explain the NGWSP.

"Michael was at Water Management before me, so I didn't select him as a colleague and he didn't select me," Leeper told me another time. "We were just there together. But he had the credentials. It's hard to out-radical Michael Benson. I think support for the San Juan settlement benefited from that because of the lunatic fringe on either side. Some of the radicals were sort of friendly and they had their position, but they understand that we all really do have the best for the Navajo Nation at heart. I think there are others that don't think that way."

From Leeper's point of view, Michael had the credentials to diffuse radical opposition. "For Michael to be a spokesman helped establish that there are times when you say, 'This is something we need to support.' And he was as radical as any of them," Leeper said. "He has helped protect the settlement from folks that were coming at it from that direction."

From the outset, the biggest objection by Navajos to the NGWSP was the inclusion of Gallup in the pipeline that would supply water to the New Mexico portion of the Navajo Nation. "Navajo resistance to Gallup participation was very strong," Leeper told me. "It would seem sometimes month to month or week to week, there would be some episode in Gallup where the wife of a Navajo president was asked to leave a restaurant for various reasons, or there was an offensive picture on the wall of a restaurant, or somebody was beaten up in some community. And those things would really, really upset the Navajo leadership and community. You'd be at meetings of the Resources Committee, and there were lots of folks who really felt the whole project was a scheme to get water to Gallup—that that's all it's about—and they all would have a long list of grievances that would back up that perception. They all had their history with the border towns, and it would get really uncomfortable at times."

Michael pushed hard for going directly to the Navajo chapters to seek support rather than dealing only with elected officials. "We wouldn't have gotten the support of the Tribal Council because initially George Arthur, the chair of the Resources Committee, was against us," he says. "John Leeper helped me put the story together that helped explain the settlement and the Navajo-Gallup Water Supply Project. I'd been going around talking about the project, and it was disjointed. John came to me and he said, "Tell people you need Gallup because the demand is there *now*, whereas a lot of the Navajo demand is in the future.' So, he helped me put the narrative together and we continued."

Lundstrom had told me that one of the biggest obstacles was that a lot of the Navajos viewed the project primarily from a racial perspective; that is, they didn't want anybody outside of their own people to get the water. "That's where Michael Benson was genius," said Lundstrom. "He was the right guy to send out to the chapters. He was funny, he was articulate, he could explain the project in terms they understood, and people trusted him. It was about trust."

On one occasion, Michael gave up trying to talk a Navajo elected official into changing his position and risked directly challenging him. "I remember one of the Navajo political leaders was complaining about the pipeline," Leeper told me. "The official was really aggressively against the project, saying 'Gallup's getting this and Gallup's getting that.' And Michael, who was very, very fluent in Navajo, stood up at the chapter house and said, 'Well, you know if you oppose this project, we can challenge you politically next time there's an election.' He said, 'This is the way this chapter is going to get a sustainable water supply and we can't have Navajo leaders fighting this project that's to serve the Navajos.' So, Michael was basically telling this political leader, 'We're going to challenge you when the election comes.' And it wasn't sort of a whim. It's like, 'We really will.' And in the end, ultimately the political leader I'm talking about supported the project in many, many different forums."

Michael and I have visited for almost two hours, so we call it a night. He leaves, and I remain in the small conference room sorting through my thoughts for a while before heading home. Again, I find myself wondering what path in life Larry Casuse would have taken if he, like Michael, had survived.

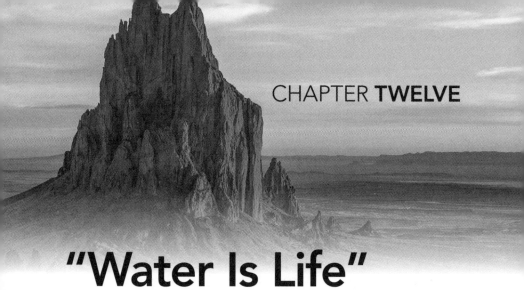

CHAPTER TWELVE

"Water Is Life"

I receive a call in June of 2004 from my hometown of Farmington. The caller says, "Mayor, we need you to come up here." The caller tells me that a Farmington city councilor, Mary Fischer, is grandstanding in a way that could mean trouble for the proposed settlement of the Navajo Nation's water rights in the San Juan River and that several Farmington-area political leaders are afraid that her public posturing might inflame public opinion to the point that a reasoned compromise may not be possible. The caller asks me to come to a special meeting of the Farmington city council regarding the settlement.

By the time I was elected mayor, most of the heavy lifting on the river settlement had already been done by Lundstrom, Leeper, and Benson and a slew of other people who had worked many years, and in some cases decades, on the NGWSP. The settlement was an indispensable cornerstone of the project. A series of formal approvals by the Navajo Nation Council and New Mexico's Interstate Stream Commission were still necessary though. By this time, approval by the Navajo Nation seemed highly probable, but opposition to the settlement in Farmington was one of the biggest obstacles to approval by the Interstate Stream Commission.

Before receiving the call from Farmington, the personal connection I'd made with George Arthur, the chairman of the Navajo Nation's

Resources Committee, during the Water Town Hall held in the first one hundred days of my term came in handy. In the lead-up to the Navajo Nation Council vote, Arthur drew the ire of Senator Domenici when the senator interpreted comments by Arthur as being critical of Gallup's inclusion in the NGWSP. Arthur called and asked me to attend the Navajo Nation's Resources Committee meeting which was a prelude to the full vote by Navajo Nation Council. Arthur and I designed mutually supportive statements prior to the committee vote designed to mollify Domenici.

Not long after the Resources Committee meeting, it was time to go to Farmington for a meeting of the city council, where I'd been asked to rebut Mary Fischer. The 120-mile drive to Farmington crosses the Navajo Nation from the south. Just before I enter the reservation, a series of chain-link fences guard a fleet of pickup trucks and trailers in various states of disrepair that were pawned at a nearby convenience store and gas station. The pawn lots are an ugly and immensely depressing sight, a testament to poverty and alcohol dependency—and the willingness of area businessmen to extract money even from the poorest of the poor.

For most of the drive, the Chuska Mountains rise to my left. On the crest of the mountain, ponderosa pines are silhouetted like soldiers standing guard. To my right, a barren plain extends as far as the eye can see.

On either side of the road, clusters of Navajo homes spread randomly. Many are half-completed with exposed plywood and blackboard. Rusted

A Navajo homesite between Gallup and Farmington next to the pipeline route. *Courtesy of Bob Rosebrough*

Navajo-Gallup Water Supply Project pipeline in the early construction phase paralleling US491 with Bennett Peak in the background. *Courtesy of Bob Rosebrough*

horse trailers and old, junked vehicles are set on blocks. Almost all the housing clusters have livestock pens, and many have basketball hoops, most on dirt courts. There are stacks of firewood, tires, and pallets. Most homes have spherical propane tanks, and many have outhouses. There are cylindrical tanks used to haul water in the beds of many of the pickup trucks.

Halfway to Farmington, near where Michael Benson grew up, the remnants of volcanic cores erupt from the surrounding plain, making it impossible to look away. A transmission line from the coal power plants near Farmington is held aloft by gigantic metal structures that resemble Yei-bi-cheis—spirits that mediate between the Diyin Dine'e (Holy People) and humans—which are frequently depicted in Navajo rugs as tall, erect human-like figures with arms extended but bent at the elbow forming a V.

On an abandoned cinder-block structure, a graffiti artist has sprayed a multicolored mural that says, "Water Is Life." It strikes me that I haven't seen water at any point on the drive.

As I near Farmington, the snowcapped La Plata Mountains have come into sight. They are the southernmost range in the San Juans and include Hesperus Peak, or Dibé Nitsaa, the northern peak among the Navajos' four sacred mountains. The vast San Juan Mountains of southwest Colorado

The snowcapped San Juan Mountains of southwest Colorado, rising above Farmington to the north, feed the San Juan River. *Courtesy of Larry Griffith*

shed the water that flows into the San Juan River, the object of this visit to Farmington.

It feels surreal to be returning as the mayor of Gallup to my hometown for a special meeting of its city council to discuss a matter in which many feel the two cities' interests are diametrically opposed. I'm nervous about the role I've agreed to take on. I know it will be controversial.

One hour later, Farmington city councilor Mary Fischer is sitting about ten feet away from me in the council chambers. The chambers are packed, and an overflow crowd of Anglo businesspeople, professionals, and ranchers extends outside into the lobby—they're looking in through a glass partition and listening by means of a sound system.

Early in the meeting Fischer says of the proposed river settlement, "I have to look and think, Is this good for Farmington? My answer is, 'No. Hell no. It's not good for Farmington.'"

Although I've heard about Fischer for years, this is the first time I've personally encountered her. She seems formidable and determined but also comfortable, almost reveling in what's about to unfold; she appears to have a clear idea of how this is going to play out. And so do I.

Seconds earlier, Fischer complained that a Navajo water staff member once said he wouldn't talk to her about the proposed settlement because a San Juan water commissioner had told him that she "wasn't going to be elected anyway." The Navajo staff member is immediately to my right. The water commissioner is sitting a few chairs over. Fischer seems to take pleasure in telling tales out of school about people in front of a crowd.

"So that's, what, ten years ago that I was elected and here I still am," Fischer says defiantly.

Also present in the council chambers today and scheduled to make presentations are Navajo Nation representatives, staff and members of the New Mexico Interstate Streams Commission, an Albuquerque water lawyer who represents the city of Farmington, and a local lawyer who is a vocal opponent of the settlement and said to be Councilor Fischer's significant other.

The proposed water rights settlement between the state of New Mexico and the Navajo Nation has been hugely controversial in Farmington, a city dominated by transplanted Texans and Oklahomans who work in the oil and gas fields of the San Juan basin. In Farmington, the San Juan, which is a major tributary of the Colorado River, is "our river" that contains "our water." It doesn't seem to matter to some of the people of Farmington that New Mexico contributes only three percent of the water in the San Juan River from its watershed, or that when the annual allotments in the upper basin of the Colorado River were established in 1948, New Mexico received a disproportionately large—11.25 percent—allocation in recognition of its need to settle water-right claims with Native tribes. In other words, New Mexico, Farmington itself, and the Navajo Nation contribute very little of the water that flows in the San Juan but get to divert much more than that.

Some project opponents in San Juan County couldn't care less that basic principles of federal water law grant Native tribes with reservations the right to enough water to establish and irrigate a homeland, or that Gallup's wells are projected to run out of water in 2025. The proposed water settlement, which is literally a life-or-death issue for the future of the Navajo Nation and Gallup, represents for many in Farmington an idea only—the theft of their water by big government for the benefit of dark-skinned hordes. The conflict is visceral.

The Navajos have been asserting that under federal water law they are entitled to have *all* of New Mexico's allocation. The settlement being considered proposes that 6.3 percent of the water in the San Juan River— 56 percent of New Mexico's allocation—will go to the Navajo Nation. The proposed settlement also includes an extensive list of specific protections for the San Juan County municipalities and non-Navajo farmers. Importantly, it also proposes congressional authorization and funding of a 100-mile-long pipeline from the river to Gallup that will provide the only chance of a renewable water source to the vast expanse of reservation in New Mexico, and to Gallup.

I know the mindset that is common in the Farmington area well. One of the city councilors at the far end of the table is a good friend and a former basketball teammate. A doctor sitting outside the glass partition was an outfielder on my Little League team. We both still bear scars on our scalps from the stitches we got after colliding while chasing a fly ball in right-center field. Many of the gray-haired people in the room are longtime friends of my parents—several of them greeted me before the meeting as "Bobby."

Mary Fischer's denunciation of the settlement is winding down. She has tossed in a few critical comments about Gallup's role in the settlement as part of a broad-based attack. Her concluding point seems to be that the huge expense of the federally funded pipeline can't be justified for a city the size of Gallup—a point that ignores the fact that the primary purpose of the pipeline is to provide water to a quarter million Navajo people, and that Gallup will play a critical role in helping to distribute water from the project to the Navajo communities east, west, and south of Gallup.

"And Gallup has how many people—20,000?" she asks. Councilor Fischer does not look at me. I'm an invited speaker with a large nameplate in front of me and I am sitting only ten feet diagonally to her right in plain view. She seems to be trying to draw me out while purposely avoiding eye contact. Many in the room look at me, wondering if I will respond. I don't.

I'm planning to take her on, but I'm going to do it at a time of my choosing, not hers. Fischer's question hangs unanswered as the mayor of Farmington perfunctorily thanks her and announces a break.

A good hour later, the mayor, by design near the end of the meeting, calls on me to speak and I address my comments to him and city councilors.

"I would like to begin by recognizing the obvious," I say. "Your obligations are not to Gallup. They're not to the Navajo Nation. They're not particularly to agricultural irrigators. You are charged with protecting the interests of the citizens of the municipality, and we appreciate the opportunity to provide input in terms of how this affects us as your neighbors.

"Gallup's situation is really pretty straightforward," I continue. "We don't have a river. We don't have surface water. We rely entirely on water wells. Our water table is dropping at the rate of 20 feet per year. By the year 2012, we are projected to have shortages in peak seasons. By the year 2020, we are projected to have daily shortages at all times of the year. The Navajo-Gallup Water Supply Project is Gallup's only chance—only potential source of renewable water. Gallup has no other alternative for a source of renewable water."

I describe the 47-year history of the project and then answer the question Councilor Fischer asked an hour ago. "The city of Gallup is a municipality of 20,000 people. The Navajo-Gallup Water Supply Project, within forty years, will provide water to over a quarter million people. I'll repeat that—over one quarter of a million people, almost entirely Navajo people."

For the last couple of weeks, Councilor Fischer has been pointedly criticizing Gallup's role in the project, so I try to dispel some of the misconceptions that have been circulating. I review the statistics about how much water flows through Farmington (1,500,000 acre-feet per year) and how much water Gallup will receive (7,500 acre-feet per year). I say, "Gallup's share is not even 1 percent. Gallup's share is a half of 1 percent." A newly elected member of Farmington's city council looks surprised when I say this. He glances around at the other councilors and the water professionals to gauge their reactions. One of them nods at him to confirm what I've said.

I explain that Gallup will have to buy water, not receive it free, and that we will use our well fields during times of shortage; then I tell the attendees, "The statement has been made that Gallup is getting all kinds of benefits. The facts are that Gallup has a lower priority than San Juan County municipalities. Our water is going to be a heck of a lot more expensive—a lot more. And we're going to have less of it than the San Juan County municipalities. Those are the facts."

I tell the mayor and councilors that the negotiations on the settlement have carried on more than a year longer than we had hoped. I congratulate the chairman on the New Mexico Interstate Streams Commission, Jim Dunlap, and the other San Juan County representatives on their negotiations, and then I list eight major benefits that the San Juan County municipalities and agricultural irrigators have gained during the extended negotiations.

I take a minute to thank the Navajo negotiators who were angered by Councilor Fischer's comments earlier and have been quietly fuming. "These guys get beat up in every meeting they go to," I say. "If you think they got beat up here, it's nothing compared to what happens to them back home. There they are criticized for not getting a much larger share of New Mexico's allocation."

I'm close to the end of my remarks when I say, "You know, we've been at this for about two-and-a-half hours and there's one point that, frankly, hasn't been made yet. That is to consider weighing the options.

"Option one: The settlement is approved, and the settlement stands. What comes out of that? Certainty and marketability of water." I repeat, "Certainty and marketability of water. I don't think that we've talked about that for two-and-a-half hours. But *that* ladies and gentlemen is going to be the benefit of this settlement for Farmington." With a settlement, Farmington will know how much water it has and will have the ability to either use its water, sell it, or lease it.

"What's the option if the settlement doesn't go through? Litigation such as Taos has faced for decades and that this community will face for decades. Some people will benefit from litigation. But will the citizens of Farmington benefit from litigation? The uncertainty and lack of marketability of water will hamstring the economics of this community and this county. The litigation between neighbors will tear people apart in this region.

"I'd like to return for a minute to a point I made early on. There may be some interests in this county—some non-Indian irrigator interests—that would prefer decades of expense, divisiveness, and the uncertainty of that litigation, but that's clearly not in the interest of a municipality whose interests have been assured through concessions in negotiations."

I have one more item on my agenda and it's time to unveil it. I've been asked to directly call out Councilor Fischer on her provocative comments, and thus give cover to those elected officials in San Juan County inclined to support the settlement, and I've agreed to do it.

I individually thank the mayor and each of the councilors except Councilor Fischer, to whom I say, "Councilor Fischer, your public comments prior to this meeting and during this meeting are alarmingly divisive and uninformed. This is not a time to play to the fears of the public and to grandstand. This is not a time to pursue hidden agendas for special interests. This is a time to think beyond ourselves to future generations. We can either litigate for decades or we can settle as neighbors and all have certainty and prosperity."

Fischer lashes back, "I don't think I need you to lecture me on what I . . ."

"I didn't need your lecture earlier either, ma'am."

We go back and forth a few times and I feel I'm on the verge of being stuck and unable to extricate myself. I turn away from Fischer, thank the Farmington mayor again and take my seat. I feel dazed and unbalanced after my attack on Councilor Fischer and her fierce response. It seems as if the attack will work as intended and that she'll be neutralized to a degree, but it's not a tactic I have any desire to repeat. And only time will tell—a final vote by the Farmington City Council is not expected for several weeks.

Seven months later, I go back to Farmington for an Interstate Streams Commission hearing on approval of the settlement agreement of the Navajo Nation's water rights claims in the San Juan River basin. As I enter the meeting, I quickly scan the room and I'm relieved that Fischer isn't present. That in itself is a victory. Thirteen days earlier, the Navajo Nation Council approved a settlement agreement, and now it's the state of New Mexico's turn, through the ISC, to consider the agreement. This meeting is the culmination of decades of work and negotiation.

This time I lead off with comments supporting the settlement: I'm followed by barrel-chested cowboy irrigators opposing the settlement, three Navajo chapter officials who support the settlement, and a wildly diverse group of speakers, including an Anglo man with pink highlights in his hair who claims the meeting was not properly noticed; a burly Legal Aid attorney in a flannel shirt who represents Navajo allottees who want more time to study the settlement; the Farmington city attorney, who says he anticipates that the Farmington city council will pass a resolution supporting the settlement at its next meeting; and a lawyer representing the state of New Mexico, who wears a ponytail but no socks and clarifies details of the settlement.

The ISC chairman brings the matter to a head. He calls for a motion, and a commissioner moves to approve the settlement. The motion is quickly seconded. He calls for discussion. There is none. He says, "All in favor? All six commissioners respond "yes."

The chairman says, "We could have kept arguing about this for five more years." He adjourns the meeting for lunch and the crowd breaks into applause.

In a conversation about the settlement sometime later, John Leeper tells me, "This is more important than the railroad, and it's more important than the Interstate. If there's going to be a Navajo Nation—a sustainable, permanent homeland for the Navajo people—this project is critical to that. It's that important."

Before heading back to Gallup, I make a call to John McBreen, Gallup's radio news reporter, and fill him in on the hearing and the Interstate Streams Commission vote to approve the settlement. After I hang up, I stop and just savor the moment. While I've only played a minor role, it feels good to be focused on an issue that seems to be on the right side of history and free from the constant fratricide of Gallup politics.

Back in Gallup, however, events seem to be conspiring to create an intramural brawl between two city councilors. As I'm finishing up a meeting in the mayor's office with Gallup's long-tenured city clerk, several days after the city manager informed us that the city is more than a decade overdue in redistricting council areas, she says without prompting, "There may be a problem with the east-side district."

In response to the threat of a suit in federal court, Gallup was forced to district its council positions in the 1980s and did. Four districts were created: East, North, South, and West. But the city didn't redistrict after the 1990 or 2000 censuses, as required. Our city manager has been pushing to redistrict to comply with the law.

A couple of months after my conversation with the city clerk, the problem becomes clear when a redistricting consultant from Albuquerque makes a presentation to the council. The bottom line is that there is no way the east-side councilor, Mary Ann Armijo, is going to be able to keep her district unless she moves from her present home, and she loves her home. Her district is way too big and there is only one way for it to shrink—the neighborhood she lives in will have to be split off in its entirety and become part of the south-side district.

This is not going to go well. When the consultant is finished, Armijo looks at him and says, "I don't think I like you."

She's joking, but barely. Being elected to an office has been a lifelong aspiration of hers and she has been the most active councilor in forming and

Harry Mendoza, an old-guard Gallup politician with a strong, loyal base of support and longtime friendships with two sitting city councilors. *Courtesy of Jeff Jones*

supporting neighborhood associations. More than any other councilor, she revels in her role. To win another term, she'll have to run in the south-side district in the midterm election against the councilor who is her best friend in city government. And they'll both have to run against Harry Mendoza, a county commissioner whose term is expiring. Mendoza, who is close with west-side councilor Frank Gonzales and north-side councilor Bill Nechero, has signaled that he'll be running for the south-side council seat.

Mendoza is an old guard Gallup politician with a domineering personality and a strong, loyal base of support. He was one of Emmett Garcia's political lieutenants, and in 1973, he'd just left City Hall after meeting with Garcia when Larry Casuse walked in. It's generally assumed that if Mendoza is elected, he will, by virtue of his friendship with Gonzales and Nechero, become the de facto mayor. Gonzales and Nechero have already sided with the county against the city's interest on a couple of issues during Mendoza's tenure on the county commission. After they do, the city manager, in jest and outside of their presence, starts referring to them as Commissioner Gonzales and Commissioner Nechero.

The redistricting goes forward and the contest for the midterm south-side council seat becomes a free-for-all. Both the incumbent south-side councilor, Pat Butler, and the east-side councilor, Mary Ann Armijo, file for the seat along with Mendoza. Mendoza, as he always does, goes negative and alleges financial mismanagement. He also criticizes our alcohol reform efforts and talks about fictional millions of dollars for trails that he says are being built for the "mayor and his buddies." He harps on the city's decision to lease, as a police substation, the building that was flooded on the second day of my term and is owned by a friend of mine, despite the fact that the lease was proposed by the north-side councilor, Mendoza's friend, and I recused myself from the decision.

Mendoza is championing the idea of an indoor arena that will seat 5,000, revised down from his original plans to seat 15,000, or 75 percent of Gallup's population. The city manager says the project will be a money pit and is pushing for a feasibility study.

The election is tight. Mendoza leads in votes with 403, Butler is second with 398 votes; and Armijo is close behind, with 376. None reach 40 percent, so a runoff is required between Mendoza and Butler. After chafing at the attacks and misinformation from Mendoza, I decide to come off the sidelines, and write a series of blistering open letters aimed at Mendoza during the runoff.

If Mendoza is elected, I write, the city will be governed by him and a group of his old-guard buddies around a table in a coffee shop. I discuss the six tax increases that were made during Mendoza's stint as County Commissioner, imply that he has plans to turn over the management of Red Rock Park to a crony, and suggest that the voters take a close look at his campaign disclosure statement if they want to know why he's keeping his plans for the park secret.

Butler, the south-side incumbent, steps up his campaign by aggressively responding to Mendoza's attacks and calling him out on his record as a commissioner. Mendoza overreaches and makes some claims against Butler that are easily and effectively refuted.

"Harry, these lies and half-truths are a prime example of the type of politician you are," Butler says in one.

The *Albuquerque Journal* takes note of the election and sends its top reporter to Gallup to do a front-page article. When the reporter comes to a regular city council meeting, State Senator Lidio Rainaldi, a political ally of Mendoza, shows up and asks to address the council. He goes into a long, rambling diatribe about my alcohol initiatives and then plays victim, telling the gathering that when he came to see me, I threatened to fight him. The senator says the alcohol problem in Gallup isn't any worse than it is elsewhere in the state. "There are only thirty drunks," he says, "that cause all the problems."

"Senator, that means there are only twelve drunks left now because the paper reported this week that eighteen people have died this winter," Armijo replies, citing a recent *Independent* article on alcohol-related exposure deaths. Undeterred, Rainaldi continues with his list of grievances and accusations.

The reporter later describes the senator as "an elderly man with exuberant eyebrows" who delivers a "tongue-lashing . . . aimed squarely at Gallup's mayor.

"Gritty and real, the western New Mexico town is a little like asparagus —you either love it or hate it," the reporter's article continues. "Its boosters like its kitschy charm, its small-town feel, and its total lack of pretension. Its critics find it dingy and drunk, with roaming clusters of homeless people and bars you wouldn't want to walk into."

The article quotes Butler as saying, "Having a little group over coffee deciding what's good for Gallup is not open government. That's what would happen if Harry's elected."

The reporter asked Mendoza for an interview, and he agreed but pointedly preferred not to sit for the interview in a coffee shop. In the *Journal* article, Mendoza touts his experience and says that advocating a new direction for Gallup implies that there is something wrong with the old Gallup.

Eddie Muñoz resurfaces and seems to target me with one of his comments, "We came back from World War II and served this community," Muñoz says. "These younger guys, they can't relate to the middle class and below."

The *Independent*'s publisher, who had a surgical hip replacement shortly before the article runs, tells the reporter he was surprised to discover the discomfort he'd been suffering was the result of a medical condition. "I thought the pain in my ass was the mayor."

The reporter gives the last word to our local bike mechanic.

"You tell people you live in Gallup and it's kind of like, why? Well," he says, "the trails are great, the town's cleaned up quite a bit, there's a handful of new restaurants. It's not quite there yet, but it's coming."

Two days after the *Journal* article appears, the voters, most of them burnt out by the extended, harsh campaign, go to the polls, and Butler, the incumbent south-side councilor, beats Mendoza 626 to 510. I'm standing with the city manager in the council chambers as the final vote tallies go up on the white board. I take a deep breath and let out a sigh of relief. Citing the progress and projects of the past two years, the city manager whispers, "It shouldn't have been this close."

I nod. Neither of us has to say it but we both know Mendoza will be back in two years to run for mayor.

During the just-completed city council election in April 2005, two unrelated Gallup stories broke, one gaining national media attention. A 32-year-old Hispanic man was dragged by rope behind a truck for two-thirds of a mile, leaving a trail of blood and skin. Not long before, a similar event had occurred in Texas and was determined to be a racially motivated hate crime. The national media wanted to know if the Gallup dragging was also a hate crime. While stunned by the cruelty of the crime, the Gallup police said they didn't think it was racially motivated. They didn't say it publicly, but they suspected it was drug related.

Shortly thereafter, I'm in a café in Durango on a skiing trip to get away from the fray for a weekend, when I overhear a fellow diner tell his companion about a second story that ran regionally. It seems a dog in Gallup had been shot in the eye with an arrow but has survived and is seen walking around with the arrow still sticking out if its eye socket. When the man finishes his story, his friend responds, "That's classic Gallup."

CHAPTER **THIRTEEN**

Best of Times, Worst of Times

"How's it going Bob?" a reporter from the *Four Corners Business Journal* asks as she begins the interview after the midterm election in 2005, just after the halfway point in my term as mayor. We're seated at the varnished maple table in the corner of the mayor's office. She has a pad of paper in front of her and pen in hand.

I start to give my standard reply—"Never a dull moment"—but I stop for a second and then say what's really on my mind. "It's the best of times and the worst of times."

And it is. I feel as if I'm riding a rollercoaster of alternating highs and lows that is exhilarating and draining. There is excitement and progress, and there is stinging disappointment and powerful resistance. At times, what talents I have are fully on display, and at other times, my weaknesses and deficits are completely exposed. There are brief elusive hints sometimes of a wonderful reality just out of reach, and sometimes the banality of evil seems omnipresent and crushing. Every day, there seems to be a moment I cherish and a moment that leaves me dispirited and exhausted.

But I don't tell the reporter all that. Instead, I go through the list of our administration's accomplishments and a list of our setbacks. And I tell her what we plan next.

A month later I pick up the *Business Journal* from a stack of mail on my desk at City Hall. The front-page headline reads: Gallup Mayor Bob Rosebrough; "Worst of Times." I feel like I've been punched in the gut but I read on. The text of the article is accurate. It's only the headline that's skewed, and I've come to expect that the press will look for an opportunity to sensationalize, especially in headlines.

A few months later, Brenda and I are invited to walk in the Navajo Nation Fair parade in Window Rock, Arizona, twenty-four miles northwest of Gallup. Brenda buys a dress from a Navajo seamstress, and I buy a traditional purple velvet pullover shirt and borrow a concho belt from a Gallup Indian trader to go with one of my bolo ties.

On the day of the parade, on a Saturday at seven in the morning, we're gridlocked in traffic three miles away in a broad valley east of Window Rock. The road ahead passes through a gap in a sandstone monocline, or hogback, much like the one that guards the eastern entrance to Gallup. The spot where we park is within yards of the location of the old Navajo Inn, the target of Larry Casuse's protests. It was bulldozed into the ground, and there is nothing left to indicate it was ever there.

A tribal police car cruising by spots us and escorts us to the front of parade entries where the other elected officials are milling around on the side of the road.

Governor Richardson is there, and given the early hour, he seems to be in an unusually good mood. I've seen him several times since the Local Empowerment District debacle, and although I don't trust him, we've established a superficial peace.

Richardson, who is Hispanic, looks intently at my wife. He seems puzzled.

"What are you?" he says.

Brenda cocks her head to the left and draws her head back—her reaction when she is puzzled or skeptical. "What do you mean?" she says. She has no idea what he is asking.

"You know. What's your nationality?" he replies.

"I'm mostly Hispanic but kind of a Heinz 57," she says. "I think a lot of other nationalities got mixed in along the way."

"You get him a lot of votes," Richardson tells her, gesturing my way.

Brenda knows that this is his attempt at a compliment, but she's taken aback at the way he filters everything through the lens of politics. When

Richardson's attention is diverted shortly after she whispers, "Is that all he cares about in a person? How many votes they can get?"

I shrug and give her a nod that says, *Yeah, probably so.*

When the parade starts, we walk behind a red truck as we hand out candy to kids. About a quarter-mile in, I get swarmed by a crowd of kids, and the reservation's plump, bald grocery king, Eddie Basha, shouts in an aggrieved voice from his perch on a battery-powered three-wheel scooter, "Hey, mayor. Get going. You're holding us up!"

As we approach the fairgrounds, the frenzy of kids looking for candy dissipates. As we continue walking, I wave and say, "Good morning." We have short, clipped exchanges with Navajo adults along the parade route who say:

"Nice shirt."

"Good job, mayor. Thanks for closing down those bars."

"We want a Chili's," one Navajo man teases in a deadpan voice.

"How about a Target too?" the man next to him joins in.

"We need water, mayor."

"I don't want any candy. Can I have your bolo?"

"How about the shirt?" another man adds. I feel at ease, even honored by their teasing. I take it as a sign of their comfort with me, and their acceptance.

"How tall are you?"

"You should say Yá'át'ééh."

"Aoo, Yá'át'ééh," I reply. Yes, Good morning.

"That's better."

Several adults come out into the parade route to take pictures of us or to have pictures taken with us. Several people come out to shake hands. One man stays seated on the curb but extends his hand, stoically demanding that I come to him to shake. I do.

We approach the end of the parade route near St. Michael and a man surprises me. He responds to my "Good morning" by saying "Good afternoon."

We've been completely immersed in the parade and it seems as though we've only been walking for about an hour and a half and that it should be about 10:30. I check my cell phone, and see the time is 12:02.

"Good afternoon," I say.

He nods approval.

A few weeks later, our city attorney, who has been tasked with managing and upgrading Gallup's small airport, asks me to come to the City Hall conference room for an evening meeting with owners of planes who rent hangars at the airport. Most plane owners in Gallup rent hangars from the city, and the rental rates haven't been increased for many years. Some of the plane owners have started using the hangars as large storage units because the rent is lower than a comparable commercial storage unit.

Under the city attorney's direction, the hangars were repainted, and the rents increased to rates comparable to those in other communities. A mass insurrection by hangar renters, most of whom are wealthy, ensued.

At the meeting, the city professional staff and I listen to hangar lessees complain for thirty minutes nonstop. My frustration builds. I'm beyond tired of hearing rich guys bellyache. One plane owner finishes a red-faced rant by saying that he's thinking about leaving Gallup because of the increased rental cost.

Leaning across the table and pointing to the door, I tell him, with emotion matching his, "On your way out of town, don't let the door hit you in the ass."

He sits stunned for a minute, and then without saying another word, he gets up and leaves. Another plane owner, also stunned, says, "Why do you have to argue so much?"

"Are you guys the only people who have the right to argue?" I say.

After the meeting the city finance director says, "God bless you, Mayor." But I'm not so happy. The constant resistance from special interests and people protecting their privileged turf is wearing on me. I'm overeating, losing sleep, and losing my temper. It's not sustainable.

After the airport hangar guys leave for the evening, I spend some time in my office, reflecting. I've lost something valuable now that I'm mayor. I'm in a bubble, and it seems people are either trying to kiss my ass or cut me off at the kneecaps. I no longer have access to the unguarded, casual comments and opinions of the people on the street. It seems like the unfiltered pulse of the community is no longer available to me. And I miss it.

And because I still work part-time as a lawyer and need to earn a living every day, I don't have the time to fight the fight the ways it needs

Navajo Nation President Joe Shirley Jr. being sworn in. *Courtesy of Jeff Jones*

to be fought. It feels as if I have one arm tied behind my back, while I'm in the fight of my life. I find myself wondering what it would be like if someone like Larry Casuse was on the scene now, someone pushing the limits of change with whom I could negotiate and play off of to find a more politically palatable middle course of progress. It seems to me that by simply pursuing progress and policies that would be considered business as usual in other places, I'm viewed as an extremist here in Gallup.

A few weeks later, Joe Shirley Jr., the president of the Navajo Nation, honors me by asking me to walk with him in the Gallup Inter-Tribal Indian Ceremonial parade, which is normally open only to Indian people. Shirley is several years older than I. He's tall, with black hair that's beginning to gray at the temples, his manner reserved and dignified. A man of few words. When I get to the parade, I find him in the staging area near several horse trailers.

"Let me show you your horse," he says. This wasn't the deal, but I go with it. I haven't ridden a horse since I was a teenager. Halfway through the parade, on Route 66, the parade stalls while a train near the railroad changing stations repeatedly goes forward and back while blowing its horn. It's hot, and my white dress shirt begins to stick to my sweaty chest. My horse starts bucking, trying to get me off its back. One of President

Shirley's aides rescues me by taking my horse and riding while I walk the rest of the parade with Shirley's entourage. At the end of the parade, President Shirley and I shake hands and I thank him for inviting me.

"Thanks for making me look good," he deadpans and we both break into a laugh.

Not long after, I have a much different experience. The Navajo Tribal Council speaker, Lawrence Morgan, a large, gruff man who resembles a barroom bouncer, calls me to complain about a three-dollar "mud fee" that a local car wash has charged him. Morgan feels that the mud fee discriminates against Navajos because so many Navajo people live far out in the county, in areas with dirt roads, and he's mad about it. He follows up with several emails demanding a refund and I call the car wash owner to try to mediate the dispute, but the owner digs in and explains in excruciating detail the costs he incurs to clean the muddy undercarriages of reservation trucks. I consider paying Morgan the three dollars out of my own pocket, but I know that won't mollify him. While the dispute seems unresolvable to me, I don't think it's the real issue anyway. I don't think Morgan would have a problem with the three-dollar mud fee if Gallup's

An early Dawn 'til Dusk 12-hour bike race in a snowstorm. *Courtesy of Brian Leddy*

pawn shops, pay day lenders, problem bars, and plasma center were to suddenly vanish.

On weekends I've been going out to the High Desert Trail system to help develop the bike trail and blow off steam. After scouting the area, several of us flagged a rough line for the trail under the guidance of the mechanic at our local bike shop. By now a sinuous line of trail has been compacted, and brush and rock cleared. I have an idea.

"Let's set a date in April," I suggest to others, "and get everyone in town who rides to come out for a twelve-hour race, with soloists, duos, and four-person teams. If we ride all day, the trail will be completely established by the next tourist season."

An event coordinator at the Chamber of Commerce gets wind of our grassroots race and asks if she can expand the idea and promote the race statewide. We call it Dawn 'til Dusk. When the race date arrives, the weather is horrendous, with gale-force winds forecasted. A fire just west of Albuquerque on I-40 closes the interstate, yet at the registration, a hundred riders who have found alternate routes to Gallup show up to ride in terrible weather. A rider from Moab wins the race and my buddy Peter Tempest places second.

Adventure Gallup is progressing on multiple fronts. We develop a hiking trail to the top of Pyramid Rock and another trail on the top of the hogback. Gamerco Associates gives us a ninety-nine-year lease for our shooting range, and we break ground. We designate sites for both a motocross park and an off-highway vehicle (OHV) park. The archery range gets a new canopy. The U.S. Forest Service starts the process to designate multiuse trails in the Zuni Mountains fifteen miles southeast of town.

The trails require little expense. Volunteers flag and ride in the trail line and Youth Conservation Corp kids, whose salaries are paid by the state, clear brush, do a little rock work, and create drainage outlets. The shooting range and OHV park, by contrast, require heavy equipment and are expensive. Yet in the coffee shops of Gallup, the constant refrain is, "The city is spending millions of dollars on trails for the mayor and his buddies." Joe Darak, one of my opponents in the mayor's race, resurfaces as a reporter for a new weekly newspaper, the *Gallup Herald*, and he writes a column criticizing the "millions of dollars being spent on trails.

Bob Rosebrough, Peter Tempest, and Hank Stokes approach the transition station during a Dawn 'til Dusk race. *Courtesy of Chuck Van Drunen*

Kahuna Rock in the Zuni Mountains. *Courtesy of Brian Leddy*

I write a letter to his publisher, citing the real numbers and demanding a retraction. The next week Darak writes a new column saying he's changed his mind and that the trails are good for the community. He doesn't correct the financial misinformation though. No one, including the coffee shop crowd, seems to have a problem with the big bucks being spent on the shooting range or the OHV park.

Around this time, I get the visit from Ursula Casuse that began this book. She arrives with an old copy of the *Independent* that features the photo of her brother's body on the front page and complains that the police are displaying the photo, framed, at the Fraternal Order of Police building. I feel morally compelled to do what I can for Ursula, although I doubt my efforts will resolve the matter with certainty.

After her visit, I ask the city attorney to set up a meeting for me at the FOP building. Two officers greet me there and give me a brief tour of a furniture-less building with stuffed animals and children's toys strewn around on the floor. I've dealt with the two officers several times before. They always seem to be nosing around City Hall, and they sometimes attend council meetings even when police matters aren't on the agenda. I

Anguish that never fully goes away. Ursula Casuse speaks at a public forum. *Courtesy of the* Gallup Independent

don't feel comfortable with them, and I have the sense that I never know what they're up to.

"We're in the middle of our Toys for Tots program," one says.

There's no sign of the photo or, for that matter, any wall hangings. I tell them what Ursula has said. They shrug, and one of them sweeps his arm around the room and says, "As you can see, there's nothing here." One of the officers reminds me that about a year before, he dropped off copies of newspaper articles about Garcia's abduction and Casuse's death at my office. I ask him why.

"I just thought you should have them," he says.

His answer strikes me as odd. I assume that something more motivated him, but I don't know what it could be and he's not going to tell me.

When I get back to my office, I spend several minutes digging through old files until I find the bundle of ten newspaper clippings from the *Independent* and the *Albuquerque Journal* about the incident that the officer left months before. One of the clippings is a very poor-quality copy of the photo of the three policemen standing over Casuse's bloody body on the sidewalk. Nothing about the size or markings on the copy suggest it was ever framed.

A few days later Ursula Casuse comes back to my office with her father. He is a quiet man with a long gray beard and long hair tucked up into an oversized cowboy hat. He lets Ursula do all the talking. I describe my visit to the FOP in detail.

"The building was a mess," I tell them. "I'm not sure if it's always like that. There weren't any photos or any wall hangings." I tell her that one of the officers reminded me about the clippings he'd given me months before and I give all the clippings to her.

Ursula thanks me and seems genuinely appreciative but also skeptical. "I think they probably still have the photo," she says, "and they'll put it up when no one else is around."

I don't know what to say. I think she may be right, but I don't know what else to do.

After a little over two years as mayor, I have a mixed scorecard on alcohol initiatives. In the face of active enforcement of the Sales to Intoxicated Persons Ordinance, two of the worst bars in Gallup have sold out after receiving multiple citations. We've gained voluntary compliance from most of the liquor licensees on banning early-morning sales and sales of fortified wines and high-alcohol malt liquors. But three of the most problematic bars and package stores have held out, and the liquor licensees successfully backdoored us with Governor Richardson, causing our Local Empowerment District to die a lingering but certain death. We've passed a city ordinance banning glass bottles larger than 23 ounces, though, and we have successfully convinced the legislature, largely through the city manager's efforts, to amend the state statute extending the period for detoxification holds from 12 to 72 hours. This allows public inebriants to dry out before going back out onto the streets. Senator Rainaldi fought the 72-hour legislation hard, but in the end, when passage seemed imminent, he switched sides and even took credit for the legislation's passage.

After the midterm election, in which our south-side councilor beats Harry Mendoza in the runoff, I keep pushing. The city manager works with our police department to establish a special unit to enforce the Sales to Intoxicated Persons Ordinance and establish uniform enforcement protocols. Albuquerque has a successful program of filing public nuisance suits against problem bars and motels, and I begin pushing for public nuisance suits in Gallup, although I know, at this point, that the city council will probably not support me.

The frustration I feel at working with the four city councilors continues to grow. It seems to me that they'd rather avoid any involvement in big-picture ideas, and that they instead relish focusing on minutiae. A multimillion-dollar revenue bond proposal to pay for water line replacements passes unanimously without a question or comment by a councilor, but a heated argument between them about how much money to pay a band for Native American Appreciation Day drags out for more than thirty minutes.

Several events add to the irritation. Up to now, although the *Independent* has been killing me on the editorial page, it's always correctly quoted me in news articles. For the first and only time since I've been mayor, the *Independent* now invents a quote that it attributes to me—and the timing is disturbing.

A deadline is approaching to award a contract to complete our Courthouse Square in downtown when I receive a call from an *Independent* reporter, Bill Donovan. I tell Donovan that no matter how much money

Joe Zecca stands in the doorway of the American Bar in downtown Gallup. *Courtesy of Brian Leddy.*

we put into the downtown, we will always have problems with our development efforts as long as the American Bar continues to open at 10 a.m.
without serving food. One of the oldest bars in town, the American Bar
is owned by Joe Zecca, a well-liked, friendly man with a booming voice.

Donovan mentions that another Gallup bar owner, Art Diaz, is thinking about opening a Bennigan's restaurant downtown. I tell Donovan that
would be good, and that the combination of food and alcohol together is
generally good for downtowns. I say that alcohol-only formats, however,
particularly those that open in the morning, are a problem.

"We can spend millions of dollars," I tell him, "but we aren't going
to be able to revitalize the downtown area as long as the American Bar is
operating as it is."

Toward the end of the *Independent's* article, which comes out on
April, 15, 2005, I read, "Rosebrough said he still hopes to convince Zecca
to change his approach and make it a downtown sandwich bar that will
attract non-Indians, much like Bennigan's or a Chili's." Donovan simply made up the words "downtown sandwich bar," "attract non-Indians,"
and "Chili's"; I never said those words, and "Bennigan's" came out of his
mouth and not mine. I call Donovan and demand a retraction. He says
he'll do a "correction," but he sounds equivocal and avoidant.

Three days after Donovan's story runs, the owner of the Silver Stallion Saloon files a lawsuit against me, the city, the city manager, and the
police chief alleging that our alcohol enforcement efforts are intended
to discriminate against him on the basis of his race. He has a Hispanic
surname but claims Pueblo Indian heritage—something I didn't know
previously. The Silver Stallion complaint repeats the invented quote in
the *Independent* word for word.

Ten days later on the *Independent's* second page a small boxed correction appears: "A recent story about the dispute between Mayor Bob
Rosebrough and the American Bar indicated that Rosebrough wanted
to get the bar's owner to transform his operation into something like a
Bennigan's and Chile's [sic] type restaurant downtown. He said this characterization came from the reporter who writing [sic] the story and not
from him." The "correction" does nothing to dispel the fiction that I am
trying to "attract non-Indians."

The liquor licensees at this point are fully engaged in their drama
drill, and with the lawsuit and the newspaper on their side, they up their

ante. There's yet another tried-and-true tactic in their bag of tricks—one that Muñoz and his key supporters experienced years before.

I start receiving calls late at night, around the time the bars close. The caller just breathes heavily into the phone. When I hang up, they call back again and again until I take the phone off the hook. The son of one of the holdouts to voluntary compliance with morning sales and fortified wines, calls City Hall while I am out, identifies himself by name and leaves a message with my secretary cursing me.

Something has shifted. The liquor licensees are no longer on the defensive; they've worked themselves into a collective frenzy. I can see it in their body language, in the tone of their voices, and in their sneers. They're a pack and they're on the hunt.

After a real-estate closing at Gallup Title, Phil Garcia, a friend who years before brokered a deal to save our downtown zoning ordinance, asks me to come into his office.

"The liquor guys are coming after you," he says. "You and I know they can still make a good living without selling to people who are already drunk, but they don't see it that way. They think you're going to drive them out of business. They're coming after you and they're talking about your family, too. You need to be careful, and you need to protect your family." My son Matt is off in college, but Mark, Megan, and Amy—ages 17, 14, and 9—are still at home. His words give me serious pause.

The city manager directs the police to put surveillance on my home at night and notifies the members of the council. None of the councilors express any support or concern publicly or even privately. A tipping point has been reached; the liquor guys and their hysteria machine have prevailed. I'm depressed and angry about the threats, but equally troubling is knowing that the council is irrevocably lost. I don't know if I want to continue serving as Gallup's mayor without a chance of curbing sales to intoxicated persons. And I don't know if I want to continue serving with four councilors I can't count on personally or publicly. I feel like quitting, giving up. I call the professional staff together and tell them what I'm thinking. They're somber and grim but not really surprised. More than anyone, other than Brenda, they know how important this issue is to me, and they realize that hope for future changes is now pretty much lost. I tell them I'm going to take a few days off and they just nod.

I walk out of City Hall and there—as if on cue—is Hank Stokes, the minister from Georgia who, after a previous dispute with the licensees, told me about his dream about the "Thwart."

After a brief discussion, in which my distress is evident, Hank asks me to get in his car. We drive to his church, where we spend a couple of hours talking in his office. I know any chance of further progress on alcohol reform during my term is now over. After some limited gains were achieved, the liquor guys, as they've done time after time in Gallup, have regrouped, fought back, and reestablished the status quo. But after talking the situation through with Hank, I know that I would regret walking away from all the other projects—quality of life, infrastructure, outdoor recreation, and water—we have in the works.

Later in the day, I run into Peter Tempest, who says, "History is not on their side, Bob," he says. I feel that he's right, but while the liquor guys might look bad decades from now, they are running rampant in the present.

I take a few days off and then go back to work, but any sense of an energy or force working through me is now decidedly gone. I am alone and on the verge of being overwhelmed.

Shortly after that low point, I receive an invitation to a weekday Korean War veteran's ceremony at the Neighborhood Center on the poor side of town.

As I walk in, thirty or forty vets, mostly Navajos, are either milling around or seated casually in metal chairs behind fold-out tables in an old linoleum-floored gym. I don't see anyone I know. A Navajo woman approaches me.

"Thank you for coming," she says, handing me a program. "We have a seat for you next to Hershey."

I'm momentarily surprised. Hiroshi H. "Hershey" Miyamura, a winner of the Congressional Medal of Honor who had been a prisoner of war in Korea, is Gallup's favorite son and our most famous citizen. I've been living in Gallup for twenty-seven years now, and I've only met Hershey once, at the dedication of our veterans' memorial in the Courtyard Square. Although we shook hands and exchanged greetings, I didn't have a chance to talk with him in any depth. Hershey, who travels widely to appear at regional and national ceremonies, rarely goes out in Gallup, and it never occurred to me that he would be at this ceremony.

The woman takes me to an empty chair next to Hershey, and he greets me casually and warmly, as if we were longtime friends.

Hershey is a Japanese American man in his mid-to-late seventies with salt-and-pepper hair. He wears a light-blue ribbon around his neck that holds a five-pointed Congressional Medal of Honor star. But nothing he says or does calls attention to the medal. He introduces me to his wife, Terry, who is seated to his left and talking with Sally Noe, a Gallup historian. Sally says that she and Hershey were classmates at Gallup High School.

For reasons I don't understand, today's event is running ridiculously behind schedule. No one seems to know why the ceremony is delayed or when it will start. Hershey doesn't seem to care though; he gives off an air of humility and infinite patience.

After waiting a bit, I ask Hershey about growing up in Gallup. I'm particularly interested in Gallup's decision not to intern Japanese citizens during World War II and whether Hershey has any memories of that time. Competing versions of the story appeared in the *Independent* a month or two before. One local rival historian seemed to be accusing Sally Noe—who had written an account of the event titled "One Town Said No"—of embellishing the facts. From what little I know, there

US Army Staff Sergeant Hiroshi H. (Hershey) Miyamura received the Congressional Medal of Honor for his actions during combat near Taejon-ni, South Korea. *Wikimedia Commons*

isn't much of a public record about the decision and several people have searched for city council minutes and records without success. The controversy, such as it is, seems to be about the person or persons in Gallup who made the decision not to intern Japanese people, and whether Gallup was the only town to say no or just one among several New Mexico communities that said no.

Hershey tells me he was in high school when the Japanese bombed Pearl Harbor, but surprisingly, the whole topic of the non-internment of Japanese citizens in Gallup doesn't seem to be of much interest to him. He does say that Terry's family, who lived in Winslow, Arizona, was interned. He doesn't have any memories about Gallup's decision not to intern, and he doesn't evince any interest in going back and trying to figure it out.

I ask Hershey how his parents came to live in Gallup, and he says that they moved here from Japan in the early 1900s but that he had an aunt who came to Gallup much earlier. Hershey's father worked as a coal weigher in Gamerco and then moved to Gallup and opened up a small hamburger diner and then a big restaurant that he named the O.K. Café on Coal Avenue downtown.

"It was strictly American food," Hershey says. The restaurant was across the street from the old courtroom where the Chihuahuita coal miners were arraigned before the riot in 1935.

Thinking back to his childhood, Hershey tells me that his parents were so busy with the restaurant that they didn't really have much time to spend with Hershey and his six siblings. He says he used to stay up too late at night.

"I could do just about anything I wanted to do," he says. "I used to like to box and we used to hold boxing matches right behind the restaurant. Our playground was the alley."

Hershey says that he wore a pair of boxing gloves around his neck and would go around challenging the other kids to boxing matches. He would fight anyone. "I just enjoyed it," he says. "But I didn't enjoy training, so I never amounted to anything."

Hershey shares with me that his childhood changed abruptly when his mother died. He was eleven years old and it changed the way he looked at life. "I just felt that loss so much," he says. "I just changed completely."

Hershey isn't sure what caused his mother's death. She was in the hospital in Gallup when Hershey left for a Japanese, Free Methodist Church conference in Palisades, California, for a week. His mother had said he should go, that it was okay. On the second day of the conference, he got word that she had passed away.

"I can't remember much after that," Hershey says. "I couldn't understand why the Lord took my mother when I was attending a church conference, and it made me bitter for many years."

Many times, Hershey said things happened in his life that he couldn't understand how and why they'd happened but that later, he discovered why they'd happened that way.

"And it's always been for the better," he says. "I like to pass that on to people I speak with." I have no doubt that he has found this to be true in his life, but I'm not feeling the same about my life at the moment. I feel that the bad guys are running roughshod over me, but I don't tell Hershey how I feel.

When the Japanese bombed Pearl Harbor, Hershey continues, life in America changed dramatically for most Japanese families. He saw Gallup as being different though. "Gallup was a town of immigrants," he says. "When the mines closed, most of the people from the mining camps moved into town and raised families. The kids grew up knowing many different types of cultures," Hershey says, "and the cultures got along well."

Hershey remembers that he couldn't understand why other towns had so many problems with other nationalities, especially during the war.

"We all looked at each other as Americans," he says. "We had no problems during the war, especially at the beginning when the Japanese bombed Pearl Harbor. We just didn't feel tension like a lot of other places that had people of Japanese ancestry."

Hershey was drafted on January 13, 1944. He wanted to volunteer earlier but couldn't because he was Japanese. He was a heavy-weapons machine-gunner in the 100th battalion, which comprised Japanese Americans.

Hershey tells me that he narrowly missed action in Europe. The day before his battalion was to ship out, he underwent a field inspection and a physical. During the physical the doctor said, "You have a hernia. Does it bother you?"

"I said, 'No sir. I don't even know what a hernia is,'" Hershey says. He underwent an operation while his friends boarded a ship and left for Europe.

"That was the last time I saw them. I lost a lot of my buddies over there," he says.

After recovering from the operation, Hershey rejoined his battalion and boarded a ship for Europe. But five days out from Naples, he and his shipmates learned the war in Europe was over.

Once back in Gallup, Hershey began working as a mechanic. He and Terry were married in 1948 and lived in a two-room home near Hershey's father, on Gallup's north side.

As a member of the reserves, Hershey was one of the first men called into service in 1950, when North Korea invaded South Korea. When I ask about the battle that caused him to be awarded the Medal of Honor, Hershey says, "Throughout the years, I've made a point to just say so much about it and that's it." I have the impression he's given this same answer many times over the years.

The only thing I know about the battle is that Hershey and his squad were manning a machine-gun nest when they were overwhelmed by a massive attack by Chinese and North Korean soldiers shortly after the Chinese joined the war.

Hershey says that after he'd been taken prisoner by the North Koreans, he told another POW who was from Clovis, "If we get out, I'm probably either going to get court-martialed or get a medal." He didn't know what his men had told the commanding officer about the battle— whether they just took off or whether he told them to leave.

I'm not sure what Hershey means by this. I think he may be saying that if his men ran off on their own, Hershey would be criticized for not maintaining discipline, but if he ordered them to leave, it would have been apparent that he was acting selflessly to protect them at his peril.

"But they finally did tell him that I told them to leave," he says. "That's why I got the medal." I would like to know more but, respecting his earlier remark, I don't press him for details.

Hershey tells me that he was one of the last men released from the POW camp. He and the other prisoners released with him at the end were in a state of shock, not believing that they'd actually been released. Seeing the American flag fluttering in the breeze after crossing the border into South Korea was what made Hershey realize they were finally free. "That's one of the most beautiful sights I ever saw."

Hershey learned he was awarded the Medal of Honor the same day he crossed the border into South Korea. He was led to a general who asked Hershey if he knew why he'd been called out of the barracks to come speak to him. He told Hershey that he'd been awarded the Congressional Medal of Honor but that the decision had been kept a secret—the army was afraid that the North Koreans might have retaliated against Hershey in the POW camp if they knew he'd been awarded a medal.

At the time of his release, Hershey weighed 98 or 99 pounds. When he arrived in San Francisco by boat days later, he was greeted by Terry and his father.

"She didn't even know I was alive the first year," says Hershey of Terry.

After a layover in California, Hershey was greeted by a surprise welcome-home ceremony when he got back to Gallup on the train. The whole town, including the children who were all let out of school, was at the train station to greet Hershey and Terry.

Hershey tells me that he still meets people today who tell him they were school kids at the ceremony.

"That really makes me feel ancient," he says laughing.

Before settling back into life in Gallup, Hershey went to Washington, DC, where President Eisenhower presented him and seven other men with the Medal of Honor.

"I don't remember too much about the ceremony itself," Hershey says, "except the president asked me, 'Are you nervous?' and I said, 'Yes sir.' And he said, 'So am I. This is one of the first Medal of Honor ceremonies I've put on at the White House.' So that made me feel a little better."

After all the pomp and ceremony were over, Hershey and Terry started to raise a family, and Hershey and a partner opened a service station on the west side of town where he worked for decades. Thirty years after the war, he overcame a late-in-life dose of post-traumatic stress disorder and settled into retirement.

My conversation with Hershey has seemed dreamlike. I had no idea that I would run into him at this ceremony, which is now almost an hour late, much less have the chance to talk with him at length the way we have. The serendipitous nature of the event makes me think there's some hidden meaning to it—something beyond the details of Hershey's story—that I'm supposed to learn. For more than an hour, I've been asking Hershey every question I can think of and now, for the first time in our conversation, there's a pause. Several people are talking to each other near the podium. A short, spry Navajo veteran of the Korean War approaches us from our right, passing out a sheet of paper.

As he hands me the page, he says, "I found this on the Internet." He nods respectfully to Hershey and puts a paper down on the table in front of Hershey and nods but doesn't speak to him. The vet continues around the room, passing out his sheets. I pick up the paper and see a dark photo of Hershey and a paragraph from his Medal of Honor citation that describes Hershey's actions in battle. The citation gives all the details that led to Hershey being honored—details he was too modest to describe himself. Hershey looks at the paper briefly without indicating either interest or displeasure.

The citation for Hershey's Medal of Honor says that on April 24, 1951, Hershey's squad was in a defensive position when the enemy attacked, threatening to overrun them. Hershey jumped from his shelter and, wielding a bayonet in hand-to-hand combat, killed approximately ten of the enemy. After returning to his position, he administered first aid to the wounded and directed their evacuation as another assault hit the line. He manned his machine gun and fired into the enemy's charge until his ammunition was expended. He ordered the squad to withdraw while he remained behind to render the machine gun inoperative. He then bayoneted his way through enemy soldiers to a second gun emplacement and assisted in its operation. He ordered his men to fall back while he remained to cover their movement. He killed more than fifty enemy soldiers before his ammunition was gone. Although severely wounded, he maintained his stand and continued to repel the attack until his position was overrun. When last seen, he was fighting alone against an overwhelming number of enemy soldiers.

I look at Hershey and get goose bumps as I realize the humble, unassuming man I've been talking with performed all these acts.

The ceremony finally begins. Several Navajo vets and their wives are bustling around a small wooden podium, testing the microphone. A color guard is assembling with its flags in a corner of the gym. We all rise to say the Pledge of Allegiance.

In the days that follow, I don't find myself thinking about Hershey's battlefield exploits or his medal. It's his humility, generous spirit, and imperturbability that stay with me. In a time of wild highs and lows in my life, when everything seems up for grabs and uncertain, Hershey seems to be an anchor, a beacon. He is a different kind of hero—a humble man who wasn't looking for glory, but who simply accepted, and stood up to, every hardship that came his way.

The date arrives for a public hearing at the El Morro Theatre on whether the council will approve the pursuing of public nuisance lawsuits against bars that regularly sell to intoxicated persons. It turns into a raucous, standing-room-only event that goes on almost until midnight.

In the days before the hearing, I sensed that the council's support, such as it was, was slipping away, and I've grown tired of lobbying them. In particular, I sensed that the mercurial south-side councilor feels the need—after receiving my unreserved public support in his midterm runoff race against Harry Mendoza—to prove that he isn't my "puppet." He's been frosty to me, and I tell a friend, "No good deed goes unpunished in politics."

And although I think I know where Frank Gonzales's heart is on the matter, I also know that his longtime friendships with the liquor guys will, when it comes time to take a position, trump everything else. I suspect that the other two councilors will just lick a finger and stick it in the air to test the wind when it's time to vote.

A conversation with the city manager in the days before the public hearing drove home the point that I couldn't count on the city councilors. At the time, Albuquerque had a highly successful program that used public nuisance lawsuits to help shut down several problem bars that regularly overserved alcohol to intoxicated persons. I invited the enforcement officer of the Albuquerque public nuisance program to Gallup and he gave a public talk on the methodology and success of the program. In a private conversation that followed the official's presentation, our city manager asked him if Albuquerque's city councilors supported public nuisance suits against problem bars. The enforcement manager seemed surprised by the question and said they did, without exception. And the real problem became unavoidably obvious.

The city manager told me what I already knew. In Gallup, our city councilors have personal relationships with liquor licensees that don't

A raucous meeting of the city council at the El Morro Theatre continued to nearly midnight on the subject of whether to pursue public nuisance lawsuits against bars that regularly serve intoxicated persons. *Courtesy of the* Gallup Independent

generally exist in the big city. While size was a factor, I knew there was more to it than that. Liquor licensees in Gallup, even those who regularly overserve, have a degree of personal and political influence here that makes them untouchable in the eyes of our city councilors.

A few days before the public hearing on nuisance suits, the bookkeeper whose office is next to my law office puts a bumper sticker on his front window, as close to my office as it can be placed, that says, "Save the Historic American Bar."

As people arrive the evening of the hearing, Gallup's political old guard—including Senator Rainaldi, Mendoza, and magistrate judge and former mayor George Galanis—waylay and lobby them as they come in. Joe Zecca, the owner of the American Bar, whips up support like no other. When it comes time for public comments, Zecca leads off by reading a lengthy, impassioned speech that extends well past the time limit of five minutes per speaker. He's carrying a large plastic bag filled with liquor bottles and cans that he says he picked up in the downtown; he takes them out of the plastic bag one at a time, telling us they were not purchased at his bar because he doesn't serve the brands he's displaying. Zecca ends his speech on an impassioned note; speaking in a loud, deep voice as he stares directly at me, he says, "Judge not lest you be judged." Zecca's lawyer speaks next and goes on a lengthy filibuster.

My accountant, who two days earlier said to me over lunch, "Bob, you're doing the right thing," stands after getting a call from Zecca, who is also one of his clients, to speak *against* the use of public nuisance suits, but he makes sure to say that it's a hard decision for him, "because Bob and I are such good friends."

One man whom I don't know and have never met gives a rambling, disjointed speech that ends with him saying to me, "I can see why your father ran you out of Farmington."

Many people, including women, speak passionately about how public drunkenness in Gallup affects their daily lives and businesses. There are cheers and applause from the competing factions after each speaker, and the two factions seem roughly equal in number and emotion, which means, given the timidity of the council, that the idea of public nuisance suits will die. And it does.

Throughout the meeting, I've taken it as it comes and not responded to attacks; as presiding officer, I've let everyone have their say. The next day, a young Hispanic man who heads the Chihuahuita neighborhood association calls and commiserates with me about the public hearing. As we are winding up, he says, "Before I go, I just want to say, I don't know how you stayed as calm as you did last night. You taught me something. You kept your peace."

I did, but I've also played my last card and lost. The council's decision means that I've come to the end of the line; it's clearer than ever to me that nothing further will be done regarding alcohol during the rest of my term as mayor.

And then two months later I get a call from Governor Richardson's DWI czar, Rachel O'Connor.

I met Rachel briefly nine months earlier at an interim legislative meeting in neighboring Grants, sixty miles east of Gallup. She struck me as the most intelligent, well-spoken person in the room that day—I wished she was up on the stage with a legislator's name card in front of her instead of sitting in the audience several rows behind me answering their questions. I learned later she was raised in Gallup.

When my secretary says Rachel is on the line, I pick up the phone quickly.

Rachel asks me to serve on a thirty-member Liquor Control Task Force that's being created by Governor Richardson to review and evaluate New Mexico's laws and regulations relating to the service of alcohol. She tells me that she hopes the task force will revisit and strengthen the regulation that makes it possible to suspend or revoke the liquor licenses of bars that have multiple convictions pursuant to Sales to Intoxicated Persons or Sales to Minors statutes.

The New Mexico statute specifies that a liquor license can be suspended or revoked for two convictions, but inexplicably a state regulation watered down the law, giving licensees five strikes per year rather than two.

I don't trust Richardson, and I'm not excited about being just one of thirty on such a broad-based task force. As I listen to Rachel, I'm also thinking that the task force will probably just be a bureaucratic game that never goes anywhere. But it's hard to say no to her, and I agree to serve.

After the first meeting of the task force, which I don't attend because of a scheduling conflict and a general lack of enthusiasm, I get another call from Rachel.

Rachel O'Connor, Governor Richardson's DWI czar, championed the three-strikes regulation that resulted in license revocations of several problem bars by the state of New Mexico. *Courtesy of Rachel O'Connor*

"The first meeting was a disaster," she says. "We really need you to come to the next meeting. I'll put you first on the agenda if you can come." Rachel says that the liquor representatives filibustered the first meeting, complaining about the severity of new criminal penalties for servers who sell to minors, and generally drowned out DWI policy advocates.

At the next meeting, I lead off and hit hard at the disparity in enforcement of DWI and Sales to Intoxicated Persons statutes in New Mexico. I say that there are 14,000 DWI convictions per year in New Mexico and 71 percent of DWI offenders are sentenced to jail. There are only thirty-nine Sales to Intoxicated Persons convictions and no one has gone to jail. Only two New Mexico liquor licenses have been revoked in the past ten years, and neither revocation was based solely on Sales to Intoxicated Persons convictions. Fifty percent of DWI offenders had last been served at a bar or restaurant and the average blood-alcohol content of those offenders was 0.17 percent, more than double the legal presumption of intoxication.

Policy advocates begin chiming in and by the end of the meeting a consensus is building to propose amending the regulation to allow the licensees just three strikes per year instead of five.

Shortly thereafter, the *Albuquerque Journal* publishes an article about the task force, quoting liquor representatives predicting imminent doom ("The regulations will shut bars down, plain and simple"), warning of prohibition ("It's almost like the temperance movement from before Prohibition is coming back online"), shedding crocodile tears for mom-and-pop bars ("There are 440 mom-and-pop operations that won't be able to hang on much longer with what the state wants to do"), and fudging the facts ("If you want two beers, and I cut you off, are you going to come back here?"). In fact, an average-size male drinking two beers in one hour would have a blood alcohol level of .02 percent, a long way from the nine drinks that would have to be served in two hours for that male's blood level to reach the .14 blood-alcohol concentration that creates a presumption for a Sales to Intoxicated Persons conviction.

The *Journal* follows the article with an editorial criticizing the proposed three-strikes regulation, and after running it by Rachel, I counter with an op-ed piece in the *Journal*'s article.

"*Here we go again,*" I write referring to the *Journal*'s article. "With each quote from an alcohol industry representative, I make another check on an all-too-familiar mental checklist and continue reading. The thought continually running through my mind is: *Here we go again.*"

I discuss the disparity between DWI and Sales to Intoxicated Persons enforcement, rebut the industry's inaccurate quotes to the press, talk about the actual legal presumptions and the amount of alcohol consumed that would justify a conviction, and discuss the political and financial influence of the alcohol industry in New Mexico.

"I've come to call the whole drama the Hysteria Machine," I write. "Every time a moderate proposal is vetted the industry rolls out the machine, flips a switch, and hysteria spews out, creating havoc, misinformation, and pain until even the proponents of reform say, 'I've had enough. Put that damn machine back in the closet.' The end result is always the same. New Mexico's problem bars operate with impunity."

To my surprise and relief, the three-strikes regulation is ultimately approved and actively enforced, resulting in the revocation of several problem-bar licenses in the state, but before the regulation becomes law, a public hearing is held at the Hispanic Cultural Center in Albuquerque.

Again, I lead off with what by then is my stump speech to a large, capacity crowd. My voice seems to have power outside Gallup. Charlie Chavez, the restaurant and lounge owner who ran for mayor against me, and one of the other licensees from Gallup are in the crowd, and we nod but don't speak. Chavez and the other licensee listen quietly for several hours slumped in their chairs, before leaving without speaking. Observing them, I realize that we've undergone a geographic role reversal. Outside the culture and code of Gallup, they're toothless, and I can tell by their body language that they know it. In Gallup, they still have power; they remain dominant. They might have to fight long and hard, but they know they'll wear down all opposition and eventually prevail. Such is the unsettling reality of the place I have embraced as my home.

CHAPTER **FOURTEEN**

"Bombs Were Bird Eggs"

"Jimmy Carter is on line two," my secretary at City Hall says. Seconds earlier Marlene, who normally buzzes me on the intercom, knocked on my door.

"Jimmy Carter—the president?" I ask.

"Yes, I think so," she says.

Several months earlier, I'd read an article about President Carter that said he spent part of his week mentoring younger elected officials by phone. I wrote President Carter a letter asking his advice about how to deal with the political tactics of Gallup's old guard and the over-the-top editorials of the *Independent*'s publisher. I'd put the letter out of my mind some time ago.

I pick up the phone and say, "President Carter?"

The Georgia drawl is instantly recognizable. It seems unbelievable to be sitting at my desk in Gallup talking to this man whose voice I've heard on TV discussing oil embargoes and hostages in Iran.

We talk for several minutes until I sense from his tone that he's on a schedule and my time is running out. I quickly describe the *Independent*'s editorial style—name calling, venomous accusations, more coffee-shop wisdom than public policy—and ask if he has any suggestions.

"I've always felt that the best way to respond to harsh criticism is with humor," he says. "I would use your good sense of humor."

With my time now up, I thank President Carter.

"Just remember you have a friend in Plains, Georgia," he says in parting.

I hang up and just sit at my desk, sorting through the conversation.

I was still undecided about whether to run for reelection when I wrote to President Carter. By the time he called, I had decided not to run, but had only spoken to Brenda about the decision.

Ironically, I've found a comfortable daily rhythm and routine as mayor just as it's time to give up the job. Early each week, I meet with the city manager, the city attorney and the economic development director at a coffee shop and we run through a list of projects and issues. I'm enjoying the fifteen-minute meetings with citizens on Open Door Friday, and on Thursdays, I do three radio shows—on the local news station, the Navajo listener station, and the public radio at the UNM branch in Gallup with Frank Bosler. I now look forward to each part of my weekly schedule, and each part of the day lifts my mood and spirit.

To my surprise, Eddie Muñoz gives me a call and we start going to lunch on occasion. For the first time, things between us seem comfortable. We just talk casually, and each of us avoids topics that might set the other off. I ask him about his early days in Gallup and he tells me stories of his political battles and personal struggles and triumphs.

A reporter from the *Independent* is pressing me for a reelection announcement. A month earlier, I told him I'd make an announcement one year before the next election.

There is not one defining moment that has led to my decision not to run again. It's a combination of things. My law office is hemorrhaging money, and I have to draw a final line before I jeopardize the financial security of my family. I *want* to run again, but I simply can't afford four more years of being a part-time lawyer. During the first year of a second term if reelected, I will have three children in college or graduate school. I keep waiting for something to happen that might miraculously change this financial reality, but time runs out.

Adding weight to the decision is the undeniable fact that my ability to effect change in Gallup is on the wane.

One month before my self-imposed announcement deadline, I enter the council chambers for a regular meeting and notice many people present who don't seem to have a connection to any of the items on the action agenda. The councilors and I usually recognize almost everyone in the room, and we can identify the issue that has prompted each person in the room to attend.

A cluster of Palestinian Muslim men, all merchants and retailers, are seated near the front left of the room, talking animatedly. Jamal Abdeljawad, a friend and client of mine who owns a Mediterranean restaurant and jewelry store on Route 66 is among them. Seated in the two back rows to the right is one of my best friends, an elderly Presbyterian minister, Don Steele, and seven or eight men and women from his congregation—all taciturn white professionals.

When Don moved to Gallup a year earlier, we instantly became close friends. I'm so comfortable with him that he feels almost like a father or older brother to me, and yet there is a mysterious, sage-like quality about him. We talk by phone and go to lunch regularly, often at Jamal's restaurant. No one here, including Don, has given me a forewarning as to why these disparate groups are here. I was out of town the weekend before the meeting, and I'm wondering what I've missed.

During a brief lull, I whisper to the south-side councilor, "Why are they here?" I don't need to explain whom I'm asking about.

"It probably has something to do with the Muhammad cartoons," he says. I've read that derogatory cartoons about the Prophet Muhammad that were published in a Danish newspaper have stirred widespread protests overseas, some violent. I have no clue why a cartoon in an overseas newspaper would prompt anyone to come to a city council meeting in Gallup. I shrug my shoulders and lift up my palms.

"The *Independent* ran the cartoons," he whispers as we resume.

At the end of the meeting, during the period of public comments, Jamal stands and approaches the podium. Reading from a statement, he opens with a prayer for greater understanding, for the meeting to be a "blessed one" and for the strength to forgive. Although he is genuinely aggrieved, I'm worried that he's on the verge of overplaying his hand.

Jamal explains that Gallup's Muslim leaders had agreed to be interviewed by *Independent* reporters in their mosque about the conflict overseas about the cartoons, and that the reporters hadn't disclosed that they planned to run the cartoons with their story.

"Instead of showing concerns for our feelings," he says, "they stabbed us in the back."

Don Steele steps forward. I've never heard him speak in public. There is a formality and authority to his speech, which projects energy and conviction. A hush falls over the room.

"The publication of these cartoons is painful and derogatory," says Don. "At best ignorant and at worst harmful. Deliberately so."

"Should there be any cartoon depicting Jesus of Nazareth, or any Navajo or Zuni spiritual figure or God," he says, "there would be a great public outcry in this community. I would suggest that harm done to any one of us is harm done to all of us.

Quoting Benjamin Franklin, Don says, "If we don't hang together, we shall all hang separately." Don talks about Gallup's tradition of supporting minorities in our community, and then says, "I ask that this council approve a resolution supporting the Muslims in our community as strong as the one that supported Japanese families in World War II."

There is a momentary stillness when Don ends his comments and then a flood of noise and activity—gasps, applause, community members talking to each other, and councilors competing to make a motion to approve a resolution. When the din dies down, the city attorney explains that we can't approve a resolution at this meeting since the matter is not on the agenda for action. I suggest that the city attorney draft a resolution for consideration at the next meeting and the south-side councilor beats the others to the draw to make a motion. The north-side and the east-side councilors then compete to second the motion, and I ask the city clerk to reflect in the minutes that the second was jointly made by both councilors. The resolution will be heard at our next meeting.

In the aftermath of the burst of enthusiasm, I'm skeptical. Will the council hold firm once the spell of Don's voice fades and the *Independent* and the coffee-shop klatches of Gallup join the discussion?

Sure enough, three days later, without forewarning, a letter appears in the *Independent* from the east-side councilor opposing the resolution. She fails to mention that she fought to second it at the meeting. At the next council meeting, the publisher of the *Independent* and three citizens show up to oppose the resolution, including the east-side councilor's husband. Fifteen citizens are there to support the resolution, however, and after extended discussion and several changes in wording, it passes.

A few days later, the *Independent* reports that rocks, with demands for an apology attached, have been thrown at its entryway, cracking the glass in one panel. With President Carter's advice about humor fresh in my mind, I send a tongue-in-check email to the *Independent*.

"Dear Editor," I say, "I need to come clean on something, I read a story in the *Albuquerque Journal* about the cartoons of the Prophet Muhammad published by the *Independent*. The article mentioned that a couple of rocks were tossed overnight at the *Independent's* entrance with scribbled, unsigned notes demanding an apology. I don't want anyone else to be wrongly accused. I need to confess that, perhaps in a moment of weakness, I tossed the rocks with the apology demand. Bob Rosebrough, Gallup."

I show the email to a couple of friends and they think it's hilarious. It occurs to me that I should give the city manager a heads-up. I take a copy of the email to him and he stares at it stone-faced. He says, "You need to retract this, right away." The finance director, also stunned, nods in agreement.

I go back to my office and write a follow-up email that says the obvious: I'm joking. The *Independent's* editor doesn't respond to either email. Several days later after I've almost forgotten about it, the *Independent* prints my first email as a letter to the editor without mentioning my retraction.

I feel as if I've handed my enemies the dagger with which to gut me. I feel humiliated and stupid—as though I don't have much of a sense of humor after all. I have no desire to fight the *Independent* to set the record straight or to initiate any kind of public explanation, as I would have early in my term; I'm just going to take my lumps and let this run its course without adding to the fiasco.

For several days, I feel overwhelmed at times, as when a friend says, "What were you thinking, Bob!" or when I see the Baptist minister glance at me from a distance, and then look away shaking his head, in what appears to be disgust or disappointment. Each time when I begin to feel overwhelmed, I stop and silently pray—no words, no request, just a silent prayer from the depths of my heart. And each time I feel a calming, protective—if only temporary—sense of spirit.

Just when I think the saga is winding down, my mother-in-law, who is now married to a Gallup liquor licensee and living in Glendale, Arizona, calls Brenda in a panic asking if I'm okay. She tells Brenda that calls are being made to an Albuquerque TV station to report my email confession. She doesn't say how she knows calls are being made when she's five hours away in Glendale, but it appears to me that the liquor guys have orchestrated a calling campaign to extend the humiliation. She hasn't seen or read the email herself, but she's heard about it and is worried about me.

Shortly thereafter, an Albuquerque TV reporter calls my cell phone on the weekend and tells me she is coming to Gallup and wants to interview me.

"You won't believe how many calls we're getting on this," she says.

"That's interesting," I say. "I haven't received calls from any other TV stations."

I meet the reporter at City Hall, and I invite her and her cameraman into my office. We are the only people in the building on a Sunday afternoon.

The camera light comes on and the interview begins. "It was an attempt by me to inject a little humor," I tell the reporter, "and it was a failed one. My family doesn't think I have a future in comedy."

I related the sequence of my two emails, but I don't criticize the *Independent*; I say that they got the better of me on this one. I don't say anything about my suspicions about the liquor dealers mounting a call-in effort to the TV station.

When the segment airs on TV, the reporter says the *Independent* declined comment.

A couple of days later, with the three-year anniversary of my election and my reelection announcement nearing, I walk into City Hall late in the afternoon and see the city attorney. He looks somber.

"Eddie Muñoz died today," he says. "He was feeding his hunting dogs and he was walking back up the hill to his house when he died of a heart attack."

I'm shocked, and I'm surprised by the depth of my sadness. In the mayor's office, Marlene hands me a pink message note.

"Mayor Muñoz came by this morning to see you," she says. "I asked if someone else could help him. He said, 'It's nothing important; I just wanted to stop by and say hello.' He left his phone number and asked for you to give him a call."

The next day, the city beat reporter from the *Independent* calls and asks me for a statement about whether I am going to run for reelection. I tell him I'm delaying the announcement until sometime after Mayor Muñoz's funeral services.

"You told me you would make an announcement at this time," he says.

"Yes, I did," I say, "but things have changed with Mayor Muñoz's death. His services are coming up and that's where the focus should be." It seems that neither of us says what's really on our minds. Privately, I'm relieved to have an excuse to not make the reelection announcement, on the heels of my rock-throwing email, and I suspect that the reporter is pressing for a statement because the *Independent* relishes the idea of an announcement from me at a time of personal embarrassment.

The Friday after Muñoz's death coincides with a monthly prayer meeting in the mayor's office with fundamentalist Christian ministers, who asked permission to hold a monthly prayer session in my office shortly after my election.

Normally five or six ministers come into my office for the Friday prayer session. I'm cordial with them but not close to any of them. After Muñoz's death, more than a dozen ministers arrive and we bring in extra chairs.

"Before we start," I say, "I'd like to go around the room and invite each of you to share your personal memories of Mayor Muñoz." I ask the pastor of the Lighthouse Church, which Muñoz and his wife Margaret attended, "Bill, can I call on you to start?"

After everyone inclined to speak says something about their experiences with Muñoz, the ministers start taking turns offering prayers.

Midway through the prayers I feel that something ineffable passes from Muñoz to me. I have the clear but counterintuitive sense that somehow the mantle of the mayorship is passing to me—which doesn't make sense. I've decided not to run for reelection and my feelings about that decision haven't changed. Besides, if there is such a thing as the mantle of the mayorship, I feel that I earned that three years earlier when I was elected. But it occurs to me that whatever may be passing to me from Muñoz was with him for many years after his mayoralty. It's not necessarily tied to the term of office, and it doesn't involve a call to action; there are no instructions or guidance but more a sense of what it is to be a leader regardless of title or office. I have the feeling that it's not necessary for me to fully understand the idea and the responsibility now but just to hold on to them.

The ministers wind up their prayers, linger to visit casually, and then trickle out of the mayor's office, giving no indication that they've sensed anything different about me.

In the following days, things begin to return to normal. With only a year left in my term, my priority is to complete pending projects. Shortly after Muñoz's death, our Aquatic Center, with a play area that features a high, spiral water slide, is scheduled for an opening ceremony.

"I'm going to wear an old suit," I tell Brenda, "and after the ribbon cutting, I'm going to go down the slide fully clothed to christen it." It seems to me that going down the slide will take some of the sting away from my rock-throwing-email faceplant with the *Independent*—and it does. The city manager and the superintendent of the Gallup McKinley County Schools, which contributed financially to the center, also go down the slide fully dressed. As I'm toweling off, a reporter from the *Independent* who covered the city beat early on during my term, whispers to me, when he knows no one else can hear, "I was proud of you for going down the slide. That was a good idea."

Bob Rosebrough christens the water slide at the ribbon cutting for Gallup's Aquatic Center. *Courtesy of Joe Kolb*, Gallup Herald

When nine months are left in my term, a federal court judge dismisses the Silver Stallion's lawsuit against the city and me. I receive word of the dismissal by phone in Scottsdale, Arizona, where I'm taking my father to a medical appointment.

In a 17-page opinion, the judge says that the Silver Stallion did not present any evidence that the enforcement of liquor laws at the saloon "was different than the enforcement at other bars owned and frequented by persons of a different race." The decision frees me up to enjoy the last months of my term without having to put in the work and time to prepare for a trial. When I return to Gallup and the mayor's office, I hoist a two-and-a-half-foot-long cardboard box full of my personal copies of correspondence, pleadings, and deposition transcripts and lug the box back to my law office for storage.

A group of citizens now wants to ban alcohol sales before noon. They gather enough petition signatures to force a referendum vote. The liquor licensees file suit to block the election, but the district court judge rules the election can proceed. The young woman spearheading the petition, who came to Gallup as a Vista volunteer, says publicly that after she appeared on a radio show, she came home and found that her answering machine was filled with half a dozen threatening and obscene messages. A few days later, when her car was in a parking lot, vandals broke the windows, dented the body, and urinated on it. Nothing of value was taken from the car—neither her CDs nor her CD player—and no other vehicles in the parking lot were damaged.

By this time, I've come to believe that the biggest political division in Gallup involves the mindset of old-guard Gallupians and that of the people who move to Gallup from the outside. Gallup draws a creative, talented, altruistic, and intelligent group of doctors, teachers, nurses, artists, traders, and entrepreneurs who are visionaries with limited experience with the historical realities of Gallup. They're excited by the diversity and energy here and see potential in Gallup. They enthusiastically but naively dive into the community only to become immensely frustrated when the brick walls rise up; then they leave as if propelled by a revolving door.

Sometimes the old guard will patiently wait for the newcomers to burn out, and sometimes they hasten the process. "You self-appointed do-gooders come and go all the time," they've been known to say. "Nothing you say means anything. In a couple of years, you'll be gone, and we will have forgotten about you. We will still be here."

There is no way a public policy initiative or project will fly without the vocal support of at least one well-regarded, born-and-raised Gallupian, and with the referendum election looming, not a single native-born Gallupian has spoken publicly in support of Not Before Noon.

Four days before the referendum, I'm at Sacred Heart Cathedral and the church is jam-packed for the funeral of Louie Chavez, the former fire chief and the brother of Charlie Chavez, the restaurant owner and liquor licensee who ran against me for mayor. Latecomers are standing in the foyer because of lack of space. Senator Rainaldi is walking up and down the center aisle shaking hands and greeting friends as he does at every funeral. Old-time Gallup is on full display, and a powerful energy fills the sanctuary. I realize something as I look around: *The referendum is going to fail.*

On election night, the council and I are in our regular meeting as the votes are being tabulated. Joe Darak, the former mayoral candidate who's now a reporter for the fledgling *Gallup Herald*, enters the council chambers carrying a sheet of paper and sits next to an *Independent* reporter. Darak is animated, almost giddy. The *Independent* reporter sees me looking at them and puts on a poker face. Darak has no clue I'm looking at him. I know from his glee that the referendum has failed. I feel deflated. Later in the meeting, the city clerk reports that the vote against banning the sale of package liquor before noon failed 976 votes to 868.

The last year of my term is highlighted by a series of ribbon-cutting events as the projects we started during my first year are coming to fruition. In addition to the Aquatic Center opening, we have ribbon cuttings lined up for the Courthouse Plaza downtown, the renovation of the El Morro Theatre, the shooting range, the downtown Veterans Memorial, the remodeled City Fitness Center, and the Second Street flood-control dam.

At one of the events, I tell a friend, "Public projects are different than private projects. It's easy to start a private project, but they take a lot of effort and money to complete. They are continuously hard for a business owner. Public projects are the opposite for an elected official. Once you establish the funding source and fight through the hoops to get approval, public projects seem to take on a life of their own."

The El Morro Theatre renovation was one of several public works projects completed in Gallup from 2003 to 2007. *Courtesy Palace of the Governors (MNM/DCA), Neg. No. 47825*

Some headaches persist however, and, predictably, they involve the *Independent*. I receive a call from the city's utility director.

"We made a mistake," he says, "by a factor of ten in setting up the *Independent's* electrical meter when the new printing press went online."

He tells me that our electrical department has been undercharging the *Independent* for almost two years. A city employee entered the wrong multiplier—24 instead of 240—into the city's computer billing system when setting up the utility account for the new printing press that we helped finance by approving Industrial Revenue Bonds back in 2004. The *Independent's* publisher got a new press that was two or three times bigger than the old press and his utility bills went *down* by 80 percent. Over the course of 22 months, the city has billed the *Independent* $12,470.52 for electrical service that should have cost $165,944.03.

The *Independent's* publisher denies that he saw a drop in his utility bills. "Absolutely not true," he says. He claims that the billing disagreement is just the city's way of retaliating against him for his editorials that criticized me and the city government. The city attorney, after months of futile negotiations, files a suit for declaratory judgment, asking the district court to resolve the dispute.

Six months before the mayoral election, I tell the city's professional staff that I'm not running for reelection. None of them seem surprised. I think they and the councilors know that if I were running, I would already have been laying the groundwork for the campaign. I read a short statement at the end of a council meeting. "It was a very difficult decision that I weighed for many months," I say. "But I'm very much at peace with it."

I take a deep breath and feel my chest expand. It feels good for the decision to be final and public, but I'm concerned about who will take my place. Harry Mendoza is still planning to run and appears to be the early favorite.

I find myself thinking about Larry Casuse and Emmett Garcia during the last months of my term. When I do, I feel deep empathy for both men. My time as mayor has stretched me thin—thinner than I imagined it would and thinner than I like to admit. My challenges may have been minor in comparison to what Casuse and Garcia faced, but at times they weighed heavily.

I imagine I know a little of how Larry Casuse felt when he saw Navajo people lying comatose, the people then in power looking the other way, as if everything was fine. And as an energetic political newcomer in Gallup rocking the boat and earning the wrath of its old-guard politicians, I feel as if I know how Emmett Garcia felt. I don't feel like I need to take sides between Garcia and Casuse. I relate to and feel genuine compassion for both. And to be completely honest, I feel fortunate to have survived my lesser travail with the same basic conflicts that they faced.

After my announcement, the tension with the liquor licensees seems to break almost instantly; I'm no longer a threat to them. One Italian licensee comes to see me in the mayor's office to tell me that during the summer while he was on a vacation in Italy, he was sitting in a roadside café watching a stage of the Giro d'Italia, Italy's version of the Tour de France. He describes the advance cars and motorcycles approaching, the surging peloton with multicolored jerseys passing just yards from where he sat, and the throng of support vehicles that followed. He tells me that he likes what we've been doing with the events and venues of Adventure Gallup and praises our efforts to create spaces for outdoor activities in Gallup.

Then he says what I assume he's been waiting for weeks to say to me, "Bob, if you really want to make Adventure Gallup a success, just put an Italian in charge of it." He laughs and gives me a pink T-shirt, cycling hat, and small stuffed animal from the Giro and leaves with a beaming smile.

On the sixty-fifth anniversary of the Japanese attack on Pearl Harbor, three months before the end of my term, Albert Smith, the president of the Navajo Code Talker's Association leaves a message for me at my law office saying he wants to see me and will come back tomorrow morning. I've been slowly weaning myself from my responsibilities at City Hall and reimmersing myself in my law practice. Even though I have three months to go, at times, I find myself thinking, *"When I used to be mayor . . ."*

When I see Albert's note, I recognize his name and think back to our silent exchange of nods three years earlier at the Silver Medal ceremony at Red Rock Park. We've seen each other at various events since and, on occasion, briefly exchanged greetings.

At 8:45 the next morning, fifteen minutes before the start of my Open Door Friday session at City Hall, my secretary knocks and says, "Mr. Smith is here."

Albert Smith comes in wearing a sweater with a caribou pattern, a red-and-blue-plaid shirt, and an Albuquerque balloon fiesta hat that rests above his wire-rim glasses. He has salt and a little bit of pepper in his hair and a thin horseshoe mustache. He is trim, alert, and cheerful.

Albert has a Gallup Joint Utilities bill in his hand, and after a few pleasantries he shows me the bill and explains that he thinks the bill is in error. I start taking notes. He's not upset at all. In fact, he almost seems amused. It appears that a $362 payment was added to the balance on the bill rather than being subtracted. I get the sense, though that the utility bill is, in part, a pretext and that Albert has something else he wants to talk about. I tell him that I'll take the bill to the city manager when I go over to City Hall at 9 for Open Door Friday.

With the Pearl Harbor anniversary fresh on my mind, I ask Albert about that day and he laughs and says that he was thirteen at the time. His laugh suggests that he's joking about his age, but I don't know what he's really getting at. I'm privately delighted to be having the conversation with a Code Talker that I wanted to have three years earlier.

Albert says that in 1942—not long after Pearl Harbor in December 1941—he went to Fort Wingate because his older brother who was in school there was going into the service and Albert wanted them to go in together. He says, "We decided to move up our ages to 17 and 19."

Albert says that he and his brother were slated to become Code Talkers from the beginning, but his brother couldn't handle the pace of the work on the code and eventually went into the artillery. Albert says the Code Talkers had two instructors, one Navajo and one Anglo. "We trained for two months," he says. "On Monday, Tuesday, Wednesday, and Thursday we learned words, and on Friday they gave us a test. We had liberty on weekends." He laughs, apparently triggered by a memory of liberty.

Albert says that learning the code wasn't hard for him.

"I just had to mesh the two Navajo and English words together," he says. "It wasn't difficult. Our language is a descriptive language."

Albert tells me that there were sixty-six characters in the code alphabet and that the code words were names of plants on the reservation, animals, minerals and parts of the body. "Planes were birds," he says. "Bombs were bird eggs. Ships were fishes." Albert says the only difficulty was when there was not an exact match on the two words and, as examples, he says the word for tank was turtle and the word for submarine was iron fish. I don't understand why his examples were not exact matches, but I'm enthralled with the conversation and don't want to interrupt his train of thought by asking him to explain.

I add the sixty-five years since Pearl Harbor with thirteen and ask him if he is seventy-eight years old.

"A few more," he says. "I have been over the hill twice." We both laugh.

Albert starts talking about basic training.

"Boy it was rough," he says. "That was a hot place—San Diego."

He remembers the white bell-bottoms worn by the Navy seamen, and the Navajo Code Talkers clustered in groups talking with each other, saying things like, "Why the heck did we get into something like this?"

Albert tells me about how the first 29 Code Talkers made the code, how subsequent Code Talkers periodically reviewed and revised it, and how he didn't tell even his wife about his service as a Code Talker after being told by Navajo elders to leave his war stories behind.

We've been talking for 45 minutes and I'm 30 minutes late for my first Open Door Friday appointment; I've never been late before. A couple of times I have made lukewarm shifts in body language with the intention of wrapping up the conversation that he seems to notice but ignore. I'm engrossed by what Albert is telling me and don't really want the conversation to end, but my sense of obligation finally overrides my feelings.

"I would enjoy talking to you all day," I say. "But I'm late and I need to get over to City Hall."

Albert nods, but clearly has something more to say. He leans forward and says that there's been a change in appearance in Gallup. Sidewalk corners are being fixed and cracks fixed.

"Gallup is a different place," he says. "I am honored to talk to you." I'm astounded that *he's* honored to talk to *me*.

"*Our town* is no longer Drunk City," he says. Though I feel that he's overstating my accomplishments, I am moved and honored by his words. I wipe tears from my eyes.

Then he reaches out with both hands and clasps my right hand, top and bottom. I put my left hand under his hand, and he places his top hand on the bottom. He begins speaking in Navajo and moves our hands in all four directions. He continues talking, switching to English. He asks that my efforts be blessed, and he moves our hands in a circle. He shifts our hands toward himself and lowers his lips to our hands. Then he moves our hands toward me, and after a pause, nods his head toward our clasped hands. I touch my lips to our hands. Albert Smith nods in approval, satisfaction, and completion. I feel a sense of completion as well.

CHAPTER FIFTEEN

"Emmett Garcia Is on Line Two"

"Who's going to win the mayor's race?" asks Don Steele over lunch. It's a month before the election and we're sitting at a sturdy wooden table in El Metate—a small home that's been converted to a one-room, tile-floored restaurant in Chihuahuita. One wall features colorful hand-painted images of a chile, a tomato, an onion, and an ear of corn. The opposite wall is wildly colored with undulating swaths of light purple, red, dark-blue and lime-green. One swath of color forms a snake whose head faces outside.

Don, who proposed the resolution in support of Gallup's Muslim citizens a couple of months earlier, is in his seventies and is short and balding. He has an insightful mind, a big heart, and an almost gnome-like presence. He seems to see the world more fully than anyone I know.

A depressing reality is settling in. "It looks pretty clear to me that Harry Mendoza is going to win," I say. "He's got all the old-guard vote, and Ralph, Mary Ann, and Larry are going to split up the rest of the vote."

I tell Don that I'm glad the projects from my term are now safely wrapped up, but I'm worried about the job security of the men and women on the city's professional staff whom I've worked with for four years.

A completely unrelated thought pops into my mind.

"Don, why are you here?" I ask. "Why did you move to Gallup?" I assume, given his wisdom and experience, that Don could live anywhere in the world and I wonder why he picked Gallup. I expect Don to reflect for a minute before answering but he responds without a pause.

"I come from the Celtic tradition," says Don. "We have a concept of places on Earth that are thin places, where the veil between heaven and Earth or between the sacred and the rest of us is thin and permeable— and I think Gallup is such a place.

"I believe Navajo culture has a similar concept," he continues. "That it is possible at times to catch a glimpse through our own version of the fog.

"If there's a thin place, it's permeable. That means you can have access to the sacred more readily, but they are places of extremes," he says. "Places of thin veil are places of struggle, where the forces of both good and evil are drawn into battle."

The idea, while new to me, *feels* true. Every word Don says seems to echo my experience here: the transcendent, ephemeral moments I've experienced in Gallup, the similar moments that others have shared with me, the never-ending struggles, and the way Gallup has always seemed both simultaneously and disproportionately wonderful and terrible to me. I find myself thinking that while some of the terrible side of Gallup is obvious to most, the wonderful side is equally real, even though it's less apparent to the outsiders.

I've recently wondered if I was drawn to Gallup by events, experiences, and feelings, rather than simply by making a reasoned decision. All of what Don describes sinks in and seems to fit. We finish our meal, pay our bill, and head outside. Before getting in my truck, I pause and stand in front of the restaurant one block from where Victor Campos's furniture was dragged out onto the street seventy-two years ago by sheriff's deputies and an eviction notice nailed to his door. I sense the struggle that's played out in this neighborhood for decades.

The next day, I call my friend Phil Garcia at the title company and pay him a visit. After sleeping on Don's words, I want to test what he's told me about Gallup being a place of thin veil with someone else, preferably someone who was born and raised in Gallup. Phil and I sit at the large conference table in the closing room at Gallup Title and I repeat my conversation with Don. Phil listens and at times nods.

When I finish, Phil says emphatically, "That's Gallup." And he adds, "But there is one other thing I would add. It's not just about good people and bad people. It's about the struggle inside each of us here. I can't tell you how many times people who have treated me terribly here later startle me with unexpected kindness. It has something to do about the good and bad in each of us here."

With the election approaching, I start organizing my personal files in the mayor's office and taking some of them to my law office. My attention is again drawn to the locked drawer in the entryway of my office that has remained locked all four years I have occupied the office. I bring a pry bar from home and break the metal clasp.

The drawer is filed with correspondence and documents from Mayor Muñoz's term. I find a press release from 1987 calling for no liquor sales before 11:00 a.m. and closure of drive-up windows on a voluntary basis, a financial impact study of NGWSP, a letter attaching legal research regarding the city's obligation to prepare a forty-year water plan, and a binder titled "Support Documentation for Alcoholism Program." Gallup's perpetual challenges—water and alcohol. Muñoz worked on them, hit a brick wall, and passed them on. Now, I'm doing the same.

A few days later, I'm walking into City Hall with a candidate, Larry, who's running against Harry Mendoza in the mayor's race, and we're talking about the strength of Gallup's political old guard. Over the last four years, I've come to know more than I'd like to know about them.

"I underestimated their strength," I say. "During my campaign, my former law partner Dolph kept telling me, 'Don't take them head-on,' and I didn't, even though I wanted to. It was inevitable that I would clash with them once I was mayor. I don't respect that they seem to have no observable interest in public policy and that they hire their friends, without regard to qualifications, instead of professionals."

Larry nods, encouraging me to continue.

"But what really bugs me is that they pretend to champion the little guy, while more times than not they're really only looking for a deal to feather their own nest or do a favor for a political buddy. But I have to admit they're effective, more so than I thought. They know how to give favors and how to call them in when they need to. One thing I didn't anticipate was their talking campaigns—they can spread a rumor like no one else."

Recently, a story has been circulating around town that the husband of one of the other mayoral candidates, the east-side city councilor, broke into a motel room in Cortez, Colorado, a few days earlier to find his wife with another man.

"I heard that," says Larry. "You mean it's not true?"

"I had coffee with her husband the day after I first heard the rumor," I say. "There's nothing to it. I didn't tell him about the rumor, but he hasn't been anywhere near Cortez recently, and things are fine at home."

"The old guard are way more effective than progressives," I add. "Progressives all view themselves as visionaries. And the problem with visionaries is that each has his or her own vision. Working with them is like trying to herd cats. The old-guard guys are like wolves. They know how to hunt together."

Earlier, I had talked with an insightful woman, a lifelong Gallupian, who used to work in City Hall, and I asked her what she thought of the old guard and why they're so effective.

"They have personal relationships that go back for generations," she said. "And they set the tone. People are fearful of change. They accept things that they know are wrong because that's the way it has always been. Even though they know they're wrong, it's comfortable and familiar."

"Why do people born here never speak out when they want change?" I asked.

"There's a code of silence," she said. "People don't want to be perceived as challenging the status quo. They don't want to be an outsider in a small town. They don't want the wrath," she says. "It's hard to break a cycle when a lot of people have made a lot of money. They see Gallup as a cash cow. They think, 'I can do what I want.'"

A month after my lunch with Don Steele, any hopes I've had for a smooth transition to a new mayor are dashed. At the council chambers for the first meeting after the election, there's a sound, not unlike swarming bees, as the four councilors and I file in and take our seats. Several people are standing in the aisle and there are many supporters of Harry Mendoza and the other mayoral candidates—people I haven't seen at a council meeting in the previous four years. They're sitting in clusters and talking feverishly. Harry Mendoza is seated three rows from the front with his campaign manager and her husband; they're huddled, talking, and looking at a sheet of paper. Mendoza's closest competitor, with several of his supporters, is seated three rows directly behind him.

I call the meeting to order. "The first item on the agenda is the presentation of the municipal election results," I say. I ask the city clerk to speak.

The city clerk explains that a canvas of the election results was completed the day before and none of the candidates received 40 percent of the vote, the amount required to avoid a runoff.

"Harry Mendoza received 1407 votes, which is 39.99 percent of the votes," she says.

"How many votes were needed for 40 percent?" I ask.

"Forty percent would be 1407.2. It would require 1,408 votes to win." She says that the other candidates received 796, 729, 316, 141, and 72 votes each. She has scheduled a runoff election between Mendoza and the second-place candidate in eighteen days.

Mendoza has been lobbying anyone who will listen for the past two days, including me, to round up his vote to 40 percent and dispense with the runoff. The city attorney then addresses the council and says, "I've researched all fifty states and there is no authority to round up election results. There is no language in our city charter, state law, or federal law that would allow rounding—40 percent means 40 percent, not 39.99 percent."

There's restlessness in the chambers and murmuring. Several clusters of people begin talking among themselves, and Mendoza is looking at one group and nodding.

Mendoza's campaign manager, a former city councilor, stands and asks to be recognized. "I'm passionate about my city," she says before launching into a rambling, emotional speech about asking her 15-year-old daughter how to round up or down, integer values, and wasting taxpayer's money on an election whose outcome is certain. She turns her back toward me and the council and addresses the second-place candidate, demanding that he concede.

"Call to order," I say. "Ms. Herrera, please address your comments to the council." I expect her to keep talking but to the council and me. She pivots, glares at me, and sits down without saying anything further, and that's fine with me.

We hold a runoff election and Mendoza wins.

The day after the runoff, at the end of my last council meeting, I'm publicly thanking my family, friends, and the city employees when a tall,

Harry Mendoza being sworn in as Gallup mayor on March 29, 2007. *Courtesy of Jeff Jones*

distinguished-looking Navajo man carrying a Pendleton blanket and a bolo tie enters the room with his wife and another Navajo man. I know them well, but I'm momentarily disoriented—I've never seen them here at City Hall or at a council meeting.

The three are Navajo Nation president Joe Shirley, his wife Vicky, and a Tribal Council delegate, Leonard Tsosie. I don't know why they've come, and I glance at the agenda to see if there's an issue related to the Navajo Nation that I've overlooked. I pause for a moment and ask if they'd like to address the council. To my surprise, they've brought the blanket and bolo tie as gifts for me. President Shirley thanks me for the working relationship we developed with the Navajo Nation during my term.

I leave my seat and stand by President Shirley, who puts the bolo tie around my neck and wraps the blanket around my shoulders.

I tell the assembly about President Shirley's bait-and-switch horse-back move at the Ceremonial parade, when he said, "Thanks for making me look good." The room breaks into laughter. "I guess this evens things up," I say, and President Shirley smiles.

When the meeting is over, a photographer from the *Independent* requests a photo. I ask Brenda and my daughter Amy to join me on the

Glad I did it and glad it's over. On the floor of the city council chambers after my last meeting as mayor. *Courtesy of the* Gallup Independent *and Brian Leddy*

floor of the council chambers and we chat as I wear my new bolo tie and hold the blanket while the photographer takes pictures. When the photographer is done, we linger silently for a moment in the now-empty chambers and then head home.

The next day, a friend tells me he was sitting behind some of Mendoza's supporters at the meeting. "They're a rough bunch and they sure don't like you," he says. "They were saying that you are moving, that they've run you out of town." I assure him I'm not going anywhere.

In the days and weeks that follow, I adapt to practicing law full-time again; I come to the office early and stay late, trying to dig out of the financial hole created by my four years as mayor. Occasionally, I find myself thinking, out of habit, that I should get up and walk across the street and down the block to the mayor's office, as I did regularly during my term, but I catch myself and realize that wouldn't go well.

Once in office, Mendoza fires the police chief, the economic development director, and the city clerk. Mendoza tells the city manager to hire the sitting north-side councilor, who is out of a job after his family's gas station closed, as an assistant city manager. When the city manager refuses, Mendoza lines up the council votes to fire him. Our finance director and city attorney resign. Mendoza hires his campaign manager's husband, who has no previous government experience, to be the new city manager—he makes his first public appearance wearing Levi's and a Bubba Gump Shrimp polo shirt.

A couple of months after my term as mayor ends, my daughter, Megan, who has just graduated from Gallup High and is getting ready for college, comes home with Brenda, laughing hysterically. Megan has a boisterous and infectious sense of humor, but she's telling me about seeing a disheveled, inebriated man who was staggering toward her and Brenda as they drove into the drugstore parking lot. I know it's not in Megan's nature to make fun of someone else's hardship and that she must be laughing at something else, so I ask her to slow down and tell me what's she's talking about.

Megan says the man was staggering directly toward their car, wearing a beige T-shirt with a colored circle on the chest.

"Dad, he was wearing one of your campaign shirts," she says. "It said, 'Bob Rosebrough for Mayor, A New Day for Gallup.'" Megan bursts out laughing again—at me and how the universe has chosen to broadcast the collapse of my aspirations. Brenda and I can't help but join her. We laugh in a way that can be easily turned to tears.

By the fall, there seems to be a shift. I am no longer in the fray. I'm fully immersed in my law practice, and the turmoil at City Hall seems to have moved on without me.

Mendoza and the *Independent*'s publisher, without me in the mix, now seem to be building to a clash. Within sixty days of Mendoza taking office, the city settled its electric-bill suit with the *Independent*, which had grown to $184,688.34, for $60,000.

I'm happy to be in my law office with papers, files, and yellow legal pads strewn on my desk, just keeping my head down and letting things run their course.

One day, the intercom buzzes, "Can you take a call?" the secretary says. "Emmett Garcia is on line two."

Although I've considered contacting Garcia over the years, I've never acted on the inclination. After his abduction, the death of Larry Casuse, and the Navajo protest marches that followed, Garcia's defeat in the 1973 mayoral election wasn't an upset. Garcia had taken the loss hard and left town, I'd been told, moving to Arizona. I'm excited to get his call. Never having crossed paths with him during the first twenty-eight years of my life in Gallup, I feel that it's time we talk.

I pick up and say, "Hi, mayor. How are you?"

Emmett tells me he's coming back to Gallup to give a couple of talks—one to Frank Bosler's high school history class at Miyamura High School and one to a political science class at UNM–Gallup. Emmett has a deep, authoritative voice—the kind of voice you would expect a powerful, big-city mayor to have.

"Are you free for lunch?" he says. "I'd like to meet with you before I give my talk," he says. He doesn't say why, and I don't ask.

A few days later, Emmett walks into the Coal Street Pub in downtown Gallup, where I'm seated, saving a table. I stand and wave to draw his attention.

Emmett is wearing a red Arizona Diamondbacks baseball cap and a heavy, lumpy sweater; he's in his early seventies, pudgy and balding. Wisps of hair on top of his head are combed back and there are hints of stubble on his prominent jowls. Emmett introduces a friend, the city's personnel director during his term as mayor, whom he's invited to join us. Emmett seems energized by his return to Gallup and his upcoming talks.

While he seems eager to tell his story, Emmett seems wary of talking to me, even though this meeting was his idea. "The truth needs to be told," he says looking at me cautiously, trying to read my reaction. I nod reassuringly; I'm eager to hear what he has to say, but I don't know where he's going with this.

"Larry Casuse was influenced by the American Indian Movement," Emmett says, "but also by my political enemies." I'm pleased that Emmett is going straight to the heart of what interests me most about him. Clearly, his life has become defined by what happened with Casuse. Emmett tells me that when he was mayor, he uncovered a fraudulent scheme by the director and an assistant director of urban renewal to skim money from urban renewal loans. "Instead of five or six or seven thousand dollars of work, they would do two thousand," he says. "Then they would sign papers to get the whole thing."

Emmett tells me that the two men were allies of Emmett's old-time Gallup political opponents, a group that included Eddie Muñoz. Emmett seems to be saying that the corrupt urban renewal administrators together with Emmett's political enemies co-opted Casuse and steered him to oppose Emmett's appointment to the UNM Regents.

Emmett is quick to form unshakable opinions. Everything seems to be black and white to him; there are no shades of gray. He seems to think that he has everything sorted out, with no unanswered questions left.

Emmett is implying that Casuse would not have taken his protest to the lengths that he did, but for the aid of Emmett's political enemies. I don't doubt that Emmett's enemies tried to co-opt Casuse, but I think Emmett is taking his theory too far. Everything I know suggests that Casuse was motivated by his own principles and that he wasn't anybody's pawn. While I can easily believe that Emmett had stirred up some serious opposition among the old-timers of his day, I seriously doubt that Larry Casuse was primarily motivated by anything that Emmett's adversaries said or did.

"Their plan," says Emmett of his enemies, "was to create publicity with Indians and the Navajo Inn. I hadn't been out there at the Navajo Inn for six years. I wanted one more term." I think that Emmett is saying that by turning over the operation of the Navajo Inn to Frank Colaianni, he would have won another term if his old-time political enemies hadn't prompted Casuse to protest his appointment to the regents.

"I started getting phone calls at home," he says, "threatening me and the kids—saying they were going to blow up my home and that my kids would have trouble at school." His statement takes me back to a time when I had also received threats, something I haven't thought about for many months. I tense as I remember the stress and fear I felt for my family.

Emmett changes the subject and talks about his appointment to the UNM Board of Regents, one of the most prized political appointments in New Mexico. Although a regent receives no salary, the position affords unparalleled influence and prestige in New Mexico political circles. At the time, Emmett's wife had been diagnosed with lupus, and he was still recovering from a head-on auto collision in Pinetop, Arizona. He says that New Mexico Governor Bruce King and his son, David King, wanted to appoint Emmett because a longtime regent from Gallup, Walter Wolf, was resigning.

"They gave me two hours to make up my mind," says Emmett.

Because of his personal circumstances, Emmett suggested that John Peña, a young Gallup professional (and the mayor who preceded me in office), be appointed in his place. But the governor's son said they would give the appointment to someone from Belen if Emmett didn't take it.

"I told him, 'I'll take it,'" says Emmett. "You would have too." I give a shrug to say, *you're probably right.*

Emmett's friend, who seems to have been invited for moral support, sits at the table listening. At times he nods his head, affirming what Emmett has said.

Emmett pauses for the first time. He's been talking nonstop for about fifteen minutes. I ask him to tell me more about the Navajo Inn.

"I built it and managed it," he says. "We had a security wagon and paddy wagon. When we closed, we looked for people lying around. We would bring them to jail for safety. I had been out for six or seven years. I left it in 1963 and became a golf pro. I hated that store. That's the most atrocious thing I did in my life." It's hard to read Emmett. I'm not sure if he really means what he is saying or whether he thinks it is now a politically correct position. His reference to the Navajo Inn as a "store" surprises me; I had only heard it referred to as a bar.

"I had no control," Emmett says of his partnership in the Navajo Inn. "I sold two thirds and kept one third because Reed Ferrari and Frank Colaianni couldn't agree. They wouldn't buy unless I kept one-third to break a tie. I gave up the management. We actually let Frank run it. Frank ran it very much differently. He ran it like a bar." Emmett's voice takes on an edge of resentment as he talks about Colaianni, who was elected to Gallup's city council four years after Garcia lost his bid for reelection and became mayor ten years after Emmett's abduction. I want to ask him more about Colaianni, but it seems to me that he is guarded every time Colaianni's name comes up and I let it pass.

"If I ran the Navajo Inn like other people, I could have made millions," says Emmett. Without saying his name, he seems to be talking about Colaianni.

"We had a program for Gallup that was one of the most comprehensive ever presented," Emmett says, tacking in another direction to talk about his time as mayor. "We had a plan right from the beginning, and we followed it. I was thirty-three when I was elected. David King wanted me to run for governor.

"I worked hard. I had an open-door policy," says Emmett. "I kept appointments and got involved. We had all these projects. I was a hands-on mayor." I don't doubt what Emmett is now saying. Everyone I've talked to about his tenure as mayor has told me that he was a hardworking go-getter.

Emmett then talks about trying to solve Gallup's public inebriation problem, saying, "I hated seeing those people drunk."

For the first time, Emmett's friend, the former personnel director chimes in. "He worked us damn hard," he says. "This guy never slept."

"I was at City Hall before anyone else," Emmett says. "I was there all the time." It occurs to me that Emmett could be describing my mayoralty. I think he and his friend probably know that without my saying it, and I think they know about the blowback I got from my version of Gallup's old guard. Perhaps that's why Emmett picked me to have this conversation.

I ask Emmett about Eddie Muñoz. Emmett knew Muñoz during Muñoz's first stint in politics, before he came back as an alcohol reformer.

"I don't even want to say what I think," says Emmett, but he obviously does want to tell me something. He says that Muñoz, who was then working as the county manager, tried to con him out of some city fire hoses by misrepresenting their condition. "When Eddie was mayor," he adds, "he had a service station and he had city equipment building it and clearing it."

Emmett also attributed the delay in the extension of I-40 through Gallup to Muñoz and his business and political ally, Al Lebeck. "I went to the State Highway Board director, Stretch Bowles, and asked, 'Why aren't you finishing the interstate?'" says Emmett. "It had been delayed for years. He showed me a letter from Eddie Muñoz and Al Lebeck that delayed the interstate for a year or so." I don't press Emmett for details about the letter, but it doesn't surprise me. When I moved to Gallup in the fall of 1979, six-and-a-half years after Emmett's term ended, the interstate was still uncompleted and traffic on Route 66 was clogged every day, thus increasing business for local service stations.

"I got the letter and said, 'I'm bringing this public,'" says Emmett. "It was a dirty trick on Gallup. Eddie Muñoz was trying to get me out of office. He was after power. He just wanted to run the show." Emmett doesn't seem to be aware of, or willing to acknowledge, the personal change Muñoz underwent prior to his second go-round as mayor when Emmett was no longer in town.

I ask Emmett about the campaign and election that followed on the heels of his kidnapping. "I couldn't get out and campaign," he says. "I had a family that was deathly afraid. I was running because I didn't want to be run out of Gallup. My wife was extremely sick. I still wasn't over the head-on collision in Pinetop."

What effect did the Indian protest marches that followed his kidnapping and the death of Larry Casuse have? I ask. "My family got me out of town because they thought I would be killed," says Emmett. "The people behind the scenes were very happy. They succeeded. They got me out." While I question whether Emmett's political adversaries had much influence over Larry Casuse, I have no doubt that they were powerful—and that they were happy with the misfortune that befell him.

Emmett says that after the election he hired a private investigator who went to UNM and talked to the people involved at the Kiva Club. While at the Kiva Club, he says, the investigator found an Urban Renewal camera that had been used to take photos of alcohol abuse at the Navajo Inn. Criminal charges were still pending against Robert Nakaidinae at the time. Emmett emphasizes the camera because, if true, it is a link between Casuse and the men Emmett was threatening to expose for fraudulent activities.

"I wrote a letter of clemency because Casuse and Nakaidinae were used," says Emmett. "Robert Nakaidinae more than Larry Casuse. Nakaidinae had only been in Albuquerque for two or three days. He was afraid."

I ask Emmett what lessons were learned from the whole affair, and he has a ready answer that surprises me. "In spite of my problems," he says, "Larry Casuse created a situation that changed a lot of things. Twenty bars were closed. Gallup is completely different. Indian people are clerks and employees; they have advanced by leaps and bounds since I left. That was a turning point." I'm puzzled by Emmett's answer; it seems as if he's just giving me an answer that he thinks sounds good. Gallup has changed, but his remark about twenty bars closing strikes me as an exaggeration. Gallup still has well over the state of New Mexico's quota of liquor licenses. And nothing Emmett has said or implied up to this point in our conversation suggests that he thinks anything positive resulted from Larry Casuse's actions.

By now, we've talked about everything I can think of—other than Emmett's abduction at City Hall, so I ask him about what happened that day. Without hesitation, Emmett shifts gears and begins talking about his kidnapping. As he recites the events, it's obvious from his cadence that he's told this story many times. I've heard and read several accounts, but some details are new to me. After an initial struggle, at the mayor's office, Emmett says Casuse tried unsuccessfully to fire his revolver. He describes Casuse cocking the gun while Emmett held him from behind. Casuse fired the gun into Garcia's desk, he says, shattering glass. Emmett realized that Casuse was too strong and released him. Then he tried to negotiate.

"He pointed the gun at me," says Emmett, "and said, 'Get on your knees.' I realized that there are different levels of fear. It was so cold. I thought he was going to kill me right there."

Shortly after Manuel Gonzales unsuccessfully tried to rescue Emmett, Casuse had Emmett cuffed and was marching him down Second Street toward Route 66 with a gun at his head. Casuse told his accomplice, Robert Nakaidinae, to turn left to go to Stearns Sporting Goods. I tell Emmett that I've always heard that Casuse intended to take him to the Indian Center across 66 and the railroad tracks, but that their path was blocked by a passing train.

"That's bullshit," says Emmett emphatically. "Everyone has a story. Their plan was always to go to the sporting goods store."

When Casuse told Nakaidinae to go left at Route 66, Emmett knew, "That's not where the sporting-goods store was. I told them to turn right."

Emmett gives a shrug that says, *I know it was crazy for me to help them with directions, but that's what I did.*

As the three approached Route 66, however, Emmett, whose nickname was Frank, or Frankie, had a revelation. "I had a feeling, *Frank, you are going to survive this,*" he says, "like someone spoke to me."

When they reached the sporting-goods store, and Casuse left Emmett with Nakaidinae while he went to the rear of the store, Emmett tells me that the feeling of calm and reassurance he got from the unspoken message gave him the courage to kick Nakaidinae and dive through the glass door with his hands cuffed behind his back.

Emmett finishes his account of the kidnapping by saying, "I still have fifty-six shotgun pellets. They come to the surface. I've taken out ten."

Our conversation has run its course now and I thank Emmett for reaching out to me and sharing his story. I briefly consider going to his talk at UNM–Gallup but decide against it. I think it's going to be painful; I don't think he realizes how hostile the crowd of native college students will be. As I linger inside the pub to visit with a friend, I glance up and see Emmett, his dark silhouette framed by the sunny large glass front of the restaurant, walking toward his car. Why do I feel so sad for him?

Throughout the conversation, I had the feeling that Emmett was flailing—grasping and searching for something lost. I was struck by the pain and loss he felt, thirty-four years later; it was palpable. As a mayor in his mid-thirties, Emmett was by all accounts a rising star. But since his abduction and surprising loss in the 1973 election, his life hasn't fulfilled its early promise. He never held an elected office again, and several business ventures failed. A couple of people have told me he has lived on financial support from his son, an immensely successful Phoenix car dealer.

I can only imagine what it would have been like to have been in Emmett's shoes. To have the people who threatened and harassed me during my time as mayor drag me out of my office and march me down the street with a gun at my head. To go through something that shattered my dreams and left me broken, confused and trying to justify actions I still felt bad about.

Again, however, I find myself feeling deep sympathy for Larry Casuse. Although I didn't share my views about Larry with Emmett, I've come to believe that Casuse encountered unrelenting pressure after his accident in which the young Navajo woman died, with his arrest, jailing, and trials, and the silent resistance of powerful men in positions of authority who wouldn't acknowledge any problem with a bar run the way the Navajo Inn was operated. I believe those are the reasons, not any connection to Emmett's old-guard adversaries, that Larry Casuse acted in the way he did.

I find myself wondering how things would have gone if the UNM Board of Regents president, Calvin Horn, had dropped in to visit Casuse, as he'd thought about doing, or if the powerful men on the senate committee had honestly acknowledged the heartlessness of what was happening at the Navajo Inn, even if they ultimately decided to make Emmett a regent. On occasion in Gallup I had found the silence of powerful men infuriating. The message it communicated: We have power and you don't; we don't even need to give you the courtesy of responding to what you say.

As Emmett drives away, my final thoughts turn to Don Casuse and how different I felt after my conversation with him, knowing that he found peace and closure years after his brother's bloody death in Gallup—the peace and closure that is still eluding Emmett. I feel unsettled and I consider going to Emmett's talk at UNM–Gallup again but quickly put the thought out of my mind. It's enough for one day.

CHAPTER SIXTEEN

"It Was a Display"

Ten years after my lunch with Emmett Garcia, I receive a call from Frank Bosler, the high-school teacher who'd given me a copy of the last letter Larry Casuse wrote to his father and the cassette tape of the shoot-out on Route 66. Bosler is now retired and living in Albuquerque. In those ten years, much has happened.

A couple of years after my term as mayor ended, the Silver Stallion bar owners who sued the city and me for racial discrimination were forced to sell their liquor license to avoid revocation, according to the three strikes regulations produced by Rachel O'Connor's task force on alcohol.

The *Independent* ran a series of twenty unrelenting editorials against Harry Mendoza, calling him such things as a "thug, master manipulator and gang rapist." The editorials were based on the fact that a 16-year-old Zuni girl had been brutally attacked and raped in Gallup on the night of June 6, 1948. Seven Gallup youths were arrested, including Mendoza. The arrest log listed Mendoza as being fifteen. One year later, five of the seven youths were convicted of rape charges. Mendoza did not stand trial. In 1949, the *Independent,* then under different ownership, reported, "Harry Mendoza who was also charged with rape in the case, was not tried since he now is in the Army."

Mendoza and the newspaper's publisher bumped into each other at a local bank while the editorials were running, and Mendoza, seventy-eight at the time, then chased the publisher around the vehicles in the parking lot trying to hit and kick him, but mostly just flailing. Security cameras captured the skirmish, which became hot news on the Albuquerque TV stations. Mendoza sued the *Independent* and the publisher for defamation over the editorials—a suit that ended in a deadlocked jury. Several jurors cried openly in the courtroom after expressing fears to the judge about retaliation from Mendoza, the publisher, and their fellow jurors.

The north-side counselor I served with, who later allied himself with Mendoza, lost his reelection bid by one vote two years into Mendoza's term, shifting the balance of power on the council against Mendoza. Mendoza's city manager was then fired.

The Navajo-Gallup Water Supply Project received congressional authorization, and President Obama included appropriations for it in his 2008 stimulus package bill; several years later, Brenda and I attended a groundbreaking ceremony at Tohlakai, near the still-expanding fenced lots north of Gallup that are filled with pawned trucks and trailers. The water pipeline was finally being built.

Our mountain-bike trails in the Zuni Mountains hosted the USA Cycling 24-Hour national championship race for two years in 2013 and 2014, bringing several hundred riders and some of the biggest names in cycling to Gallup. Peter Tempest and I paired up to ride as a duo team, a race classification not eligible for a national championship, and with Peter pushing the pace, we finished in first place.

A retired Gallup businessman, who looks and talks like Willie Nelson, defeated Harry Mendoza's reelection bid and was successful in getting legislation that gives Gallup the option to limit early-morning sales of alcohol. The *Independent* began running editorials calling the new mayor our Pretend Mayor, claiming that he was just going through the motions without any real accomplishments.

Gamerco Associates sold its forty square miles of property in and around Gallup to a businessman from Chicago living in Shanghai. The new owner approved a public recreation lease for Gallup's north-side property, the location of Pete's Wicked Trail. The lease fell apart, however, when the same cowboy who had the old grazing lease, again raised a ruckus. The new owner's management team got cold feet, and the one

The Navajo-Gallup Water Supply Project pipe is laid in the ground near the base of Ford Butte halfway between Gallup and Farmington. *Courtesy of Bob Rosebrough*

Adventure Gallup project that we'd sought from the very beginning continued to elude us.

Several months after the ban on early morning sales of alcohol went into effect following the city council's vote to exercise the legal option, I started to notice heavy pedestrian traffic in the alley behind my law office in the morning. I asked our office manager, who rented a small home overlooking the alley, what was going on. She said, "There's a guy one block east in the alley who is bootlegging."

Gallup's liquor licensees remained cordial. Joe Zecca waves and says "Hi," whenever I see him. When Brenda and I went out to dinner one evening, we saw Frank Colaianni and his family in a large booth, and he waved and said "Hi." When it was time to leave, the waiter told us Frank had paid for our meal. Though fading and beginning to wear around the edges, the "Save the Historic American Bar" bumper sticker is still up on my business neighbor's front window.

Fourteen years after I met Gary Stuart, the author of *The Gallup 14,* I drove down to Tempe, Arizona, to sit in on the writing class that he taught at the Arizona State University School of Law. After the class, we

A rider in the "24 Hours in the Enchanted Forest Race" during the National Championships in 2014. *Courtesy of Brian Leddy*

Howard "Bobcat" Wilson on the old Ceremonial grounds with performers.
Courtesy of Octavia Fellin Public Library, Gallup, New Mexico

had lunch at a crowded, upscale university cafeteria and then returned to the law school where we found a private room to talk about the 1935 coal riot and the trial that followed.

For years I'd been struggling to understand the trial of the ten coal miners that followed the riot where Sheriff Carmichael was killed and Deputy Bobcat Wilson seriously wounded. I still didn't understand why Bobcat Wilson never testified. And I didn't understand why the miners were charged with first-degree murder when the prosecution never called a witness who identified a miner as shooting Carmichael.

I pressed Stuart, who had meticulously researched the trial for his historical novel, *The Gallup 14*, and he did not hold back. During the trial, the prosecution never produced the murder weapon. A sheriff's deputy's gun, a 1917 model .45 Smith & Wesson, was identified as the weapon that killed Carmichael and severely wounded Wilson, but the gun was missing. The inference was that the deputy who was attacked and beaten by the miners lost his gun and a miner had picked it up and shot the sheriff.

Yet in the final chapter of *The Gallup 14* titled, "Bobcat Speaks: May 13, 1987," Stuart describes Bobcat Wilson being in possession of the .45 Smith & Wesson and displaying it to an insurance evaluator who was making a video as part of an appraisal of three or four hundred guns that

Howard "Bobcat" Wilson (second from left) in the old Ceremonial stands with Ceremonial directors. *Courtesy of Octavia Fellin Public Library, Gallup, New Mexico*

Bobcat owned. At one point on the video, Bobcat says that the deputy who purportedly lost the .45 told him, "If you testify, Bobcat. I'm going to Old Mexico." The fact that Bobcat had the missing gun was completely inconsistent with the theory that a rioting miner scooped up the deputy's gun and killed Carmichael and wounded Bobcat.

Bobcat's final statement on the video about the riot was ambiguous. He says, "You got to remember we had the mines going. There were a lot of people in town. There was very good people and some very rough people." Even years later, there was clearly something that Bobcat was holding back.

Stuart never had the chance to interview Bobcat Wilson, but he was high school friends with Bobcat's son, Larry, and talked with Larry Wilson at length while researching the book. Stuart told me that his book's description of the video was factual and that Larry Wilson played the video for him.

After revisiting the facts of the riot and the record of the trial, I asked Stuart who he thought shot and killed Sheriff Carmichael. He told me that Larry Wilson believed that the other deputy who was attacked by the miners panicked and fired the shot that wounded his dad. That's what his dad told him, he said, and that's why they didn't want to testify. Stuart didn't say one way or the other whether the deputy also fired the shot that killed Carmichael, but it seemed clear that he did. Expert testimony at the trial had established that both Bobcat and Carmichael were shot by the deputy's missing gun. Bobcat was one of only three law enforcement witnesses, but inexplicably he wasn't called to testify. The gun that fired the bullets that killed Carmichael hadn't been introduced at trial, yet here was the gun in Bobcat's possession and, if that wasn't enough, Bobcat had told his son that the deputy—not a coal miner—shot him.

After the interview, I walked out to the covered ASU parking structure and sat in my Jeep. Ten coal miners had been tried on first degree murder charges for Sheriff Carmichael's death, which had been caused by friendly fire from a deputy. As I sat in my Jeep thinking about Bobcat Wilson displaying the .45 Smith & Wesson to the insurance evaluator and his son's conversations with Stuart, the thought running through my mind was: *There must be a deep-seated need to selectively share long-kept secrets before going to the grave.*

Around the same time I met with Stuart in Tempe, an elderly official from the Fort Defiance Chapter of the Navajo Nation, Louise Nelson, called me and asked me to play a role in the chapter's annual Navajo Treaty Day reenactment on the first weekend of each June. I play President Andrew Johnson, who signed the treaty, and although I only have one line, I look forward to the reenactment every year.

Ursula Casuse came to my law office fourteen years after she came to see me at City Hall. I was out, but she left her number with my new law partner. I called her and asked her to come back in. Ursula brought her daughter with her, and we sat in a small conference room and talked for more than an hour. A few weeks later, she invited me to her house, and we talked at length and made the personal connection I had hoped for fourteen years earlier. Before I left, Ursula drew a map to show me how to get to her brother Larry's gravesite near Mexican Springs.

I'm still practicing law in the same office, down the street from City Hall, riding my bike and hiking our trails with Chuck—the friend who put together a campaign pamphlet for me—and a group of friends, most of whom are twenty years younger than me. Matt, Mark, and Megan, who have finished their schooling, are working in Albuquerque and Amy is in graduate school in Tucson. We have our first grandchildren, Matt's daughters, Addie and Ellie. Brenda is nearing her twentieth year as a speech therapist with the Gallup schools and continuing to unconditionally support me on each wild tangent I pursue.

In our phone conversation, Frank Bosler tells me he wants to give me his collection of documents and recordings about the Garcia abduction. He asks if I'll be coming to Albuquerque anytime soon. By now, Emmett Garcia, Manuel Gonzales, and Robert Nakaidinae have all passed away. Shortly after Emmett Garcia died, a local author who was paid by Garcia to write a biography for him, delivered a collection of photographs, personal papers, and newspaper clippings to me, with no note or phone call, that he and Garcia had collected. The story of Larry Casuse and Emmett Garcia continued to follow me.

I retrieve a large, overflowing tub from Bosler, who gives me an overview of its contents and hands it over to me. He seems to be relieved.

Back in my office in Gallup, I listen first to a CD of a conversation between Garcia, Robert Nakaidinae, and Nakaidinae's lawyer that took place forty-four years earlier as a prelude to the fifteen-month sentence Nakaidinae received, which was later reduced to eight months.

The exchange between Garcia and Nakaidinae is extremely awkward. Nakaidinae gives short, clipped answers to Garcia's questions, expressing doubt and uncertainty. He pauses before answering, but Garcia bores in with long, pointed questions. He seems to be trying to get Nakaidinae to support the official version that Larry Casuse committed suicide after he was seriously injured. Eventually, after a deep sigh, Nakaidinae says, "You know—like myself, you know—I don't actually know whether he did shoot himself or not, you know. There's still some question in my mind, you know, how actually he did die."

Nakaidinae's lawyer diverts the conversation by bringing up a song Nakaidinae wrote, and he asks him to sing it. Nakaidinae starts playing his guitar and singing a song with lyrics that include "heroes dying killing," "town of corruption," "shot down before blind pride," "lying on the pavement," and "blood was in the gutter." One of the chorus lines is "Ride Red and the Dynamite Kid." I assume Red is Larry Casuse whose Austrian mother had bright red hair and the Dynamite Kid is Nakaidinae, who carried a homemade bomb into city hall.

After Nakaidinae stops singing, there is a long awkward pause. Nakaidinae's lawyer says, "A little militant. I thought you might like to hear it." The recording of the conversation ends. The whole conversation seems to me to confirm Don Casuse's suspicions that Nakaidinae wasn't telling the whole story at the time.

Going through Bosler's collection of materials, I also come across an issue of the *Navajo Times* with three articles about Garcia's and Gonzales's talk at UNM–Gallup. There's an interview with Nakaidinae by a *Times* reporter, in which Nakaidinae is more forthcoming than he was on the recording.

"He [Casuse] got shot five times, four times by a pistol and one by a shotgun, when the mayor escaped," Nakaidinae is quoted as saying. "Once he got shot, the first time, he was an open target and he was hit four other times, and he went down. We talked a bit and it was a heavy discussion. But I left him, and he was alive.

"There was all this tear gas," Nakaidinae says. "They threw me on the ground, and I heard another shot. While I was still on the ground, police officers came out and said, 'This one's done.' They were referring to Larry."

Continuing to go through the collection, I find DVDs that Bosler made at the talks Garcia and Gonzales gave at his Miyamura High School class back in 2008, the afternoon of the day I met with Garcia in the pub and at UNM–Gallup later that evening, a talk that drew a large, raucous crowd of Indian activists. The UNM–Gallup talk was reported in the *Independent,* though the paper didn't cover the high school talk.

On the DVDs, Garcia, then 71, scores poorly for both style and appearance. He is heavy, rumpled, and his large belly flows over his belt; he comes across as if he is making a pitch rather than laying out the facts. Gonzales, then 83, is balding, with short gray hair on the sides. His stomach is flat, and he's crisply dressed. Garcia tries to sell the story of how his political adversaries had co-opted Casuse, but as I had anticipated, he couldn't have picked worse audiences. The high school kids couldn't care less and the older students and Indian activists at UNM–Gallup are overtly hostile and argumentative.

Gonzales, in comparison, doesn't appear to be trying to sell anything. Early in the DVD of the Miyamura talk, Gonzales is off-camera but Bosler's mic picks him up saying, "Don't put words in my mouth" to either Garcia or Bosler, or both. On camera, he is matter-of-fact, not

Manuel Gonzales and Emmett Garcia confer during a public talk at UNM–Gallup in 2008. *Courtesy of Jeff Jones*

defensive, and resigned in his presentation; at times he deftly lightens the mood by taking gentle jabs at Garcia's weight and jokes that Garcia is even heavier than he looks because of the pellets in his back he still carries from Nakaidinae's shotgun blast.

At Miyamura High, Gonzales says he was talking to Casuse and Nakaidinae from his position outside Stearns Sporting Goods and trying to get them to release Garcia and end the standoff.

"I was telling them to knock it off," he says. "When the mayor got away, this is the time to end it," Gonzales says. "I ordered all the police officers, every one of them, 'Open fire on the building.' And I'm sure that is what killed Casuse.

"Some people think that he committed suicide," says Gonzales. "My story is that he was killed when police opened fire."

At the UNM–Gallup talk, Gonzales went further in his comments about Casuse and his death—which inexplicably were not mentioned in the *Independent*'s article. He says he knew Casuse for a year or two before Garcia's abduction. Casuse had applied for parade permits in Gallup and had held four demonstrations. Gonzales says there had been no problems with Casuse at the demonstrations.

"I got to know him," says Gonzales who goes on to describe Garcia's escape and the fusillade that followed.

"And that's when all hell broke loose," Gonzales says. "The minute they saw the mayor was safe, everybody, everybody opened fire into that store—shotguns, rifles, thirty-aught-sixes, pistols. And one fellow got killed by that barrage—and that was Casuse." At UNM–Gallup, Gonzales doesn't say he gave an order to open fire.

"The guy that was with Casuse came out the door," Gonzales continues, "and he said, 'Please help Casuse. He's hurt. He's bleeding. He's on the floor.' So, with that, a couple of officers went in and brought him out. He was dead.

"But anyway, I wasn't at the police department too long after that," says Gonzales. "I didn't want to go through something like that again. I lost some good friends, Larry being one of them." The words "good friends, Larry being one of them," seem to be a stretch. From his wistfulness the words seem not really true but rather what he wishes were true.

"But that's what happens when you pull serious crimes like that," he says. "They're going to make sure that you never do it again." I assume that "they" are the Gallup police—in particular, the police at the sporting goods store, but the word choice is striking since earlier in the day, Gonzales had said that he gave the order to open fire. It makes me wonder whether he really gave such an order or just said he did so later, to provide cover for his men. I remember that the eyewitness who talked to Don Casuse said that after Garcia escaped, the policemen shouted, "Kill him! Kill Him!" without any mention of Gonzales giving an order.

Then slowly and deliberately, Manuel Gonzales, in a tired, resigned voice, slowly says, "There's other police officers that are going to make sure that you never do that again. It's not the right way to think, but that's the way it is. Courts don't do it. Courts are too lenient. And sometimes a police officer knows what he can do and what he can't do. But if he gets the opportunity, he's going to do what has to be done to eliminate the problem. A lot of prosecutors are sympathetic to a police officer when he behaves that way.

"You've been a good audience," Gonzales says in conclusion, and he pauses. "If you have any questions, ask him." Gonzales nods toward Garcia, and the audience laughs, breaking the tension of the moment. Gonzales steps away from the podium. Stunningly, his complete candidness and lack of defensiveness wins over the hostile audience, at least for the moment.

After reviewing the documents and listening to the recordings in Bosler's collection, there's one word I can't get out of my mind—and one photo. The word belonged to the conversation I had with my buddy Hank Stokes, the minister from Georgia who spent an afternoon with me when I was considering resigning as mayor because of threats to me and my family over the enforcement of liquor regulations. He had just had that dream in which he saw the ominous figure that he called a Thwart.

"In the dream," he had said, "I saw this giant, dark metallic creature that rose up out of the sand and its hands and feet were shaped like wedges. It could stop anything that gained forward momentum in the city. And I asked an angelic being that was present in the dream, 'What is this thing?' And it said, 'It's a Thwart, and it can stop any good in this town. And you need to pray against it. It's been here for many, many years.'"

I feel there *is* a thwarting presence or spirit in Gallup, and over the years it's forced me to swing back and forth between periods of political activism and periods of withdrawal. I've pushed at times in my life here, and I've gone out on a limb, and each time I have, I've eventually had to back off. I know, as much as I can know anything, that if I reached a certain point and didn't back off, I would have been crushed.

The photo, of course, is the photo of Larry Casuse's body lying on the sidewalk in front of Stearns Sporting Goods. What clues does it hold to what really happened that day? I ask my buddy, Chuck, whose judgment and insight I trust, sometimes more than my own, to drop by my office, and when he does, I hand him a copy of the newspaper with the photo of Larry Casuse's bloody body lying on the sidewalk surrounded by police. I ask him what he sees, what his impressions are.

"First, it's incredibly disrespectful," he says. "From the blood marks on the sidewalk you can tell that Casuse was dragged by his heels and laid out on the sidewalk. Why would you do that? Why would you disturb a crime scene like that? Why would you drag a dead body from inside a building and put it on a sidewalk on the main street of Gallup? It's for display. That's what this is, a display. And it's incredibly disrespectful."

I ask Chuck what he sees in the officers and their bearing. "The guy in the back with the rifle on his hip looks almost like he's flinching," he

Policemen surround the body of Larry Casuse, which was dragged out onto the sidewalk. Casuse's body has been blacked out in this photograph. *Courtesy of the* Gallup Independent

says. "And look at Chief Gonzales's hand. The way he's holding his hand out over Casuse's body."

"It looks protective," I say. "Like he is protecting Casuse."

"I don't think he is protecting Casuse or the body," Chuck says, "I think it's a reaction to the photographer approaching. I think the police are reacting to the photographer. They didn't expect a photographer to capture their display and it alarms them."

As I look at the photo, I see what Chuck is saying—it *was* a display. A display that demonstrates that thwarting presence and spirit in Gallup. A spirit that says, don't mess with us; this is what you will get if you do. And that was why the photo struck so viscerally among the Navajos, unleashing, for a time, an emotional response that for Navajos is normally

In the spring of 2017, memorial posters featuring Larry Casuse's image began appearing in Gallup after city officials removed a downtown planter with an image of Casuse. *Courtesy of Bob Rosebrough*

deeply buried—a response that shook Gallup until the status quo could eventually be restored.

And yet I know, and I've felt, that there is a competing spirit in Gallup, one that says: This place is wonderful, or at least it *can* be. A spirit that says: Help make this place all that it can be and should be. A spirit that tells us how wonderful it can be to reach out to people who are different from us. A spirit that tells us that these historic barriers that we keep bumping into can be learned from and overcome.

Epilogue

One Sunday afternoon in May, not long after perusing Frank Bosler's materials on Larry Casuse and Emmett Garcia and talking with Chuck about the photo of Casuse's body, I grab a small daypack and head off to hike up to the lookout on Gallup's north side where Tim and Jay took me forty years earlier when I was interviewing for my first job in Gallup. I've been back to the lookout hundreds of times over the years by various means and routes. This time I drive to a dead-end street and walk through trash: Miller Lite and Bud Light cans, a dirty Levi's shirt turned inside out and lying in a heap, a crushed Styrofoam soft-drink cup, and a Canadian Fireball Whisky miniature bottle.

I hop over a locked metal gate and cross the newly graded right-of-way of a lateral NGWSP water line heading east toward the Navajo chapters of Church Rock and Iyanbito. I hike through a brushy area on two-track roads. Surface seams of black coal are occasionally exposed on both sides of my path. I head to the right, toward tailings piles of an old underground coal mine. This mine, the Biava mine, closed when a fire spontaneously ignited. It is one of four underground coal mine fires still smoldering decades after the last underground mine closed.

The tailings piles near the mine are laced with the tire tracks of dirt bikes—they appear to have been used for jumps. Rusted metal pipes of various sizes are strewn randomly. Aiming for a ridge, I scramble up a short sandstone cliff scattered with old, burned-black roof beams from a small structure at its base. At the top of the cliff, I hike by one of several small vents, no bigger than my daypack, that provides oxygen to the smoldering fire buried below, and I smell the invisible sulfur-tinged smoke.

Half a mile out from my Jeep, I gain the ridge, and now I'm in natural terrain, gaining elevation by climbing higher through layers of thick tan sandstone, thin coal seams, and broad deposits of clay. I spot deer and bobcat prints on the intermittent trail I'm following. The junipers and cedars are now fuller and more densely grouped, and to my left are vertical pillars of hard clay topped with sandstone caps. One impossibly large sandstone oval is balanced on a thin neck of clay.

Smoke from an underground coal-mine fire rises through vents in the earth above the Biava mine north of Gallup.
Courtesy of Bob Rosebrough

Another mile farther, I stand and take in the view over Gallup. Not much has changed in forty years. Interstate 40 is now paved. The mall built in the early '80s lies to the west. Miyamura High School, built ten years ago, is visible on the east end of town, and there are three large water tanks that are part of the Navajo-Gallup Water Supply Project. There appear to be a few more new buildings than when I stood here forty years ago, but none I can identify from this distance.

A precariously balanced cap rock north of Gallup, below the overlook.
Courtesy of Bob Rosebrough

Like many before me and many who will come in the future, I've wanted to make my mark in Gallup, and to a limited degree, I have. But from this vantage point, nothing I've done is visible. It's all too small. While a few old Gallup anchors, like the Gallup Indian Medical Center, Sacred Heart Cathedral, and the courthouse are large enough to be seen from here, none of the projects completed when I was mayor can

The gap in the hogback, through which transcontinental traffic flows on a railroad line, Route 66, and I-40. *Courtesy of Bob Rosebrough*

be spotted from this distance. Fifty years after my first visit to Gallup, forty-six years after Larry Casuse was shot dead, and forty years after I moved here, the view of the town is essentially the same.

As always, my gaze is drawn east toward the serrated, multicolored layers of sandstone that erupt from the earth to form the hogback and the three sets of cliffs beyond—the yellow cliffs to my left, the White Cliffs rising above the hogback in the center, and the red rocks to the distant right. This stunning landscape draws me back to this point time after time.

I look to the 200-yard-wide natural gap in the hogback through which history has flowed. Native people migrated through this gap, early surveyors established stagecoach and railroad routes through here, U.S. soldiers marched in, and starving Navajos walked out to the eastern plains of New Mexico and then back. And travelers through the decades have passed through this gap on historic Route 66, America's "mother road." It is a conduit of history, where nature has conspired to create a collision of cultures and people.

As I stand on the overlook forty years after my first visit to this spot, I ponder the future of Gallup. I doubt the city and surrounding area will ever undergo the kind of transformation I've hoped for and sought. But the story is far from over. And the struggle is far from over. There is a lot left to play out here—in ways both terrible and wonderful—and it will be interesting to see what comes next.

Acknowledgments

Writing this book has been a long journey for me. I received help, some unexpected, from many people. After a chance encounter, Kyra Ryan Ochoa taught me how to interweave my personal experiences with Gallup's larger story. Anne Nolan, a longtime friend, helped me with finishing touches. The Guadanogli family—Shan Guadanogli, Beverly Guadanogli Davis, Roy Davis, and Amanda Shanel Davis—generously shared rare photos from the historic Tom Mullarky collection, and Bob Zollinger gave permission to use important images from the *Gallup Independent*. Aaron Downey, Rio Nuevo Publishers' skilled editor, ultimately put it all together into a finished product.

Spanning a period of more than twenty years, many other people have given me interviews, shared photos, provided documents, reviewed early drafts, and offered suggestions, including: Alfred Abeita, Aurelio Baca, Michael Benson, Frank Bosler, Theo Bremer-Bennett, Barry Butler, Brenda Byerley, Gabe Campos, Ursula Casuse Carillo, Don Casuse, Phyliss Casuse, Richard Chavez, Judy Conejo, Chris Dahl-Bredine, Bill Donovan, Joe Esparza, Tim Folger, Alice Franey, Emmett Garcia, Michael Haederle, Elizabeth Harden-Burrola, Tom Hartsock, Adriel Heisey, Levon Henry, Dirk Hollebeck, Eric Honeyfield, Chris Hoover, Jeff Jones, Marianne Joyce, Kenji Kawano, Joe Kolb, Brian Leddy, Bill Lee, John Leeper, Martin Link, Leslie Linthicum, Karl Lohmann, Patty Lundstrom, Paul McCollum, Lionel McKinney, Hershey Miyamura, Tammie Moe, Herb Mosher, George Muñoz, Margaret Muñoz, Rachel O'Conner, David Pike, Craig Pirlot, Larry Price, Peter Procopio, Karla Rivera, Tom Robinson, Lisa Rodriguez, Amy Rosebrough, Mark Rosebrough, Matt Rosebrough, Megan Rosebrough, Ben Sorrel, Don Steele, Hank Stokes, Ernie Stromeyer, Gary Stuart, Peter Tempest, Lane Towery, Earl Tully, Chuck Van Drunen, Margo Manaraze Waggoner, and Joe Zecca. I'm deeply grateful to each of you.

About the Author

After finishing his education at the University of New Mexico, Bob Rosebrough moved to Gallup in 1979. He is a lawyer, outdoorsman, and author or co-author of four previous books.

Courtesy of Bob Rosebrough

Index

Page numbers in *italics* indicate photos or photo captions.